Myth and Southern History

Volume 1: The Old South

Myth and Southern History

Volume 1: The Old South

Second Edition

Edited by **Patrick Gerster**
and **Nicholas Cords**

University of Illinois Press

Urbana and Chicago

Illini Books edition, 1989
©1974, 1989 by Patrick Gerster and Nicholas Cords
Manufactured in the United States of America
P 5 4 3 2

This book is printed on acid-free paper.

Library of Congress Cataloging-in-Publication Data

Myth and Southern history / edited by Patrick Gerster and Nicholas
  Cords. —2nd ed.
     p.   cm.
  Includes bibliographies and indexes.
  Contents: v. 1. The Old South—v. 2. The New South.
  ISBN 0-252-06024-5 (v. 1). ISBN 0-252-06025-3 (v. 2)
    1. Southern States—History. 2. Southern States—Historiography.
  I. Gerster, Patrick. II. Cords, Nicholas.
  F209.M95 1989   88-4871
  975'.0072—dc19   CIP

For
Mark, Jennifer, Jason, James,
John, Nicholas, and Daniel

It's all *now* you see. Yesterday won't be over until tomorrow and tomorrow began ten thousand years ago. For every Southern boy fourteen years old, not once but whenever he wants it, there is the instant when it's still not yet two o'clock on that July afternoon in 1863, the brigades are in position behind the rail fence, the guns are laid and ready in the woods and the furled flags are already loosened to break out and Pickett himself with his long oiled ringlets and his hat in one hand probably and his sword in the other looking up the hill waiting for Longstreet to give the word and it's all in the balance, it hasn't happened yet, it hasn't even begun yet, it not only hasn't begun yet but there is still time for it not to begin against that position and those circumstances which made more men than Garnett and Kemper and Armstead and Wilcox look grave yet it's going to begin, we all know that, we have come too far with too much at stake and that moment doesn't even need a fourteen-year-old boy to think *This time. Maybe this time* with all this much to lose and all this much to gain: Pennsylvania, Maryland, the world, the golden dome of Washington itself to crown with desperate and unbelievable victory the desperate gamble, the cast made two years ago; or to anyone who ever sailed even a skiff under a quilt sail, the moment in 1492 when somebody thought *This is it:* the absolute edge of no return, to turn back now and make home or sail irrevocably on and either find land or plunge over the world's roaring rim.

WILLIAM FAULKNER, *Intruder in the Dust*

Contents

Acknowledgments

As is the case with any project based on secondary sources, we have incurred many debts. Because this work is thematic, we are especially indebted to all those historians whose works have contributed either directly or indirectly to our developing interest in the relationship between myth and history. The work being regional in focus, we are most indebted to southern historians' contributions, and most particularly to those whose works are included herein. We also extend our thanks to Lawrence Malley, editor in chief, University of Illinois Press, who early developed a sustaining interest in the project. It is gratifying to note that he was instrumental in bringing the first edition from dream to reality and again plays a crucial role in this second edition. Further, he gave consistent encouragement during the book's long odyssey between editions. We would like also to thank Theresa Sears, our manuscript editor. Finally, we express deep gratitude to our wives and children for their usual support and diversions, however directly or indirectly they contributed to this edition.

Introduction to the Second Edition

The enthusiastic response to *Myth and Southern History* makes this second edition possible. In receiving both words of praise and suggestions for improvement from users of the first edition, our conviction about the relevance of a mythic perspective on the American South has, if anything, become even more firm. We feel secure in saying that perception of a mythic dimension to southern history has proven itself viable, as scholars continue to explore its frontiers and probe its subtleties. The mythological approach to southern history continues to be both relevant and exciting. It most assuredly has come of age, or at least it has assumed its proper place alongside the more traditional perspectives on the southern past.

Since the publication of the first edition of *Myth and Southern History*, we have had occasion to comment further—in classroom lectures, when presenting professional papers, and with the publication of articles, books, and reviews—on the elusive relationship of myth and southern history. What the intervening experiences have effected, in fact, is an even broader awareness of the reality myth contains. We continue to see myth and reality as complementary elements of the historical record. Indeed, even though southern myths may well emanate from historical inaccuracies, they are deeply imbedded in the fundamental explanations the South continues to hold about the mandates of its traditions. Their most important role is their persistent ability to control continuing social and political realities. In short, we stand convinced of our earlier stated belief, that many historical myths are factually false and psychologically true at one and the same time; and that their psychological truth is by far the more important.

Given the opportunity to completely revise *Myth and Southern History,* as editors we would have insisted on gender-neutral language and substitution of "black" for "Negro." We have found, however, good reason to retain the basic style of the first edition in the interests of sustaining the integrity of selections as originally published. Moreover, it is inevitable and proper, given the dynamic nature of southern scholarship, that we would add a number of new selections and drop several others. We have been guided by a desire to choose essays that voice our mythological theme in a scholarly way yet are readable and interesting.

This second edition contains new selections that deal with slavery in a colonial context, the nature of the slave debate (in both a historical and a historiographical sense), antebellum southern women, patterns of abolitionism and unionism in the Civil War era, the matter of the South's (indeed the nation's) reconstruction, the postbellum development of a civil religion, the role of the North in southern mythology, as well as new perspectives on such traditionally debated issues as the so-called Savage South, twentieth-century southern women both black and white, and the South's persistent Edenic impulse in the context of a continually emerging New South.

Introduction to the First Edition

Students of the southern past have long sought to identify a central theme in southern history. It was out of such a concern, for example, that historian Ulrich B. Phillips spoke of the sustained southern commitment to white supremacy; journalist Wilbur J. Cash sought to tap the inner workings of "the mind" of the South; and others have concluded the inner logic of southern history to be climate, geography, or its seemingly distinctive economic, political, social, or religious patterns. Indeed the debate over the central theme of southern history is a continuing one, with the only consensus being that there does exist a common thread of experience somewhere in the deep recesses of the southern past.

In 1964, while in pursuit of this central theme, George B. Tindall isolated "mythology" as a "new frontier" in southern history.[1] Acknowledging the work of earlier historians such as Francis Pendelton Gaines (*The Southern Plantation: A Study in the Development and Accuracy of a Tradition,* 1925), and anticipating the verdict of southern historians to come, Tindall's essay enthusiastically endorsed mythology as a tool for analyzing the rather blatant ambiguities, ironies, and paradoxes inherent in the southern past. The lens of myth had indeed been applied to the South before Professor Tindall's seminal work, but it was left for him to suggest that such an approach might well result in a new synthesis and a perspective worthy of sustained application. In short, Tindall's article posed the question: Is myth indeed one of the more important psychological determinants of southernism?

To what extent George B. Tindall's suggested approach to southern history will withstand the long-term erosion of historical scholarship is a question only future generations of scholars can answer with any full degree of certitude. It is the opinion of the editors, however, that an affirmative yet tentative judgment is now possible given the body of historical literature which has arisen clearly vindicating the Tindall thesis. An impressive array of southern scholars prior to and since Tindall's seminal essay have sought to determine the parameters of myth within what C. Vann Woodward has labeled "that twilight zone between living memory and written history." This volume brings together a sampling of their findings. Such scholars

---

[1] George B. Tindall, "Mythology: A New Frontier in Southern History," in Frank E. Vandiver (ed.), *The Idea of the South: Pursuit of a Central Theme* (Chicago, 1964).

are representative of an expanding and distinguished group of American historians who have come to see important distinctions between what might be termed "history as actuality" and "history as perceived."[2]

But perhaps further clarification and explanation are needed before this work can indeed provide the measure of historical insight which the "new frontier of mythology" potentially holds. The term "myth," as presented in this set of readings, is viewed in two ways. In the first instance, some of the authors seem to have Thomas A. Bailey's definition in mind as they speak of the myths of southern history: "a historical myth is . . . an account or belief that is demonstrably untrue, in whole or substantial part."[3] Those reflecting this definition tend to emphasize the negative aspects of myth, to isolate, and when the occasion warrants to debunk the results of misguided scholarship. Second, others appear more consistent with Henry Nash Smith's view of myth as "an intellectual construction that fuses concept and emotion into an image."[4] Briefly stated, one school seeks to emphasize historical inaccuracies while the other approaches the problem from the vantage point of social psychology. One sees myth as the by-product of historical scholarship (or lack of it), while the other shows a marked concern for the ways in which myth serves the decidedly positive function of unifying experience providing, in the words of Mark Schorer, "a large controlling image that gives philosophical meaning to the facts of ordinary life. . . ."[5] Certainly, at times both definitions are present—on occasion they tend to blend to the point of becoming almost indistinguishable. Both notions of myth are germane to the South and its history.

It is also important to note that the existence of a southern mythology in no way sets the South apart as distinctive or unique. It has been demonstrated in other quarters that much behavior and belief based on myth survives, and in fact thrives, in the contemporary world. The preeminent mythic scholar, Mircea Eliade, has observed that "certain aspects and functions of mythical thought are constituents of the human being."[6] Fundamental to the "human condition," myths in their infinite variety and complexity serve a supportive role to the dreams, ideals, and values of every society. Accordingly, "southern mythology" must be seen as differing from

[2] For a view of myth in its larger American context see Nicholas Cords and Patrick Gerster (eds.), *Myth and the American Experience*, 2 vols. (New York and Beverly Hills, 1973).

[3] Thomas A. Bailey, "The Mythmakers of American History," *The Journal of American History*, 55 (June 1968), p. 5.

[4] Henry Nash Smith, *Virgin Land: The American West as Symbol and Myth* (New York, 1950), p. v.

[5] Mark Schorer, "The Necessity of Myth," in Henry A. Murray (ed.), *Myth and Mythmaking* (New York, 1960), p. 355.

[6] Mircea Eliade, "Survivals and Camouflages of Myth," *Diogenes*, 41 (Spring 1963), p. 1.

its American equivalent only in degree not in kind, just as "American mythology" stands in relation to that of the world at large. Paul M. Gaston concurred with this judgment in his recent work, *The New South Creed: A Study in Southern Mythmaking:*

> What does distinguish the South, at least from other parts of the United States, is the degree to which myths have been spawned and the extent to which they have asserted their hegemony over the Southern mind.[7]

In this sense, at least, the American South has successfully transcended the strictures of regionalism.

Finally, the identification of myth as an important element in the historical process demonstrates anew that history is the dual product of documentation and imagination—both the record of the past *and* the dialogue among historians. The basic documents and the personal and professional prejudices of the historian (for Wendell H. Stephenson, "the fallacies of assumptions and methods") all find their way into the historical "record." The historian cannot dismiss the controlling images or myths of the society within which he writes. Because the serious historian must factor for all of these as he engages his discipline, this volume is as much a commentary on the writing of southern history—that is to say historiography—as it is on the viability of myth in the historical process. In these pages there is much support of the observation that "myth[s] have been used for centuries in writing history as well as making it."[8] The reader will find that "mythology" has provided, as well as suggests, new realms of scholarly speculation. More specifically, it becomes evident that such an approach applied to the South has come of age. It is an approach to southern history both relevant and exciting, deserving to *take its stand* beside the more traditional and validated perspectives long provided by historians of the marketplace, the political and diplomatic arenas, and the social record.

Some years ago Wilbur Cash wrote of the importance of the South's frontier experience: ". . . the history of the roll of frontier upon frontier—and on to the frontier beyond."[9] Given George B. Tindall's scholarly directive and the focus provided by the following selections, perhaps the South's enigmatic frontiers of the past—even that elusive central theme—can now find clearer explanation and synthesis in terms of her "new frontier of mythology."

---

[7] Paul M. Gaston, *The New South Creed: A Study in Southern Mythmaking* (New York, 1970), p. 8.

[8] Alfred Stern, "Fiction and Myth in History," *Diogenes,* 42 (Summer 1963), p. 98.

[9] Wilbur Cash, *The Mind of the South* (New York, 1941), p. 4.

1

Mythology: A New Frontier in Southern History

George B. Tindall

The "reality" of history, irrespective of time or place, remains an
elusive commodity, especially as regards the American South. Indeed, as George B. Tindall, Professor of History at the University
of North Carolina, Chapel Hill, argues in the selection which follows, the basic problem of distinguishing *objective reality* from *perceived reality* is ever present for the historian. Historical reality
involves not only that which is demonstrably true but also that
which one believes to be true. As such, the historian has a dual
role: he remains at once a "custodian of the past and keeper of the
public memory." The role of the historian involves both countering
misguided scholarship and identifying the public dreams which do
so much to orchestrate human behavior. Both of these facets of the
historical enterprise inevitably lead the historian into the province
of myth. Thus, in determining the dimensions of the southern experience, the historian must reckon not only with peculiar regional
characteristics but also the myths which have conditioned them. As
a significant unit of the region's experience, myth supplies an internal structure and a sustaining symmetry to our understanding
of the South. Professor Tindall's exploration of this new frontier of
mythology does much to establish the context—the perspective and
technique—for this entire work.

From George Tindall, "Mythology: A New Frontier in Southern History," in Frank
E. Vandiver (ed.), *The Idea of the South: Pursuit of a Central Theme,* pp. 1–15.
Reprinted by permission of the author and the University of Chicago Press. Copyright © 1964 by William Rice University. All rights reserved. Published 1964. Composed and printed by the University of Chicago Press, Chicago, Illinois, U.S.A.

The idea of the South—or more appropriately, the ideas of the South—belong in large part to the order of social myth. There are few areas of the modern world that have bred a regional mythology so potent, so profuse and diverse, even so paradoxical, as the American South. But the various mythical images of the South that have so significantly affected American history have yet to be subjected to the kind of broad and imaginative historical analysis that has been applied to the idea of the American West, particularly in Henry Nash Smith's *Virgin Land: The American West as Symbol and Myth.* The idea of the South has yet to be fully examined in the context of mythology, as essentially a problem of intellectual history.

To place the ideas of the South in the context of mythology, of course, is not necessarily to pass judgment upon them as illusions. The game of debunking myths, Harry Levin has warned us, starts "in the denunciation of myth as falsehood from the vantage-point of a rival myth."[1] Mythology has other meanings, not all of them pejorative, and myths have a life of their own which to some degree renders irrelevant the question of their correlation to empirical fact. Setting aside for the moment the multiple connotations of the term, we may say that social myths in general, including those of the South, are simply mental pictures that portray the pattern of what a people think they are (or ought to be) or what somebody else thinks they are. They tend to develop abstract ideas in more or less concrete and dramatic terms. In the words of Henry Nash Smith, they fuse "concept and emotion into an image."[2]

They may serve a variety of functions. "A myth," Mark Schorer has observed, "is a large, controlling image that gives philosophical meaning to the facts of ordinary life; that is, which has organizing value for experience."[3] It may offer useful generalizations by which data may be tested. But being also "charged with values, aspirations, ideals and meanings,"[4] myths may become the ground for belief, for either loyalty and defense on the one hand or hostility and opposition on the other. In such circumstances a myth itself becomes one of the realities of history, significantly influencing the course of human action, for good or ill. There is, of course, always a danger of illusion, a danger that in ordering one's vision of reality, the myth may predetermine the categories of perception, rendering one blind to things that do not fit into the mental image.

---

[1] Harry Levin, "Some Meanings of Myth," in Henry A. Murray (ed.), *Myth and Mythmakers* (New York, 1960), p. 106.

[2] Henry Nash Smith, *Virgin Land: The American West as Symbol and Myth* (Vintage ed., New York, 1957), p. v.

[3] Mark Schorer, "The Necessity for Myth," in Murray (ed.), *Myth and Mythmakers,* p. 355.

[4] C. Vann Woodward, "The Antislavery Myth," *American Scholar,* XXXI (Spring, 1962), 325.

Since the Southern mind is reputed to be peculiarly resistant to pure abstraction and more receptive to the concrete and dramatic image, it may be unusually susceptible to mythology. Perhaps for the same reason our subject can best be approached through reference to the contrasting experiences of two Southerners—one recent, the other about forty-five years ago.

The first is the experience of a contemporary Louisiana writer, John T. Westbrook.

> During the thirties and early forties [Westbrook has written] when I was an English instructor at the University of Missouri, I was often mildly irritated by the average northerner's Jeeter-Lester-and-potlikker idea of the South. Even today the northern visitor inertia-headedly maintains his misconception: he hankers to see eroded hills and rednecks, scrub cotton and sharecropper shacks.
>
> It little profits me to drive him through Baton Rouge, show him the oil-ethyl-rubber-aluminum-chemical miles of industry along the Mississippi River, and say, "This . . . is the fastest-growing city of over 100,-000 in America. We can amply substantiate our claim that we are atomic target number one, that in the next war the Russians will obliterate us first. . . ."
>
> Our northerner is suspicious of all this crass evidence presented to his senses. It bewilders and befuddles him. He is too deeply steeped in William Faulkner and Robert Penn Warren. The fumes of progress are in his nose and the bright steel of industry towers before his eyes, but his heart is away in Yoknapatawpha County with razorback hogs and night riders. On this trip to the South he wants, above all else, to sniff the effluvium of backwoods-and-sand-hill subhumanity and to see at least one barn burn at midnight. So he looks at me with crafty misgiving, as if to say, "Well, you *do* drive a Cadillac, talk rather glibly about Kierkegaard and Sartre . . . but, after all, you *are* only fooling, aren't you? You do, don't you, sometimes, go out secretly by owl-light to drink swamp water and feed on sowbelly and collard greens?"[5]

The other story was the experience of a Southern historian, Frank L. Owsley, who traveled during World War I from Chicago via Cincinnati to Montgomery with a group of young ladies on the way to visit their menfolk at an army camp. He wrote later that, "despite everything which had ever been said to the contrary," the young ladies had a romantic conception of the "Sunny South" and looked forward to the journey with considerable ex-

    John T. Westbrook, "Twilight of Southern Regionalism," *Southwest Review,* XLII (Summer, 1957), 231.

citement. "They expected to enter a pleasant land of white columned mansions, green pastures, expansive cotton and tobacco fields where negroes sang spirituals all the day through." Except in the bluegrass basins of central Kentucky and Tennessee, what they actually found "were gutted hillsides; scrub oak and pine; bramble and blackberry thickets, bottom lands once fertile now senile and exhausted, with spindling tobacco, corn, or cotton stalks . . . ; unpainted houses which were hardly more than shacks or here and there the crumbling ruins of old mansions covered with briars, the homes of snakes and lizards."[6] The disappointment of Dr. Owsley's ladies was, no doubt, even greater than that of Mr. Westbrook's friend in Baton Rouge.

There is a striking contrast between these two episodes, both in the picture of Southern reality and in the differing popular images that they present. The fact that they are four decades apart helps to account for the discrepancies, but what is not apparent at first is the common ancestry of the two images. They are not very distant cousins, collateral descendants from the standard image of the Old South, the plantation myth. The version of Owsley's lady friends is closer to the original primogenitor, which despite its advancing age and debility, still lives amid a flourishing progeny of legendary Southern gentility. According to Francis Pendleton Gaines, author of *The Southern Plantation,* the pattern appeared full-blown at least as early as 1832 in John Pendleton Kennedy's romance, *Swallow Barn.*[7] It has had a long career in story and novel and song, in the drama and motion picture. The corrosions of age seem to have ended its Hollywood career, although the old films still turn up on the late late. It may still be found in the tourist bait of shapely beauties in hoop skirts posed against the backdrop of white columns at Natchez, Orton, or a hundred other places.

These pictures are enough to trigger in the mind the whole euphoric pattern of kindly old marster with his mint julep; happy darkies singing in fields perpetually white to the harvest or, as the case may be, sadly recalling the long lost days of old; coquettish belles wooed by slender gallants in gray underneath the moonlight and magnolias. It is a pattern that yields all too easily to caricature and ridicule, for in its more sophisticated versions the figure of the planter carries a heavy freight of the aristocratic virtues: courtliness, grace, hospitality, honor, *noblesse oblige,* as well as many no less charming aristocratic vices: a lordly indifference to the balance sheet, hot temper, profanity, overindulgence, a certain stubborn obstinacy. The old-time Negro, when not a figure of comedy, is the very embodiment of

[6] Frank L. Owsley, "The Old South and the New," *American Review,* VI (February, 1936), 475.

[7] Francis Pendleton Gaines, *The Southern Plantation: A Study in the Development and Accuracy of a Tradition* (New York, 1925), p. 23.

loyalty. And the Southern belle: "Beautiful, graceful, accomplished in social charm, bewitching in coquetry, yet strangely steadfast in soul," Gaines
has written, "she is perhaps the most winsome figure in the whole field of
our fancy."[8] "The plantation romance," Gaines says, "remains our chief
social idyl of the past; of an Arcadian scheme of existence, less material,
less hurried, less prosaically equalitarian, less futile, richer in picturesque-
ness, festivity, in realized pleasure that recked not of hope or fear or un-
rejoicing labor."[9]

But there is still more to the traditional pattern. Somewhere off in the
piney woods and erosion-gutted clay hills, away from the white columns
and gentility, there existed Po' White Trash: the crackers; hillbillies; sand-
hillers; rag, tag, and bobtail; squatters; "po' buckra" to the Negroes; the
Ransy Sniffle of A. B. Longstreet's *Georgia Scenes* and his literary descendants like Jeeter Lester and Ab Snopes, abandoned to poverty and degeneracy—the victims, it was later discovered, of hookworm, malaria, and
pellagra. Somewhere in the pattern the respectable small farmer was lost
from sight. He seemed to be neither romantic nor outrageous enough to
fit in. His neglect provides the classic example in Southern history of the
blind spots engendered by the power of mythology. It was not until the
1930's that Frank L. Owsley and his students at Vanderbilt rediscovered
the Southern yeoman farmer as the characteristic, or at least the most
numerous, ante bellum white Southerner.[10] More about the yeoman presently; neglected in the plantation myth, he was in the foreground of another.

In contrast to the legitimate heirs of the plantation myth, the image of
John T. Westbrook's Yankee visitor in Baton Rouge seems to be descended
from what might be called the illegitimate line of the plantation myth, out
of abolition. It is one of the ironies of our history that, as Gaines put it, the
"two opposing sides of the fiercest controversy that ever shook national
thought agreed concerning certain picturesque elements of plantation life
and joined hands to set the conception unforgettably in public consciousness."[11] The abolitionists found it difficult, or even undesirable, to escape
the standard image. It was pretty fully developed even in *Uncle Tom's
Cabin*. Harriet Beecher Stowe made her villain a Yankee overseer, and has
been accused by at least one latter-day abolitionist of implanting deeply in
the American mind the stereotype of the faithful darkey. For others the
plantation myth simply appeared in reverse, as a pattern of corrupt opulence resting upon human exploitation. Gentle old marster became the ar-

[8] *Ibid.*, p. 16.
[9] *Ibid.*, p. 4.
[10] Frank L. Owsley, *Plain Folk of the Old South* (Baton Rouge, 1949).
[11] Gaines, *The Southern Plantation*, p. 30.

rogant, haughty, imperious potentate, the very embodiment of sin, the central target of the antislavery attack. He maintained a seraglio in the slave quarters; he bred Negroes like cattle and sold them down the river to certain death in the sugar mills, separating families if that served his purpose, while Southern women suffered in silence the guilty knowledge of their men's infidelity. The happy darkies in this picture became white men in black skins, an oppressed people longing for freedom, the victims of countless atrocities so ghastly as to be unbelievable except for undeniable evidence, forever seeking an opportunity to follow the North Star to freedom. The masses of the white folks were simply poor whites, relegated to ignorance and degeneracy by the slavocracy.

Both lines of the plantation myth have been remarkably prolific, but the more adaptable one has been that of the abolitionists. It has repeatedly readjusted to new conditions while the more legitimate line has courted extinction, running out finally into the decadence perpetrated by Tennessee Williams. Meanwhile, the abolitionist image of brutality persisted through and beyond Reconstruction in the Republican outrage mills and bloody shirt political campaigns. For several decades it was more than overbalanced by the Southern image of Reconstruction horrors, disarmed by prophets of a New South created in the image of the North, and almost completely submerged under the popularity of plantation romances in the generation before Owsley's trainload of ladies ventured into their "Sunny South" of the teens. At about that time, however, the undercurrents began to emerge once again into the mainstream of American thought. In the clever decade of the twenties a kind of neoabolitionist myth of the Savage South was compounded. It seemed that the benighted South, after a period of relative neglect, suddenly became an object of concern to every publicist in the country. One Southern abomination after another was ground through their mills: child labor, peonage, lynching, hookworm, pellagra, the Scopes trial, the Fundamentalist crusade against Al Smith. The guiding genius was Henry L. Mencken, the hatchet man from Baltimore who developed the game of South-baiting into a national pastime, a fine art at which he had no peer. In 1917, when he started constructing his image of "Baptist and Methodist barbarism" below the Potomac, he began with the sterility of Southern literature and went on from there. With characteristic glee he anointed one J. Gordon Coogler of South Carolina "the last bard of Dixie" and quoted his immortal couplet:

> Alas, for the South! Her books have grown fewer—
> She never was much given to literature.

"Down there," Mencken wrote, "a poet is now almost as rare as an oboe-player, a dry-point etcher or a metaphysician." As for "critics, musical composers, painters, sculptors, architects . . . there is not even a bad one between the Potomac mud-flats and the Gulf. Nor an historian. Nor a sociologist. Nor a philosopher. Nor a theologian. Nor a scientist. In all these fields the south is an awe-inspiring blank. . . ."[12] It was as complete a vacuity as the interstellar spaces, the "Sahara of the Bozart," "The Bible Belt." He summed it all up in one basic catalogue of Southern grotesqueries: "Fundamentalism, Ku Kluxry, revivals, lynchings, hog wallow politics—these are the things that always occur to a northerner when he thinks of the south."[13] The South, in short, had fallen prey to its poor whites, who would soon achieve apotheosis in the Snopes family.

It did not end with the twenties. The image was reinforced by a variety of episodes: the Scottsboro trials, chain gang exposés, Bilbo and Rankin, Senate filibusters, labor wars; much later by Central High and Orval Faubus, Emmett Till and Autherine Lucy and James Meredith, bus boycotts and Freedom Riders; and not least of all by the lush growth of literature that covered Mencken's Sahara, with Caldwell's *Tobacco Road* and Faulkner's *Sanctuary* and various other products of what Ellen Glasgow labeled the Southern Gothic and a less elegant Mississippi editor called the "privy school" of literature. In the words of Faulkner's character, Gavin Stevens, the North suffered from a curious "gullibility: a volitionless, almost helpless capacity and eagerness to believe anything about the South not even provided it be derogatory but merely bizarre enough and strange enough."[14] And Faulkner, to be sure, did not altogether neglect that market. Not surprisingly, he was taken in some quarters for a realist, and the image of Southern savagery long obscured the critics' recognition of his manifold merits.

The family line of the plantation myth can be traced only so far in the legendary gentility and savagery of the South. Other family lines seem to be entirely independent—if sometimes on friendly terms. In an excellent study, "The New South Creed, 1865–1900," soon to be published, Paul M. Gaston has traced the evolution of the creed into a genuine myth. In the aftermath of the Civil War, apostles of a "New South," led by Henry W. Grady, preached with almost evangelical fervor the gospel of industry. Their dream, Gaston writes, "was essentially a promise of American life for the South. It proffered all the glitter and glory and freedom from guilt that inhered in the American ideal."[15] From advocacy, from this vision of

[12] Henry L. Mencken, "The Sahara of the Bozart," in *Prejudices: Second Series* (New York, 1920), pp. 136, 137, 139.

[13] Henry L. Mencken, "The South Rebels Again," in Robert McHugh (ed.), *The Bathtub Hoax and Other Blasts & Bravos from the Chicago Tribune* (New York, 1958), p. 249. From a column in the Chicago *Tribune,* December 7, 1924.

[14] William Faulkner, *Intruder in the Dust* (New York, 1948), p. 153.

[15] Paul Morton Gaston, "The New South Creed, 1865–1900" (Ph.D. dissertation, Department of History, University of North Carolina, 1961), p. 193.

the future, the prophets soon advanced to the belief that "their promised land [was] at hand, no longer merely a gleaming goal." "By the twentieth century . . . there was established for many in the South a pattern of belief within which they could see themselves and their section as rich, success-oriented, and just . . . opulence and power were at hand . . . the Negro lived in the best of all possible worlds."[16]

As the twentieth century advanced, and wealth did in fact increase, the creed of the New South took on an additional burden of crusades for good roads and education, blending them into what Francis B. Simkins has called the "trinity of Southern progress": industrial growth, good roads, and schools. When the American Historical Association went to Durham in 1929 for its annual meeting, Robert D. W. Connor of the University of North Carolina presented the picture of a rehabilitated South that had "shaken itself free from its heritage of war and Reconstruction. Its self-confidence restored, its political stability assured, its prosperity regained, its social problems on the way to solution. . . ."[17] Two months before Connor spoke, the New York Stock Exchange had broken badly, and in the aftermath the image he described was seriously blurred, but before the end of the thirties it was being brought back into focus by renewed industrial expansion that received increased momentum from World War II and postwar prosperity.

Two new and disparate images emerged in the depression years, both with the altogether novel feature of academic trappings and affiliations. One was the burgeoning school of sociological regionalism led by Howard W. Odum and Rupert B. Vance at the University of North Carolina. It was neither altogether the image of the Savage South nor that of industrial progress, although both entered into the compound. It was rather a concept of the "Problem South," which Franklin D. Roosevelt labeled "the Nation's Economic Problem No. 1," a region with indisputable shortcomings but with potentialities that needed constructive attention and the application of rational social planning. Through the disciples of Odum as well as the agencies of the New Deal, the vision issued in a flood of social science monographs and programs for reform and development. To one under-graduate in Chapel Hill at the time, it seemed in retrospect that "we had more of an attitude of service to the South as the South than was true later. . . ."[18]

The regionalists were challenged by the Vanderbilt Agrarians, who de-

[16] *Ibid.*, pp. 195, 216.

[17] Robert D. W. Connor, "The Rehabilitation of a Rural Commonwealth," *American Historical Review*, XXXVI (October, 1930), 62.

[18] Alexander Heard, quoted in Wilma Dykeman and James Stokely, *Seeds of Southern Change: The Life of Will Alexander* (Chicago, 1962), p. 303.

veloped a myth of the traditional South. Their manifesto, *I'll Take My Stand,* by Twelve Southerners, appeared by fortuitous circumstance in 1930 when industrial capitalism seemed on the verge of collapse. In reaction against both the progressive New South and Mencken's image of savagery they championed, in Donald Davidson's words, a "traditional society . . . that is stable, religious, more rural than urban, and politically conservative," in which human needs were supplied by "Family, bloodkinship, clanship, folkways, custom, community. . . ."[19] The ideal of the traditional virtues took on the texture of myth in their image of the agrarian South. Of course, in the end, their agrarianism proved less important as a social-economic force than as a context for creative literature. The central figures in the movement were the Fugitive poets John Crowe Ransom, Donald Davidson, Allen Tate, and Robert Penn Warren. But, as Professor Louis Rubin has emphasized, "Through their vision of an agrarian community, the authors of *I'll Take My Stand* presented a critique of the modern world. In contrast to the hurried, nervous life of cities, the image of the agrarian South was of a life in which human beings existed serenely and harmoniously." Their critique of the modern frenzy "has since been echoed by commentator after commentator."[20]

While it never became altogether clear whether the Agrarians were celebrating the aristocratic graces or following the old Jeffersonian dictum that "Those who labor in the earth are the chosen people of God . . . ," most of them seemed to come down eventually on the side of the farmer rather than the planter. Frank L. Owsley, who rediscovered the ante bellum yeoman farmer, was one of them. Insofar as they extolled the yeoman farmer, the Agrarians laid hold upon an image older than any of the others—the Jeffersonian South. David M. Potter, a Southerner in exile at Stanford University, has remarked how difficult it is for many people to realize that the benighted South "was, until recently, regarded by many liberals as the birthplace and the natural bulwark of the Jeffersonian ideal. . . ."[21] The theme has long had an appeal for historians as well as others, Frederick Jackson Turner developed it for the West and William E. Dodd for the South. According to Dodd the democratic, equalitarian South of the Jeffersonian image was the norm; the plantation slavocracy was the great aberration. Dodd's theme has been reflected in the writing of other his-

[19] Donald Davidson, "Why the Modern South Has a Great Literature," *Vanderbilt Studies in the Humanities,* I (1951), 12.

[20] Louis D. Rubin, Jr., "Introduction to the Torchbook Edition," in Twelve Southerners, *I'll Take My Stand* (Torchbook ed.; New York, 1962), pp. xiv, xvii. See also Herman Clarence Nixon, "A Thirty Years' Personal View," *Mississippi Quarterly,* XIII (Spring, 1960), 79, for parallels in recent social criticism.

[21] David M. Potter, "The Enigma of the South," *Yale Review,* LI (Autumn, 1961), 143.

torians, largely in terms of a region subjected to economic colonialism by an imperial Northeast: Charles A. Beard, for example, who saw the sectional conflict as a struggle between agrarianism and industrialism; Howard K. Beale, who interpreted Reconstruction in similar terms; C. Vann Woodward, defender of Populism; Arthur S. Link, who first rediscovered the Southern progressives; and Walter Prescott Webb, who found the nation divided between an exploited South and West on the one hand, and a predatory Northeast on the other. Jefferson, like the South, it sometimes seems, can mean all things to all men, and the Jefferson image of agrarian democracy has been a favorite recourse of Southern liberals, just as his state-rights doctrines have nourished conservatism.

In stark contrast to radical agrarianism there stands the concept of monolithic conservatism in Southern politics. It seems to be a proposition generally taken for granted now that the South is, by definition, conservative—and always has been. Yet the South in the late nineteenth century produced some of the most radical Populists and in the twentieth was a bulwark of Wilsonian progressivism and Roosevelt's New Deal, at least up to a point. A good case has been made out by Arthur S. Link that Southern agrarian radicals pushed Wilson further into progressivism than he intended to go.[22] During the twenties Southern minority leadership in Congress kept up such a running battle against the conservative tax policies of Andrew Mellon that, believe it or not, there was real fear among some Northern businessmen during the 1932 campaign that Franklin D. Roosevelt might be succeeded by that radical Southern income-taxer, John Nance Garner![23] The conservative image of course has considerable validity, but it obscures understanding of such phenomena as Albert Gore, Russell Long, Lister Hill, John Sparkman, Olin D. Johnston, William Fulbright, the Yarboroughs of Texas, or the late Estes Kefauver. In the 1960 campaign the conservative image seriously victimized Lyndon B. Johnson, who started in politics as a vigorous New Dealer and later maneuvered through the Senate the first civil rights legislation since Reconstruction.

The infinite variety of Southern mythology could be catalogued and analyzed endlessly. A suggestive list would include the Proslavery South; the Confederate South; the Demagogic South; the State Rights South; the Fighting South; the Lazy South; the Folklore South; the South of jazz and the blues; the Booster South; the Rapacious South running away with Northern industries; the Liberal South of the interracial movement; the White Supremacy South of racial segregation, which seems to be for some

[22] Arthur S. Link, "The South and the 'New Freedom': An Interpretation," *American Scholar,* XX (Summer, 1951), 314–24.

[23] A. G. Hopkins to Sam Rayburn, July 29, 1932; Rayburn to J. Andrew West, October 26, 1932, in Sam Rayburn Library, Bonham, Texas.

the all-encompassing "Southern way of life"; the Anglo-Saxon (or was it the Scotch-Irish?) South, the most American of all regions because of its native population; or the Internationalist South, a mainstay of the Wilson, Roosevelt, and Truman foreign policies.

The South, then, has been the seedbed for a proliferation of paradoxical myths, all of which have some basis in empirical fact and all of which doubtlessly have, or have had, their true believers. The result has been, in David Potter's words, that the South has become an enigma, "a kind of Sphinx on the American land."[24] What is really the answer to the riddle, what is at bottom the foundation of Southern distinctiveness has never been established with finality, but the quest for a central theme of Southern history has repeatedly engaged the region's historians. Like Frederick Jackson Turner, who extracted the essential West in his frontier thesis, Southern historians have sought to distill the quintessence of the South into some kind of central theme.

In a recent survey of these efforts David L. Smiley of Wake Forest College has concluded that they turn upon two basic lines of thought: "the causal effects of environment, and the development of certain acquired characteristics of the people called Southern."[25] The distinctive climate and weather of the South, it has been argued, slowed the pace of life, tempered the speech of the South, dictated the system of staple crops and Negro slavery—in short, predetermined the plantation economy. The more persuasive suggestions have resulted from concentration upon human factors and causation. The best known is that set forth by U. B. Phillips. The quintessence of Southernism, he wrote in 1928, was "a common resolve indomitably maintained" that the South "shall be and remain a white man's country." Whether "expressed with the frenzy of a demagogue or maintained with a patrician's quietude," this was "the cardinal test of a Southerner and the central theme of Southern history."[26] Other historians have pointed to the rural nature of Southern society as the basic conditioning factor, to the prevalence of the country gentleman ideal imported from England, to the experience of the South as a conscious minority unified by criticism and attack from outside, to the fundamental piety of the Bible Belt, and to various other factors. It has even been suggested by one writer that a chart of the mule population would determine the boundaries of the South.

More recently, two historians have attempted new explanations. In his

[24] Potter, "The Enigma of the South," p. 142.

[25] David L. Smiley, "The Quest for the Central Theme in Southern History," paper read before the Southern Historical Association, Miami Beach, Florida, November 8, 1962, p. 2.

[26] Ulrich B. Phillips, "The Central Theme of Southern History," in E. Merton Coulter (ed.), *The Course of the South to Secession* (New York, 1939), p. 152.

search for a Southern identity, C. Vann Woodward advances several crucial factors: the experience of poverty in a land of plenty; failure and defeat
in a land that glorifies success; sin and guilt amid the legend of American
innocence; and a sense of place and belonging among a people given to
abstraction.[27] David M. Potter, probing the enigma of the South, has found
the key to the riddle in the prevalence of a folk society. "This folk culture,
we know, was far from being ideal or utopian," he writes, "and was in fact
full of inequality and wrong, but if the nostalgia persists was it because
even the inequality and wrong were parts of a life that still had a relatedness and meaning which our more bountiful life in the mass culture seems
to lack?"[28]

It is significant that both explanations are expressed largely in the past
tense, Potter's explicitly in terms of nostalgia. They recognize, by implication at least, still another image—that of the Dynamic or the Changing
South. The image may be rather nebulous and the ultimate ends unclear,
but the fact of change is written inescapably across the Southern scene. The
consciousness of change has been present so long as to become in itself
one of the abiding facts of Southern life. Surely, it was a part of the inspiration for the symposium that resulted in this volume. As far back as the
twenties it was the consciousness of change that quickened the imaginations
of a cultivated and sensitive minority, giving us the Southern renaissance
in literature. The peculiar historical consciousness of the Southern writer,
Allen Tate has suggested, "made possible the curious burst of intelligence
that we get at a crossing of the ways, not unlike, on an infinitesmal scale,
the outburst of poetic genius at the end of the sixteenth century when commercial England had already begun to crush feudal England."[29] Trace it
through modern Southern writing, and at the center—in Ellen Glasgow, in
Faulkner, Wolfe, Caldwell, the Fugitive-Agrarian poets, and all the others
—there is the consciousness of change, of suspension between two worlds, a
double focus looking both backward and forward.

The Southerner of the present generation has seen the old landmarks
crumble with great rapidity: the one-crop agriculture and the very pre-
dominance of agriculture itself, the one-party system, the white primary,
the poll tax, racial segregation, the poor white (at least in his classic connotations), the provincial isolation—virtually all the foundations of the
established order. Yet, sometimes, the old traditions endure in surprising
new forms. Southern folkways have been carried even into the factory,

[27] C. Vann Woodward, "The Search for a Southern Identity," in *The Burden of
Southern History* (Baton Rouge, 1960), pp. 3–25.

[28] Potter, "The Enigma of the South," p. 151.

[29] Allen Tate, "The New Provincialism," *Virginia Quarterly Review,* XXI (Spring,
1945), 272.

and the Bible Belt has revealed resources undreamed of in Mencken's philosophy—but who, in the twenties, could have anticipated Martin Luther King?

One wonders what new images, what new myths, might be nurtured by the emerging South. Some, like Harry Ashmore, have merely written *An Epitaph for Dixie.* It is the conclusion of two Southern sociologists, John M. Maclachlan and Joe S. Floyd, Jr., that present trends "might well hasten the day when the South, once perhaps the most distinctively 'different' American region, will have become . . . virtually indistinguishable from the other urban-industrial areas of the nation."[30] U. B. Phillips long ago suggested that the disappearance of race as a major issue would end Southern distinctiveness. One may wonder if Southern distinctiveness might even be preserved in new conditions entirely antithetic to his image. Charles L. Black, Jr., another *émigré* Southerner (at Yale Law School) has confessed to a fantastic dream that Southern whites and Negroes, bound in a special bond of common tragedy, may come to recognize their kinship. There is not the slightest warrant for it, he admits, in history, sociology, or common sense. But if it should come to pass, he suggests, "The South, which has always felt itself reserved for a high destiny, would have found it, and would have come to flower at last. And the fragrance of it would spread, beyond calculation, over the world."[31]

Despite the consciousness of change, perhaps even more because of it, Southerners still feel a persistent pull toward identification with their native region as a ground for belief and loyalty. Is there not yet something more than nostalgia to the idea of the South? Is there not some living heritage with which the modern Southerner can identify? Is there not, in short, a viable myth of the South? The quest for myth has been a powerful factor in recent Southern literature, and the suspicion is strong that it will irresistibly affect any historian's quest for the central theme of Southern history. It has all too clearly happened before—in the climatic theory, for example, which operated through its geographical determinism to justify the social order of the plantation, or the Phillips thesis of white supremacy, which has become almost a touchstone of the historian's attitude toward the whole contemporary issue of race. "To elaborate a central theme," David L. Smiley has asserted, is "but to reduce a multi-faceted story to a single aspect, and its result . . . but to find new footnotes to confirm revealed truths and prescribed views."[32] The trouble is that the quest for the central

---

[30] John M. Maclachlan and Joe S. Floyd, Jr., *This Changing South* (Gainesville, Fla., 1956), p. 151.

[31] Charles L. Black, Jr., "Paths to Desegregation," *New Republic,* CXXXVII (October 21, 1957), 15.

[32] Smiley, "The Quest for the Central Theme in Southern History," p. 1.

theme, like Turner's frontier thesis, becomes absorbed willy-nilly into the process of myth making.

To pursue the Turner analogy a little further, the conviction grows that the frontier thesis, with all its elaborations and critiques, has been exhausted (and in part exploded) as a source of new historical insight. It is no derogation of insights already gained to suggest that the same thing has happened to the quest for the central theme, and that the historian, *as historian,* may be better able to illuminate our understanding of the South now by turning to a new focus upon the regional mythology.

To undertake the analysis of mythology will no longer require him to venture into uncharted wilderness. A substantial conceptual framework of mythology has already been developed by anthropologists, philosophers, psychologists, theologians, and literary critics. The historian, while his field has always been closely related to mythology, has come only lately to the critique of it. But there now exists a considerable body of historical literature on the American national mythology and the related subject of the national character, and Smith's stimulating *Virgin Land* suggests the trails that may be followed into the idea of the South.

Several trails, in fact, have already been blazed. Nearly forty years ago, Francis Pendleton Gaines successfully traced the rise and progress of the plantation myth, and two recent authors have belatedly taken to the same trail. Howard R. Floan has considerably increased our knowledge of the abolitionist version in his study of Northern writers, *The South in Northern Eyes,* while William R. Taylor has approached the subject from an entirely new perspective in his *Cavalier and Yankee.* Shields McIlwaine has traced the literary image of the poor white, while Stanley Elkins' *Slavery* has broken sharply from established concepts on both sides of that controversial question.[33] One foray into the New South has been made in Paul Gaston's "The New South Creed, 1865–1900." Yet many important areas —the Confederate and Reconstruction myths, for example—still remain almost untouched.

Some of the basic questions that need to be answered have been attacked in these studies; some have not. It is significant that students of literature have led the way and have pointed up the value of even third-rate creative literature in the critique of myth. The historian, however, should be able to contribute other perspectives. With his peculiar time perspective he can seek to unravel the tangled genealogy of myth that runs back from the modern Changing South to Jefferson's yeoman and Kennedy's plantation.

[33] Howard R. Floan, *The South in Northern Eyes, 1831–1860* (Austin, 1958); William R. Taylor, *Cavalier and Yankee: The Old South and American National Character* (New York, 1961); Shields McIlwaine, *The Southern Poor White from Lubberland to Tobacco Road* (Norman, Okla., 1939); Stanley M. Elkins, *Slavery: A Problem in American Institutional and Intellectual Life* (Chicago, 1959).

Along the way he should investigate the possibility that some obscure dialectic may be at work in the pairing of obverse images: the two versions of the plantation, New South and Old, Cavalier and Yankee, genteel and savage, regionalist and agrarian, nativist and internationalist.

What, the historian may ask, have been the historical origins and functions of the myths? The plantation myth, according to Gaines and Floan, was born in the controversy and emotion of the struggle over slavery. It had polemical uses for both sides. Taylor, on the other hand, finds it origin in the psychological need, both North and South, to find a corrective for the grasping, materialistic, rootless society symbolized by the image of the Yankee. Vann Woodward and Gaston have noted its later psychological uses in bolstering the morale of the New South. The image of the Savage South has obvious polemical uses, but has it not others? Has it not served the function of national catharsis? Has it not created for many Americans a convenient scapegoat upon which the sins of all may be symbolically laid and thereby expiated—a most convenient escape from problem solving?[34] To what extent, indeed, has the mythology of the South in general welled up from the subconscious depths? Taylor, especially, has emphasized this question, but the skeptical historian will also be concerned with the degree to which it has been the product or the device of deliberate manipulation by propagandists and vested interests seeking identification with the "real" South.

Certainly any effort to delineate the unique character of a people must take into account its mythology. "Poets," James G. Randall suggested, "have done better in expressing this oneness of the South than historians in explaining it."[35] Can it be that the historians have been looking in the wrong places, that they have failed to seek the key to the enigma where the poets have so readily found it—in the mythology that has had so much to do with shaping character, unifying society, developing a sense of community, of common ideals and shared goals, making the region conscious of its distinctiveness?[36] Perhaps by turning to different and untrodden paths we shall encounter the central theme of Southern history at last on the new frontier of mythology.

[34] "In a sense, the southern writer has been a scapegoat for his fellow Americans, for in taking his guilt upon himself and dramatizing it he has borne the sins of us all." C. Hugh Holman, "The Southerner as American Writer," in Charles Grier Sellers, Jr. (ed.), *The Southerner as American* (Chapel Hill, 1960), p. 199.

[35] James G. Randall, *The Civil War and Reconstruction* (Boston, 1937), pp. 3–4.

[36] Josiah Royce's definition of a "province" is pertinent here: "... any one part of a national domain which is geographically and socially sufficiently unified to have a true consciousness of its own ideals and customs and to possess a sense of its distinction from other parts of the country." Quoted in Frederick Jackson Turner, *The Significance of Sections in American History* (New York, 1932), p. 45.

2

The Colonial Search for a Southern Eden

Louis B. Wright

It is commonly accepted among historians that America has been, to a large degree, an extension of the European imagination—"the dream of Europe." Perhaps less tenable, but nevertheless widely accepted, is the belief that the English were more motivated by imaginative, edenic, even utopian strains of thought than other Europeans. In this article, the late Louis B. Wright, former Director of the Folger Shakespeare Library in Washington, D.C., and History Consultant to the National Geographic Society, focuses on the edenic impulse prompting colonial settlement to the south of Virginia. As settlement proceeded, Mr. Wright argues, and although imaginative visions would at times be altered greatly by economic realities, a highly favorable and temperate climate together with the development of lucrative overseas trade worked to sustain lingering dreams of prosperity. It would seem that The South was fast becoming a state of mind. Indeed, as myth and reality repeatedly intersected in these formative years, many southerners learned that the latter could be as elusive and uncontrollable as the former. Viewed within a wider historical context, however, this utopian thrust carried with it even greater implications for the future. Born of such an impulse, and despite the fiction and delusion often involved, the southern colonies were thus intellectually conditioned to becoming a land at ease with myth and legend. Professor Wright's article supports the premise that within the matrix of myth is to be discovered the soil in which southern history found its roots.

From "Eden and Utopia South of Virginia" in *The Colonial Search for a Southern Eden,* by Louis B. Wright. University, Alabama: University of Alabama Press, 1953. Reprinted by permission of the author.

The notion that the earthly paradise, similar to if not the veritable site of the Scriptural Eden, might be found in some southern region of the New World was widely held in the seventeenth and early eighteenth centuries. Explorers from Virginia expected to find the Great South Sea somewhere to the southwest and they believed its shores would be a land like Eden. In the summer of 1650, Edward Bland, an English merchant resident in Virginia, and Abraham Wood, a militia captain and Indian trader, led an expedition from the site of Petersburg to a point in southwest Virginia where they discovered a river which they believed ran west into the South Sea.[1] The next year Bland printed in London *The Discovery of New Britain* (1651), which carried a preface extolling the land and urging all who desired "the advancement of God's glory by the conversion of the Indians [and] the augmentation of the English commonwealth in extending its liberties" to consider "the present benefit and future profits" of settling the new territory lying between thirty-five and thirty-seven degrees of north latitude.

This geographical position carried a mystical significance. Bland's book reprinted a passage attributed to Sir Walter Raleigh's *Marrow of History,* pointing out that God had placed Eden on the thirty-fifth parallel of north latitude.[2] This location guaranteed an ideal climate of perpetual spring and summer, a garden shaded by palm trees, described by Raleigh as the greatest blessing and wonder of nature. Other earthly paradises, the passage implied, would be found along the thirty-fifth parallel, presumably also shaded by palm trees and producing dates, raisins, spices, and everything else which Adam had had for his comfort. This location would put paradise along a line connecting Newbern and Fayetteville, North Carolina, with Chattanooga and Memphis, Tennessee.

When Lieutenant Governor Alexander Spotswood of Virginia in 1716 led an exploring expedition across the Blue Ridge Mountains, he discovered a river which we now call the Shenandoah but which Spotswood and his company named the Euphrates, after one of the four rivers of Eden, because the country looked to them like paradise. The explanation of why this spot appeared so rosy at that time may be found, however, in an account of the expedition, which must have been one of the most convivial on record. On the very crest of the ridge, the explorers stopped to drink the health of King George I, and the opportunity seemed appropriate to celebrate still further. "We had a good dinner," reported John Fontaine, chronicler of the expedition, "and after it we got the men together, and

---

[1] A part of this first appeared in Louis B. Wright, "The Westward Advance of the Atlantic Frontier," *The Huntington Library Quarterly,* XI (1948), 261–275.

[2] *The First Explorations of the Trans-Allegheny Region by the Virginians, 1650–1674,* ed. Clarence W. Alvord and Lee Bidgood (Cleveland, Ohio, 1912), pp. 112–113.

loaded all their arms, and we drank the King's health in champagne, and fired a volley; the Princess' health in burgundy, and fired a volley; and all the rest of the royal family in claret, and fired a volley. We drank the Governor's health and fired another volley: We had several sorts of liquor, viz., Virginia red wine and white wine, Irish usquebaugh, brandy, shrub, two sorts of rum, champagne, canary, cherry punch, water, cider, etc."[3] After these potations, the driest river bed in Arizona, much less the Valley of Virginia, would have seemed a land flowing with milk and honey.

When William Byrd II of Westover, Virginia, set out to promote the sale of a large tract of land which he had acquired on the Dan River near the border between North Carolina and Virginia, he called his property the Land of Eden and supplied notes to a German-Swiss land agent named Jenner who published in Switzerland in 1737 an alluring promotional tract under the title of *Neu-gefundenes Eden* [New Found Eden]. The description of Byrd's property was intended to leave no doubt in the reader's mind that here indeed was the earthly paradise.

Because promoters had lately been recommending South Carolina and Georgia to hopeful Swiss emigrants as lands of fertility and felicity, Byrd's agent goes to some pains to prove that this particular Eden far surpasses any other. "I am pleased to have the opportunity to make it known to my fellow countrymen, the Swiss," Jenner remarks with an air of objectivity, "that they [may] turn their thoughts to this beautiful, healthful and fertile land, and renounce miserable and unhealthful South Carolina, since [there] they will find after all nothing but poverty, sickness, and early death. . . ." South Carolina, Jenner argues, is trying to create a fortress on its southern border, or Georgia, and wants settlers in that unwholesome spot. And he cites what he says is an English proverb, "Whoever desires to die soon, just go to Carolina."[4]

The exact reverse is Byrd's Land of Eden. There the climate is perfect, the air is pure, the water is as sweet as milk, and the sun shines every day of the year. When it rains, it rains gently at night sufficient to keep the heavenly place well-watered. In this mild and beneficent land, disease is practically unknown and Europeans who come ailing soon find themselves restored to health, and "what is much more miraculous, the old people receive quite new strength, feel as if they were wholly born anew, that is, much stronger, much more light-footed, and in every way much more comfortable than before. . . ."[5]

[3] *Memoirs of a Huguenot Family,* ed. Ann Maury (New York, 1872), pp. 288–289.

[4] Richmond C. Beatty and William J. Mulloy (eds.), *William Byrd's Natural History of Virginia or The Newly Discovered Eden* (Richmond, Va., 1940), pp. 11, 14.

[5] *Ibid.,* pp. 2–3.

The products of this Eden, we will not be surprised to learn, are practically all those which a settler—or the British Board of Trade—might desire. At last, in the Dan River bottoms, if one believes this tract, the production of silk and wine is assured, along with other good things. "One could make silk also very easily," the author asserts, "because the land is full of mulberry trees, and requires little exertion. People have already tried this, and obtained very beautiful silk. The English, however, do not want to go to any trouble in this. Cotton grows in sufficiency in this land. One can merely pick it and spin it, and make all kinds of materials from it for use. It is also a very good ware in trade." Flax, hemp, indigo, grains, fruits, and herbs of all descriptions flourish. Grapes grow in great abundance and have already proved their utility and "therefore nothing is lacking but good grape people."[6] Especially valuable is the sugar maple tree: "This is the most useful tree in the whole world, because one makes wine, spirits, vinegar, honey, and sugar from it, which comes from its juice."[7] Verily nothing was lacking in Eden but a happy people to consume its products. Unfortunately the ship loaded with the Swiss emigrants who heeded the siren words of the promoter wrecked off the coast of North Carolina and only a handful survived to reach the promised land. For all the fine promises, William Byrd never succeeded in turning the rich bottom lands along the Dan River into the paradise his agent pictured. To this day the land is reasonably fertile but its products have always been such prosaic things as corn, cotton, and tobacco.

Notwithstanding William Byrd's low opinion of South Carolina, as indicated in the *New Found Eden,* and an equally low opinion of North Carolina, which he had expressed in *The History of the Dividing Line,* the Carolinas proved highly profitable to the empire and won the approval of merchants, bankers, and politicians in London. Although their products were not precisely the ones which the mercantilists had originally intended, they fulfilled perfectly the current idea of the proper relation between colony and mother country. Even that irascible and hard-to-please agent of the Crown, Edward Randolph, surveyor-general of His Majesty's Customs for North America, had only words of praise in a report which he made to the Board of Trade in London on March 16, 1699. "The great improvement made in this Province is wholly owing to the industry and labour of the Inhabitants," he wrote. "They have applied themselves to make such commodities as might increase the revenue of the Crown, as Cotton, Wool, Ginger, Indigo, etc. But finding them not to answer the end, they are set upon making Pitch, Tar, and Turpentine, and planting of rice, and can

---

[6] *Ibid.,* p. 33.
[7] *Ibid.,* p. 35.

send over great quantityes yearly, if they had encouragement from England, . . ."[8]

The Carolinas, Randolph reported, are a much better source for naval stores than New England: "My Lords, I did formerly present Your Lordships with proposals for supplying England with Pitch and Tar, Masts and all our Naval Stores from New England. . . . But since my arrival here I find I am come into the only place for such commodities upon the Continent of America."[9] By this statement he meant the *best* place, not literally the only place. The value of the tar, pitch, masts, and other supplies helped to bring prosperity to the Carolinas and security to the Royal Navy.

In other ways the Carolinas, especially South Carolina, pleased the mercantilists. A constant stream of raw materials poured out of Charleston and into English channels of industry and commerce. For instance, South Carolina developed a great trade in deerskins needed by the leathermakers and glovers. Furs from the backcountry also added to the revenue. Unlike the Chesapeake Bay colonies, which depended upon tobacco for their money crop, the Southeast developed a diverse commerce centered in Charleston, and of this commerce, the deerskin and fur trade contributed much to colonial and imperial prosperity.

So much attention has been lavished on the fur trade of other regions that we forget the importance of the South in this connection. Louisiana is still the largest fur-producing region in North America. Throughout the eighteenth century Charleston, South Carolina, was the great skin and fur market. Some of the toughest characters in all North America brought their pack trains of deerskins and furs to Charleston each spring. The tinkle of the packhorse bells and the clatter of hoofs on the cobble stones of the Battery brought Charlestonians to their windows to view picturesque traders, some well-known and famous as Indian fighters.

The caravans often brought long strings of Indian captives to be sold as slaves to Barbádos and other islands of the West Indies. We must also remember this dark chapter in the history of commerce. Charleston was an important slaving port. Captured Indians by the hundreds were sold to ship captains headed for the West Indies, and Negroes by the thousands were brought into Charleston from Africa. Indian slaves were not dependable in the Carolinas, for they might escape to the forests and make their way back to their tribes, but African Negroes had no such hope. They proved useful laborers in the pine forests and hot fields of the coastal plain. The traffic in slaves and the commodities which they produced made rich

---

[8] Alexander S. Salley, Jr. (ed.), *Narratives of Early Carolina, 1650–1708* (New York, 1911), p. 207.

[9] *Ibid.*, p. 208.

the merchants and shipowners of London and Bristol as well as their agents in Charleston.

South Carolina gave promise late in the seventeenth century of becoming the dream colony of the English mercantilists. Some of the inhabitants wrote to London in the year 1691 that "We are encouraged with severall new rich Comodityes as Silck, Cotton, Rice and Indigo, which are naturally produced here."[10] Silk remained a delusion, but rice, indigo, and eventually cotton became indeed "rich commodities." The first of these to be grown extensively was rice, which flourished in the alluvial swamp lands of the coastal region. Although colonists even in Virginia had experimented with rice, not until the last decade of the seventeenth century, in South Carolina, was it grown extensively. The legend that a shipmaster from Madagascar, accidentally touching at Charleston in 1696, left a half-bushel of rice seed from which grew the Carolina rice industry, is apparently only a half-truth,[11] but from that date until the mid-nineteenth century rice was an increasingly important article of commerce with England.

To an extraordinary woman, Eliza Lucas, South Carolina owed the development of the production of indigo, a vegetable dye much in demand in the eighteenth century when clothing of this hue was especially fashionable. In the year 1739, Eliza Lucas, then just sixteen, found herself established as manager of a plantation on the west side of the Ashley River above Charleston. Her father, Lieutenant Colonel George Lucas, was stationed at Antigua in the West Indies, but since his wife was sickly and could not endure that climate, he moved his family to South Carolina and put this remarkable girl in charge of the family plantation. In a letter to her father written in July 1739, she reported that she was trying "to bring the Indigo, Ginger, Cotton, and Lucern and Casada [cassava] to perfection and had greater hopes from the Indigo (if I could have the seed earlier next year from the West Indies) than of ye rest of ye things I had try'd."[12] After many discouragements, not only in raising the plants, but in producing the dye, Eliza achieved success. By 1747–48, the production was such that the port of Charleston exported 138,334 pounds of the dyestuff. When the British government offered a bounty in 1748 for the production of the dye in the British-American colonies, some growers found it so profitable that they doubled their capital every three or four years.[13]

The production of indigo within the empire was important, for the

---

[10] Lewis C. Gray and Esther K. Thompson, *History of Agriculture in the Southern United States* (Washington, D. C., 1933), I, 278; quoted from the *Calendar of State Papers, America and West Indies, 1677–1680*, p. 59.

[11] *Ibid.*, I, 278–279.

[12] *Ibid.*, I, 290.

[13] *Ibid.*, I, 292.

source of most of the dye would otherwise have been the French West Indies. Since England was at war with France through a good part of the eighteenth century, it was imperative that she not buy this useful commodity from the enemy. The power of fashion was such, however, that the clothiers and dyers would have obtained the dye even if they had been obliged to deal in the enemy's black market. The solution of course was to stimulate production in the tropical and semi-tropical areas of the British dominions, an operation which proved highly successful.

The production of cotton, another article which England had bought outside the empire, was less successful than indigo and rice, but some cotton was produced in the various Southern colonies and in the West Indies in the period before the Revolution. Few of us stop to realize the importance of cotton in the social progress of mankind. The importation into England of cheap cotton textiles from India, brought about by the expansion of the East India Company's activities in the seventeenth century, for the first time made it possible for Englishmen of average means to be reasonably clean. Up to that time linen was the only available fabric for undergarments, and linen, then as now, was expensive.[14]

The East India Company brought in chintzes, muslins, calicoes, and other fabrics. The word calico comes from the name of an Indian town, Calicut. Though the importation of cotton from India gave English merchants an article of trade much in demand on the continent of Europe, the East India Company had to pay out cash for its textiles. If raw cotton could be produced within the empire and woven at home, this would be an advantage to both the industry and commerce of Great Britain.

Although efforts continued throughout the colonial period to stimulate the production of raw cotton, only small amounts reached the markets. In the year 1768, Virginia led the South by exporting 43,350 pounds of ginned cotton. In the same year South Carolina exported only 3,000 pounds, and Georgia, only 300 pounds.[15] During most of the period, planters lacked confidence in the stability of cotton prices—an old complaint—and they found other crops more profitable. The separation of the lint from the seed was also a troublesome problem. Although roller gins were known and used in the colonial period, not until Eli Whitney invented the saw gin in the last decade of the eighteenth century was this problem solved.

By the end of the century South Carolina and Georgia were producing several million pounds of cotton. Although the colonies were now politically free of Great Britain, trade retained many of its old characteristics. The South continued to supply raw materials for English industry; and of

[14] James A. Williamson, *The Ocean in English History* (Oxford, 1941), p. 107.

[15] Gray & Thompson, *History of Agriculture*, I, 184. See also *Ibid.*, II, 680 ff.

these raw materials, cotton rapidly increased in importance. By the mid-nineteenth century, cotton spinning and weaving had become one of Great Britain's most valuable industries, and raw cotton from the plantations of the Southern states was an essential of international trade. By a curious irony of history, cotton textiles of English manufacture in the nineteenth century ruined the native weaving industry of India, which had first supplied cottons to Britain. And by another reversal of the process, the cheap labor in the Indian cotton mills in the twentieth century ruined the English textile industry by destroying its Asiatic market for cotton goods.

Paralleling the British emphasis on trade in the eighteenth century was a growing spirit of humanitarianism. As in the United States in the twentieth century, the brotherhood of man and the acquisition of material property were somehow equated. As humanitarians and mercantilists, often one and the same, viewed the southern American colonies, they warmed with enthusiasm over the prospect of discovering there at last the perfect paradise where all men could be happy and prosperous as they produced the commodities which served the best interests of the British Empire. Occasionally the humanitarians contemplated the institution of slavery, which seemed to be necessary for prosperity, and found it disturbing; but usually they salved their consciences by thinking of the boon of Christianity which slavery had brought to the heathen whom they imported from Africa. George Whitefield, the evangelist, for example, wept over man's sins and distress, but he recommended slavery for Georgia and helped pay the expenses of Bethesda, his orphan home, from the profits of a South Carolina plantation worked with slaves.

As the humanitarian planners contemplated the opportunities in the South, they had visions of new Edens in which the poor and oppressed of England would find a refuge; there the erstwhile indigents would work out their salvation and keep a steady stream of profitable raw materials pouring into the home ports. Some of the planners had read More's *Utopia,* Bacon's essay "Of Plantations," James Harrington's *The Commonwealth of Oceana* (1656), or some other treatise on ideal commonwealths. The spirit of social experiment was in the air. Furthermore the atmosphere was also heavily charged with the excitement of speculation. During 1719 and the early part of 1720, men and women rushed to buy stock in the South Sea Company which doubled, trebled, quadrupled and further multiplied in value as they watched it. Before the bubble burst in August 1720, other speculations promised similar incredible profits. It was an age of "projectors," or promoters, some of whom picked the region embracing this very spot as the scene of their activities. No scheme seemed impossible, not even Swift's satirical project to extract sunbeams from cucumbers.

For reasons not difficult to comprehend, the hope of finding a fruitful land in the South appealed strongly to Scots. No country could have been more unlike the hills of Scotland than the coastal plains and river bottoms of the Carolinas and Georgia. Perhaps that was its greatest attraction. During the eighteenth century Scots were among the most important immigrant groups received in the Southern colonies. Because we usually think of the Scots as a practical and thrifty people, convinced that destiny has already settled the affairs of man in accordance with the theology of John Calvin, it may be a surprise to find that some of the most fantastic of the Utopian projects were dreamed up by Scots.

One of the better known and most colorful schemes was hatched in the mind of a Scottish baronet, Sir Robert Montgomery of Skelmorly, who in 1717 published *A Discourse Concerning the design'd Establishment Of a New Colony To The South of Carolina, In The Most delightful Country of the Universe.* This was a plan to establish a colony in the country embraced between the mouths of the Savannah and Altamaha rivers and extending westward to the Great South Sea [the Pacific Ocean]. That included most of the present state of Alabama, not to mention the states westward to the California coast.

Sir Robert described this country, which he named Azilia, as "our future Eden," and he further declared that English writers "universally agree that Carolina, and especially in its Southern Bounds, is the most amiable Country in the Universe: that Nature has not bless'd the World with any Tract, which can be preferable to it, that Paradise, with all her Virgin Beauties, may be modestly suppos'd at most but equal to its Native Excellencies."[16] This territory which exceeded Paradise itself in excellence was claimed by South Carolina, but the Lords Proprietors were more than glad to encourage Scottish settlers who would serve as a protection against the Spaniards in Florida and the French in Louisiana. Accordingly they granted permission to Sir Robert and his colleagues to settle Azilia.

In a literary genre characterized by optimism, Sir Robert Montgomery's *Discourse* is surely one of the most hopeful ever printed. Azilia, as he describes it, "lies in the same Latitude with Palestine Herself, That promis'd Canaan, which was pointed out by God's own Choice, to bless the Labours of a favourite People. It abounds with Rivers, Woods, and Meadows. Its gentle Hills are full of Mines, Lead, Copper, Iron, and even some of Silver. 'Tis beautified with odiferous Plants, green all the Year. . . . The Air is healthy, and the Soil in general fruitful, and of infinite Variety; Vines, naturally flourishing upon the Hills, bear Grapes in most luxurious Plenty. They have every Growth which we possess in England, and almost every Thing that England wants besides. The Orange and the

---

[16] J. Max Patrick (ed.), *Azilia: A Discourse by Sir Robert Montgomery, 1717, Projecting a Settlement in the Colony Later Known as Georgia,* Emory University Publications: Sources and Reprints, Series IV (Atlanta, 1948), p. 18.

Limon thrive in the same common Orchard with the Apple, and the Pear-Tree, Plumbs, Peaches, Apricots, and Nectarins bear from Stones in three years growing. The Planters raise large Orchards of these Fruits to feed their Hogs with."[17] To Scots and Englishmen, who knew oranges from Seville and lemons from Portugal merely as symbols of luxury, this country, in the same latitude as Palestine, must have appeared indeed as a new Canaan.

To help him in the colonization of Azilia, Montgomery had as associates Aaron Hill, a theatrical poet who claimed to have an invention for making potash, and Amos Kettleby, merchant and politician of London, whom the South Carolina Assembly had dismissed in the previous year from his post as colonial agent. Montgomery was to have the title of Margrave, with a great palace at the exact center of the district where he would reside. There he would live in splendor and rule over a feudal principality peopled with a hierarchy of gentry, tenants, and slaves. Aaron Hill and Amos Kettleby appear to have been more concerned with the financial returns from the venture than with the glories of title.

The chapter in Montgomery's tract headed "Of some Designs in View for making Profit" assures the reader that at long last imperial and mercantilist ambitions are about to be realized in Azilia. "Our Prospects in this Point are more extensive than we think it needful to discover," Montgomery remarks with an air of mystery. "It were a shame shou'd we confine the Fruitfulness of such a rich and lovely Country to some single Product, which Example first makes common, and the being common robs of Benefit. Thus Sugar in Barbadoes, Rice in Carolina, and Tobacco in Virginia take up all the Labours of their People, overstock the Markets, stifle the Demand, and make their Industry their Ruin, . . ." Azilia, however, will not be a one-crop country. Instead it will produce the very commodities which England still has had to buy from foreigners. Montgomery makes this explicit: "Coffee, Tea, Figs, Raisins, Currants, Almonds, Olives, Silk, Wine, Cochineal, and a great Variety of still more rich Commodities which we are forc'd to buy at mighty Rates from Countries lying in the very Latitude of our Plantations: All these we certainly shall Propagate, . . . mean while we shall confine our first Endeavours to such easy Benefits as will (without the smallest waiting for the Growth of Plants) be offer'd to our Industry from the spontaneous Wealth which overruns the Country."[18] With Aaron Hill's alleged invention in mind, Montgomery promises that potash will be a source of immediate profit.

The happy Margravate of Azilia, alas, was doomed to be a delusion. To transport colonists, to clear land, to build a palace, and even to make

[17] *Ibid.*, p. 18.
[18] *Ibid.*, p. 23.

potash required capital. There were also political complications. Discouraged at frustrations and delays, Sir Robert Montgomery sold his interest late in 1718 to Aaron Hill the poet. But after the failure of the South Sea Company in 1720, not even Aaron Hill's literary style was sufficiently purple to lure investors in Azilia, and the scheme collapsed. Yet such was the hopefulness of the projectors that one of them, possibly Hill, published two further pamphlets late in 1720, one of which was entitled *A Description of the Golden Islands, with an Account of the Undertaking Now on Foot for Making a Settlement There.* This tract outlined a plan for making a paradise of the sea islands along the coast of Georgia and producing there not only silk and almonds, but "many more Fruits and Drugs, growing in Persia, in India about Lahore, in China, and in Japan."[19] But the public had its fingers too thoroughly burned on the South Sea Company stock to take an interest in the Golden Islands. The Azilian project is worth detailed consideration, however, because it epitomizes the search for Eden which had obsessed British thinking since the beginning of the colonial effort and which was to continue to the end.

Another Scottish baronet, Sir Alexander Cuming of Coulter, even more erratic than Sir Robert Montgomery, conceived a project to settle three hundred thousand Jews on the Cherokee tribal lands in the backcountry of South Carolina. This proposal for a Zion on the Carolina frontier had as its object the relief of oppressed Jewish families in Europe by taking them out of crowded ghettos and establishing them on the land where they could turn their talents and industry to farming and the production of commodities useful to the British Empire. If the government would underwrite the enterprise, Sir Alexander promised, it would presently be able to retire a large portion of the national debt from the profits.

Sir Alexander attributed his zeal for colonial affairs to a vision of his wife's which suggested that he make a journey to the backcountry of South Carolina. Considering the Scot's peculiarities, we cannot escape the suspicion that his wife's vision was a clever ruse to procure a little peace at home. But whatever the motive, Sir Alexander set out in 1729 on a self-appointed mission to Carolina and the Cherokees. Surely the Scottish baronet had read books similar to those which had sent Cervantes' good knight of La Mancha on his adventures, for his travels read like a chapter from *Don Quixote.* Leaving Charleston on March 13, 1730, Sir Alexander travelled during the following month nearly a thousand miles through the Cherokee tribes. Armed to the teeth and boasting of the power and brilliance of his King, George II, the baronet astonished his Indian hearers and persuaded them that he was a great chief representing a king whose power reached even to the hills of South Carolina. At a tribal council he

[19] *Ibid.,* p. 12.

persuaded the chiefs to kneel and swear allegiance to King George—or so he thought—and he had himself acclaimed the King's viceroy. So persuasive was Sir Alexander's eloquence that he induced six Cherokees, a minor chief and five warriors, to set out with him for London and the King's court. Near Charleston they picked up another stray Indian. When they all reached England, the chief was a king and the other Indians were described as generals or chiefs. On June 18, 1730, King George received the Scot and his Indian protegés. During the next three months the Cherokee "king" and his fellow "chiefs" were the sensation of London. They were entertained, feted, and taught English vices. On September 28, the play of *Orinoco* was performed in their honor at Lincoln's Inn Fields, and so great was the public excitement over the Indians that the theatre's box office receipts trebled that night. When they returned to their tribesmen, the Indians' report of the glories of the English nation probably helped to keep the Cherokees loyal to England in the succeeding wars with France.[20]

Fantastic as were Sir Alexander Cuming's schemes for Cherokee-Jewish Utopias in the foothills of Carolina, the publicity which they received helped to focus further interest on the Southern colonies. The settlement of Georgia itself was a manifestation of the freshly aroused humanitarian, mercantilist, and imperialistic interest in expansion south of the Carolina settlements.

During the summer of 1730, about the time the Cherokees were exciting the London populace, General James Oglethorpe and some of his friends were petitioning the King to make them a grant of land south of the Carolina border "for settling poor persons of London."[21] The plan, as every school child knows, was prompted by a desire on the part of this philanthropic group to provide relief for imprisoned debtors. It received favorable consideration from the government for other reasons. The need for a bulwark against Spain and France from the South and southwest was greater than ever. And once more the merchants and bankers of London were dreaming of a source for those raw materials which they still found it necessary to buy from their enemies. Moved by so many worthy reasons, the King granted a charter to Oglethorpe and his fellow trustees on June 9, 1732. This time a Utopian scheme was to succeed, but not precisely as Oglethorpe or the government planned it. For few debtors ever came to Georgia and once more the vision of exotic produce was a mirage. Nevertheless Georgia did become a useful colony and an element in the imperial organization.

[20] Verner W. Crane, *The Southern Frontier, 1670–1732* (Durham, N. C., 1928), p. 280.

[21] E. Merton Coulter, *Georgia: A Short History* (Chapel Hill, N. C., 1947), pp. 17–18.

The Trustees tried earnestly to make Georgia the combination of Eden and Utopia which they had envisioned. They opened the country to oppressed folk not only of England but of the Continent as well. They passed regulations aimed at keeping the commonwealth pure by excluding rum and forbidding slavery. And they were determined to produce silk, wine, olives, and other good things which had always eluded Englishmen. A poet writing in the *South Carolina Gazette* in 1733 pictured the new colony as a garden of Hesperides. Its silks would clothe England's beauties; its wine would flow unstinted, "refreshing Labour and dispelling Woe"; and its orchards and groves would be fruitful with dates, lemons, oranges, citrons, limes, almonds, tea and coffee.[22] The trustees included some hardheaded businessmen who knew such beneficence would not be spontaneous, even in Paradise, in the rational eighteenth century. They therefore encouraged Swiss and other Continental silkworkers to come to Georgia; they ordered every recipient of a grant of land to plant mulberry trees; and they encouraged experimentation with other exotic commodities. But it was all to no avail. Georgia followed South Carolina in depending upon rice, the skin and fur trade, and upon naval stores for the basis of its economy.

The search for an exotic Eden did not end with the settlement of Georgia. The ink on the Treaty of Paris was hardly dry in 1763 before Archibald Menzies of Megerny Castle, Perthshire, devised a plan to people Florida with Armenians, Greeks, and Minorcans, who would be expert in growing olives, grapes, and silk worms. Nothing came of his proposal but four years later a brother Scot, Dr. Andrew Turnbull, and two English associates, Sir William Duncan and Sir Richard Temple, formed a partnership to settle other Greeks, Italians, and Minorcans in Florida. They succeeded actually in establishing a group at New Smyrna on the coast below St. Augustine, but quarreling and fighting among the settlers quickly ruined the enterprises in which the promoters had pinned such hope. When a Scot takes leave of practical matters and begins to spin ingenious plans, the extent of his fantasy is illimitable

The faith in a Southern Utopia persisted and manifested itself in numerous projects throughout the colonial period and afterward. Time will not permit even the mention of various schemes to create a paradise in the lands south of Virginia. Perhaps the most visionary of all was a project of a sentimental and mystical German from Saxony, one Christian Gottlieb Priber, who devised a plan for a Utopia among the Cherokees on the headwaters of the Tennessee River. A precursor of Rousseau, Priber's state represented a fusion of ideas from Plato's *Republic,* current doctrines of humanitarianism, and concepts of the noble savage which

[22] *Ibid.*

had cropped up from time to time. His efforts to found a communistic state among the Cherokees and to teach them to resist the inroads of the whites and the knavery of traders aroused the antagonism of Georgians who succeeded in arresting Priber in 1743. He was kept a political prisoner and died at Frederica on St. Simon's Island a few years later. Among his manuscripts was one describing his projected Utopian state as the "Kingdom of Paradise." In the opinion of his captors it was "extremely wicked" because "he enumerates many whimsical privileges and natural rights, as he calls them, which his citizens are to be entitled to, particularly dissolving marriages and allowing community of women, and all kinds of licentiousness."[23] His greatest sin, however, lay in his success in winning the friendship of the Indians and developing an organization which threatened the expansion of the British.

The British Empire profited immensely from the Southern colonies, but the mercantilists never succeeded in making these colonies the source of all the exotic commodities they yearned to produce within the empire. The economic planners, then as now, never grasped all of the factors involved in their schemes. For example, they never realized that silk production required both skilled and cheap labor, which the colonies always lacked, a lack which indeed has always been a serious problem in the New World.

The dream of making the South the source of many of the luxuries which mankind requires has never died. In modern times we have seen a certain realization of these hopes in the expansion of the textile industry. If we do not produce worm silk in the South, we at least have manufactories of rayon, nylon, and other chemical substitutes. A Japanese economist was in my office recently lamenting the shift in fashion and production, which had ruined the silk industry of Japan.

Not far from where Swiss and Italian colonists in the eighteenth century sought to establish new industries on the upper Savannah River the United States government is today building a great plant to transform hydrogen into energy. The end product of that effort is yet unknown. Some believe that ultimately the release of energy from such an abundant source will solve most of the problems of mankind. Others, more gloomy, see in it the destruction of civilization. But we are witnessing one more effort to establish Utopia, even at the risk of universal destruction.

[23] Verner W. Crane, "A Lost Utopia of the First American Frontier," *Sewanee Review*, XXVII (1919), pp. 48–61.

3

Slavery and the Meaning of America

David Brion Davis

Early American history strongly reflects a European climate of opinion which for centuries had been nurtured by mythical predispositions toward a New World. It was within a utopian and mythical atmosphere that the transoceanic expeditions and geographic discoveries of Christopher Columbus and others took place. Long before settlement, America served as a useful fiction, providing Europeans with an imaginative escape into a dreamworld of social, political, and religious alternatives. It seems plausible to argue, then, that this broadly based European utopian mentality spawned the ideas and sentiments necessary to the development of an American mythology. Born in the romantic dreams of Europeans, reared in a tradition of glory and heroism, America soon became a land particularly receptive to the mythic. Contemporaneous with these utopian-mythical visions of and for America, however, were the beginnings of what a later scholar would see as the core of an American dilemma—black slavery. According to David Brion Davis of Yale University, the simultaneous development of utopianism and slavery has given the nation a paradoxical heritage. The presence of slavery in the Promised Land of the New World suggests many important questions about the ultimate meaning of America. Much of the English utopian vision of North America was directed toward what is now the American South—toward the "Southern Eden." Davis's paradox is magnified and intensified there simply by virtue of the growing number of slaves. It is a fact that slavery became legal in all the English colonies and that trade in that commodity

Reprinted from David Brion Davis, *The Problem of Slavery in Western Culture*. Copyright © 1966 by Cornell University. Used by permission of Cornell University Press.

became an economic mainstay in New England. Still, the "American dilemma" would come to be seen as a southern phenomenon writ large—not easily swept away by George Bancroft's tide of democracy, including his racial rationale.

From the time of the first discoveries Europeans had projected ancient visions of liberation and perfection into the vacant spaces of the New World. Explorers approached the uncharted coasts with vague preconceptions of mythical Atlantis, Antillia, and the Saint Brendan Isles. The naked savages, living in apparent freedom and innocence, awakened memories of terrestrial paradise and the Golden Age described by the ancients. Even the practical-minded Columbus fell under the spell of the gentle natives on the Gulf of Paria, who wore golden ornaments and lived in a land of lush vegetation and delicious fruits. He concluded in August 1498, that he had arrived on the "nipple" of the earth, which reached closer to Heaven than the rest of the globe, and that the original Garden of Eden was nearby.[1] Seventeen years later, when Sir Thomas More began writing *Utopia,* he naturally chose the Western Hemisphere as his setting.

Columbus's successors pursued elusive visions of golden cities and fountains of youth; their narratives revived and nourished the utopian dreams of Europe. From antiquity Western thought had been predisposed to look to nature for the universal norms of human life. Since "nature" carried connotations of origin and birth as well as of intrinsic character, philosophers often associated valid norms with what was original in man's primeval state. They contrasted the restraints, prejudices, and corrupting tastes of civilized life with either a former age of virtue or a simpler, more primitive state of society.[2] Many of the explorers and early commentators on America drew upon this philosophic tradition; in the New World they found an Elysium to serve as a standard for criticizing the perverted manners of Europe. Catholic missionaries, being dedicated to ideals of renunciation and asceticism, saw much to admire in the simple contentment of the Indians, whose

[1] Samuel Eliot Morison, *Admiral of the Ocean Sea: A Life of Christopher Columbus* (Boston, 1942), pp. 556–557.

[2] Arthur O. Lovejoy, Gilbert Chinard, George Boas, and Ronald S. Crane, *A Documentary History of Primitivism and Related Ideas,* I (Baltimore, 1935), pp. 12–18, 109–111.

mode of living seemed to resemble that of the first Christians. As Gilbert Chinard has pointed out, the *voyageurs* and Jesuit priests who compared the evils of Europe with the freedom, equality, and felicitous life of the American savages, contributed unwittingly to the revolutionary philosophy of the eighteenth century.[3]

Some writers, to be sure, described the Indians as inferior degenerates or as Satan's children and presented a contrary image of America as an insalubrious desert. Antonello Gerbi has documented the long dispute over the nature of the New World— "mondo nascente o neonato, mondo deserto e misero."[4] Howard Mumford Jones has recently shown that America was conceived at once as an idyllic Arcadia and as a land of cannibalism, torture, and brutality, where extremities of human greed and cruelty were matched by the unexpected terrors and monstrosities of the wilderness.[5] But in Hebrew and Christian thought the idea of wilderness had long been linked with rebirth and fulfillment. After being delivered from slavery in Egypt, the children of Israel had crossed the Red Sea and had wandered in the wilderness for forty years before finding the Promised Land. The desert was a place of refuge and purification, of suffering and perseverance; and no matter what hardships it offered, there was the assurance that a fertile paradise would ultimately emerge from its desolate wastes. Thanks to the researches of George H. Williams, we know what an important part such imagery played in Christian ideas of redemption.[6] The wilderness might be thought of as a purely spiritual state, or as the abode of monks, hermits, or persecuted sects. But early American colonists could hardly escape the symbolic implications of a baptismal crossing of the Atlantic, or of dwelling in a land which could be seen as either desert or primeval garden. The New World, like the wilderness in both the Old and New Testaments, was a place of extraordinary temptation, obligation, and promise.

[3] Gilbert Chinard, *L'Amérique et le rêve exotique dans la littérature française au XVIIe et au XVIIIe siècle* (Paris, 1913), pp. v–vii, 119–150, 431. See also Lois Whitney, *Primitivism and the Idea of Progress in English Popular Literature of the Eighteenth Century* (Baltimore, 1934), pp. 40–48 and *passim;* Maren-Sofie Røstvig, *The Happy Man: Studies in the Metamorphoses of a Classical Ideal, 1600–1700* (Oslo, 1954), pp. 16, 41–46 and *passim;* Hoxie Neale Fairchild, *The Noble Savage: A Study in Romantic Naturalism* (New York, 1928), pp. 10–13 and *passim.*

[4] Antonello Gerbi, *La disputa del Nuovo Mondo: storia di una polemica, 1750–1900* (Milano, 1955).

[5] Howard Mumford Jones, *O Strange New World! American Culture: The Formative Years* (New York, 1963), pp. 35–70.

[6] George H. Williams, *Wilderness and Paradise in Christian Thought: The Biblical Experience of the Desert in the History of Christianity and the Paradise Theme in the Theological Idea of the University* (New York, 1962), pp. 10–137.

While a growing literature celebrated America as a symbol of nature, free from the avarice, luxury, and materialism of Europe, promoters and colonizers saw the virgin land as a place for solving problems and satisfying desires. This was true of the conquistadores who tried to recreate the age of chivalric romance; it was true of the Jesuits who followed Manuel da Nóbrega to Brazil, determined to purify morals and spread the faith; it was true of the English Puritans who sought to build a New Jerusalem as a model of piety for the rest of the world; it was true of the drifters and ne'er-do-wells, the bankrupts and sleazy gentlemen, who fluttered to the New World like moths drawn to a light. In America things would be better, for America was the Promised Land. It could be said, of course, that America was an asylum for scoundrels, adventurers, and religious fanatics. But in time much of the magic of the virgin continent seemed to rub off on its conquerors. French humanitarians, for example, found it easy to shift their enthusiasm from noble savage to peace-loving Quaker. In Saint-John de Crèvecoeur's *Letters from an American Farmer* we see perhaps the clearest picture of the American idyll, a skillful weaving together of primitivist, pastoral, and democratic themes, the portrayal of a land in which individual opportunity and social progress are somehow merged with the simple, self-denying virtues of Seneca and Vergil.

This long tradition, based on a mixture of biblical and classical sources, helped to shape the American's image of himself as the new Adam of the West, a being unencumbered by the fears and superstitions of a moldering civilization, a wise innocent dwelling in a terrestrial paradise. He was at once the Happy Husbandman, content to enjoy the serene blessings of a simple, rural life, and an adventurous pioneer, expansive and supremely confident of his ability to improve the world. Such an image contained an intrinsic contradiction which contributed to severe tensions in the face of rapid social and economic change. But if Americans were often inclined to see Satan fast at work corrupting their new Eden, this only enhanced the moral importance of their mission. And by the time of the Revolution many European liberals looked to America as the hope of mankind, for it was there that institutions seemed most clearly modeled on nature's simple plan. By reconciling nature and human progress, the newly independent states appeared to have fulfilled the ancient dream of a more perfect society.[7]

[7] For discussions of the themes of innocence, moralism, and the American mission, see Charles L. Sanford, *The Quest for Paradise: Europe and the American Moral Imagination* (Urbana, Ill., 1961), pp. 34–55, 86, 106–110; R. W. B. Lewis, *The American Adam: Innocence, Tragedy and Tradition in the Nineteenth Century* (Chicago, 1955), pp. 4–34 and *passim;* Perry Miller, *The New England Mind: The Seventeenth Century* (Cambridge, Mass., 1954), pp. 463–491; Miller, *Errand into the Wilderness* (Cambridge,

. . . Yet slavery had been linked from the very beginning with what Edmundo O'Gorman had called "the invention of America." The African voyages promoted by Prince Henry of Portugal prepared the way for the first crossing of the Atlantic; and when Columbus arrived in Lisbon in 1477 the trade in Negro slaves was a flourishing enterprise. The same Columbus who identified the Gulf of Paria as the gateway to the Garden of Eden had no compunction about sending hundreds of Indians to be sold in the slave marts of Seville, although some two hundred died on the first voyage and had to be thrown into the sea.[8] It was thus the discoverer of America who initiated the transatlantic slave trade, which moved originally from west to east.

It was soon apparent, however, as the Spanish came close to exterminating the native inhabitants of Hispaniola, that successful colonization would require a fresh supply of laborers. Negro slaves arrived in the New World at least as early as 1502, and by 1513 the sale of licenses for importing Negroes was a source of profit for the Spanish government.[9] Following the Guinea current and trade winds, Portuguese ships provided the colonists with a mounting supply of slaves but seldom with enough to meet the insatiable demand. As Negro labor became indispensable for Spanish and then Portuguese colonization, European traders and African chieftains slowly built a vast commercial system which brought a profound transformation in African culture and stunted the growth of other commerce between Europe and the Dark Continent.[10]

For three centuries the principal maritime powers competed with one another in the lucrative slave trade and carried at least fifteen million Africans to the New World.[11] Historians have long been inclined to regard this vast movement of population as an unfortunate but relatively minor incident in American history. Interest in national and sectional history has often obscured the significance of Negro slavery in the overall development of the Americas. But if the institution was of little

Mass., 1956), pp. 1–15; Edward McNall Burns, *The American Idea of Mission: Concepts of National Purpose and Destiny* (New Brunswick, N.J., 1957), pp. 61–86; Henry Nash Smith, *Virgin Land: The American West as Symbol and Myth* (Cambridge, Mass., 1950).

[8] Morison, *Admiral of the Ocean Sea*, pp. 32, 291, 486–493.

[9] Elizabeth Donnan, ed., *Documents Illustrative of the History of the Slave Trade to America* (Washington, 1930–35), I, 14–16.

[10] Basil Davidson, *Black Mother: The Year's of the African Slave Trade* (Boston, 1961), pp. 44–48, 82–112, 117–162; Alexander Marchant, *From Barter to Slavery: The Economic Relations of Portuguese and Indians in the Settlement of Brazil, 1500–1580* (Baltimore, 1942), pp. 73–79, 131.

[11] It is impossible, of course, to make more than an informed guess, but this estimate is on the conservative side. See Davidson, *Black Mother,* pp. 79–81, and Frank Tannenbaum, *Slave and Citizen: The Negro in the Americas* (New York, 1947), pp. 31–32.

economic importance in Massachusetts or Nova Scotia, it nevertheless extended from Rio de la Plata to the Saint Lawrence and was the basic system of labor in the colonies most valued by Europe. In the most profitable colonies Negro slaves were employed in mines and in clearing virgin land or on the great plantations which provided Europe with sugar, rice, tobacco, cotton, and indigo. The northern colonies that were unsuited for the production of staple crops became dependent, early in their history, on supplying the slave colonies with goods and provisions of various kinds. As a stimulus to shipbuilding, insurance, investment, and banking, the slave trade expanded employment in a diversity of occupations and encouraged the growth of seaports on both sides of the Atlantic. Africa became a prized market for iron, textiles, firearms, rum, and brandy. Investments in the triangular trade brought dazzling rewards, since profits could be made in exporting consumer goods to Africa, in selling slaves to planters, and especially in transporting sugar and other staples to Europe. By the 1760s a large number of the wealthy merchants in Britain and France were connected in some way with the West Indian trade; and capital accumulated from investment in slaves and their produce helped to finance the building of canals, factories, and railroads. Even after the United States had achieved independence and a more diversified economy, her principal export was slave-grown cotton, which was the chief raw material for the industrial revolution.[12]

Without exaggerating the economic significance of Negro slavery, we may safely conclude that it played a major role in the early development of the New World and in the growth of commercial capitalism. Given the lack of an alternative labor supply, it is difficult to see how European nations could have settled America and exploited its resources without the aid of African slaves. Yet slavery had always been more than an economic institution; in Western culture it had long represented the ultimate limit of dehumanization, of treating and regarding a man as a thing. How was one to reconcile the brute fact that slavery was an intrinsic part of the American experience with the image of the New World as uncorrupted nature, as a source of redemption from the burdens of history, as a paradise which promised fulfillment of man's highest aspirations? . . .

The European thinkers . . . had somewhat ambivalent views on the moral influence of the New World. George Bancroft, the most popular

---

[12] Paul Mantaux, *The Industrial Revolution in the Eighteenth Centrury* (rev. ed., tr. by Marjorie Vernon (New York, 1929), pp. 105–111; Eric Williams, *Capitalism and Slavery* (Chapel Hill, 1944), pp. 36–38, 46–58, 92–107; Davidson, *Black Mother*, pp. 60–65; Frank W. Pitman, "Slavery on British West India Plantations in the Eighteenth Century," *Journal of Negro History*, XI (October 1926), 584–587.

and nationalistic of early American historians, had not the slightest doubt that the influence had been all for the good. Limiting himself to the area included in the United States, he set out to explain how in only two centuries the happiest and most enlightened civilization in history had arisen from the wilderness to become a model for the rest of the world. But when he grappled with the problem of slavery—how it was related to the American mission, whether it was integral to American development, and whether its extension to the New World was a retrogression from the course of progress—he resorted to a curious mixture of assumptions which reflected inconsistencies prevalent in American thought from late colonial times to the twentieth century.

As a loyal Democrat and patriotic American, writing at a time when his party supported the expansion of slave territory, Bancroft went out of his way to emphasize the antiquity and universality of an institution which, one might conclude, was not so "peculiar" after all. . . . He found no continuing contest between liberty and bondage in the ancient world: "In every Grecian republic, slavery was an indispensable element." Nor was the practice wholly incompatible with virtue and religion, for "the light that broke from Sinai scattered the corrupting illusions of polytheism: but slavery planted itself even in the promised land, on the banks of Siloa, near the oracles of God."[13] It was true that the extreme harshness of the Roman slave law had hastened the Empire's fall; but Bancroft's picture of the ancient world suggested that slavery might be planted in other promised lands without blighting their mission.

He adopted, however, the conventional view of Christianity slowly sapping the foundations of bondage in Europe. If slavery had not detracted from the splendor of Grecian republics, it was still incompatible with human progress and would have disappeared entirely among civilized nations had not an outside force intervened. In Bancroft's eyes this outside force was not America but the continuing wars between Islam and Christianity, which had nourished bigotry and revenge. Angered by the raids of Saracen corsairs, Christians had felt justified in capturing any Moor they could lay hands upon, and they had classified all Africans as Moors.[14] In any event, the Negroes themselves had always accepted slavery, and when the Portuguese had commenced trading along the western coast of Africa, they had simply appropriated a commercial system which the Moors of the north had established centuries before. Bancroft admitted that the Portuguese were guilty of

[13] George Bancroft, *History of the United States, from the Discovery of the American Continent,* 14th ed. (Boston, 1850–74), I, 159–161. The first volume was originally published in 1834.

[14] *Ibid.,* I, 163–164.

"mercantile cupidity,"[15] but in a certain sense it was Africa that had corrupted Europe.

The Spanish, who had also been brutalized by wars with the Moslems, had endeavored to enslave the Indians, or, as Bancroft called them, the "freemen of the wilderness." Even Columbus had participated in this unnatural act, though such a lapse was presumably redeemed by his contribution to the advance of liberty; and, as Washington Irving had said, "the customs of the times . . . must be pleaded in his apology."[16] Slavery, however, was totally alien to American soil, and in order to rivet the system on their colonies, the Spanish had been forced to import a more docile and submissive race. The significant point about Bancroft's interpretation is that he considered slavery basically extraneous to the New World and contrary to the natural development of Europe. It was thus a kind of abnormal excrescence which had been fastened on America by Europeans whose avarice and brutality had been stimulated by their contact with Africa.

When Bancroft turned to the founding of the North American colonies, he underscored the fundamental conflict between slavery and the very meaning of the New World. "While Virginia," he wrote, "by the concession of a republican government, was constituted the asylum of liberty, by one of the strange contradictions in human affairs, it became the abode of hereditary bondsmen." Monarchy, aristocracy, and priestcraft had no motive to cross the Atlantic — "Nothing came from Europe but a free people. The people, separating itself from all other elements of previous civilization; the people, self-confiding and industrious; the people, wise by all traditions that favored popular happiness—the people alone broke away from European influence, and in the New World laid the foundations of our republic."[17] As part of this classic picture of American innocence and separateness, Bancroft stressed the original and deep antipathy that the people felt for slavery. His argument that slavery was essentially foreign to America appeared to stumble a bit when, discussing South Carolina, he seemed to adopt Montesquieu's belief in the primacy of climate; he even asserted that the contrast between Carolina and New York was due to climate and not to the superior humanity of the original Dutch colonists.[18] Yet he thought that

---

[15] David Levin has pointed out a significant ambivalence in Bancroft's view of commerce, which he at times associated with greed and materialsm and at other times with progress and natural principles. See Levin, *History as Romantic Art: Bancroft, Prescott, Motley and Parkman* (Stanford, 1959), p. 42.

[16] Washington Irving, *The Life and Voyages of Christopher Columbus,* in *The Works of Washington Irving,* (New York, 1897), VI, 375.

[17] Bancroft, *History,* I, 159; II, 451.

[18] *Ibid.,* II, 170–171, III, 303.

the people and legislation of every colony had favored freedom and that Massachusetts, especially, had opposed the introduction of slaves from the beginning. In Rhode Island, if Providence and Warwick had failed to enforce their law of 1652 against slavery, "the principle lived among the people."[19]

How, then, could one account for the survival and growth of an institution so repugnant to the desires of a free people? Bancroft's answer was one which Americans had long resorted to; it was founded on a sharp moral distinction between the original cause of American slavery—the selfish greed of European merchants and governments—and the conditions which led to its perpetuation. If the type of servitude fastened on America had been the same as that which Europeans had long endured, the problem would soon have been solved "by the benevolent spirit of colonial legislation." But from the beginning, America had been plagued with racial incompatibility: "The negro race, from the first, was regarded with disgust, and its union with the whites forbidden under ignominious penalties."[20]

Thus racial dissimilarity could be offered as an excuse for laws and practices which simply made the best of an unfortunate situation. And when Bancroft took a larger perspective, he had to admit that America's burden was not, after all, without its rewards. In his native continent the African would have remained in "unproductive servitude"; in America at least his labor contributed greatly to the wealth of nations. Adopting for the moment one of the favorite theories of southern apologists, Bancroft concluded that "in the midst of the horrors of slavery and the slave trade, the masters had, in part at least, performed the office of advancing and civilizing the negro."[21]

While Bancroft saw a basic contradiction between slavery and America's mission, he resolved the dilemma in a manner that was apparently satisfactory to most of his countrymen. The institution was alien to the true nature of the New World; it had been imposed on the people against their will, and the guilt thus fell upon an already guilt-sickened Europe. Yet in a larger view, even slavery appeared as part of the providential plan for the redemption of the human race. In Bancroft's eyes the first ship that brought Negroes to America was a "sure pledge" that in due time ships from the New World would carry the blessings of Christianity to Africa. Even selfishness and injustice had a role to play in the historical unfolding of truth and liberty. Americans could comfort themselves with the thought that Negro slavery, a vestige of Old World

[19] *Ibid.*, I, 175, 190; III, 408.
[20] *Ibid.*, I, 177.
[21] *Ibid.*, III, 408.

corruption, was only a temporary irritant which could gradually disappear under the beneficent pressure of democratic institutions. The history of the slavery controversy in the United States well testifies that Bancroft was not alone in this optimistic belief.

We have suggested that Negro slavery, a product of innumerable decisions of self-interest made by traders and princes in Europe and Africa, was an intrinsic part of American development from the first discoveries. The evolution of the institution was also coeval with the creation of the ideal of America as a new beginning, a land of promise where men's hopes and aspirations would find fulfillment. The dreams and ideals embodied in various images of the New World would not necessarily conflict with the enslavement of a foreign people unless there were already tensions over slavery in the system of values which Europeans applied to America. That there were such tensions remains to be shown. For the moment it will suffice if we note that the problem of slavery in the New World could be conceptualized as part of a general conflict between ideals and reality in the course of human history. Thus the Abbé Raynal hinted that the discrepancy between natural law and colonial slavery was so great that revolution might be necessary to bring the ideal and reality of America into harmony. For Henri Wallon and Auguste Comte, America itself was something of an anomaly, since it represented a disturbing retrogression from the course of historical progress. Yet Wallon's faith in the power of Christianity and Comte's confidence in the inexorable laws of history led them to expect the imminent triumph of freedom. To some extent all three of these thinkers associated the paradox of modern slavery with America itself, but to George Bancroft servitude was fundamentally extrinsic to the New World, whose very meaning lay in the emancipation of mankind. Although Bancroft recognized that the Negro had played a vital part in the founding of certain colonies, he felt that slavery was so contrary to America's destiny that it would evaporate from the sheer heat of triumphant democracy.

4

The Southern Ethic in a Puritan World

C. Vann Woodward

Of those forces said to have been instrumental in forging the
American character, "Puritanism" and its concomitant the
Protestant Ethic are generally granted singular importance.
Though subject to considerable myth in its own right, not all have
come to grant Puritanism such exalted status. Arguments in favor
of seeing the distinctiveness of a southern culture quite at odds
with "Puritan" theory and practice have long prevailed on both
sides of the Mason-Dixon line. While speaking of the entire
range of the southern experience, C. Vann Woodward, emeritus
Sterling Professor of History at Yale, here attempts to analyze the
Puritan ethic and its southern counterpart, and to judge their
relationship. By isolating the leisure-laziness myth, a basic
ingredient of the "southern ethic," Professor Woodward
attempts not its destruction but rather a serious critique. While
essentially a review article examining the impact of recent
historical scholarship as it relates to this theme, it remains as
well a status report on a staple of southern mythology: leisure
as a mythical element which continues to pervade the "real
life" of the South. Finally, the article suggests that the southern
inclination toward a leisured and mannered society had sufficient
grounding in the colonial era to allow southerners largely
to escape the extremes of the Puritan ethic.

Myths that support the notion of a distinctive Southern culture tend to
be Janus-faced, presenting both an attractive and an unattractive counte-
nance. The side they present depends on which way they are turned and

who is manipulating them. The reverse side of Chivalry is Arrogance, and the other side of Paternalism is Racism. The Plantation myth is similarly coupled with the Poor White myth, the myth of Honor with that of Violence. Graciousness, Harmony, and Hospitality also have their less appealing faces. And for Leisure there is its long-standing counterpart, Laziness—together with the synonyms, idleness, indolence, slothfulness, languor, lethargy, and dissipation.

Early and late Southerners and their friends and critics have worried the Leisure-Laziness myth. It began with Captain John Smith's jeremiad against "idleness and sloth" at Jamestown and continued with Robert Beverley's disquisition on industrious beavers and William Byrd's lamentations on the slothful Carolinians of "Lubberland." An impressive literature on the subject has proliferated over the centuries. Leisure, the brighter side of the coin, has been repeatedly praised as an ideal, a redeeming quality of the Southern way that sets it off against the ant-like busyness and grubby materialism of the Northern way, another adornment of the Cavalier to shame the Yankee. Laziness, the darker face of the legend, has been deplored, denied, lamented, and endlessly explained. The explanations include climate, geography, slavery, and the staple crop economy, not to mention pellagra and a formidable list of parasites. No matter which face of the myth is favored and which explanation is stressed, agreement is general that this is a fundamental aspect of Southern distinctiveness.

As much as they deplored laziness, even exponents of the New South and the Northern way of bustle and enterprise often retained a fondness for the reverse side of the stereotype and clung to leisureliness as an essential mark of regional identity. Although Walter Hines Page scorned many characteristics of the old regime and urged a program of industrialization for the South, he cherished "the inestimable boon of leisure," hoped that "in the march of industrialism these qualities of fellowship and leisure may be retained in the mass of people," and thought that "no man who knows the gentleness and dignity and the leisure of the old Southern life would like to see these qualities blunted by too rude a growth of sheer industrialism."[1]

At the opposite pole from Page on the matter of industrialization for the South, John Crowe Ransom, arch-champion of agrarianism and "the old-time life," also fixed upon leisure as the essence of the Southern Ethic. Whatever the shortcomings of the Old South, "the fault of being intemperately addicted to work and to gross material prosperity" was hardly among them, he says. "The South never conceded that the whole

[1] Walter Hines Page, *The Rebuilding of Old Commonwealths* (New York, 1902), 111, 114, 141.

duty of man was to increase material production, or that the index to the degree of his culture was the volume of his material production." The arts of the South were "arts of living and not arts of escape." All classes participated in these arts and their participation created the solid sense of community in the South. "It is my thesis," he writes, "that all were committed to a form of leisure, and that their labor itself was leisurely."[2]

Between Page and Ransom, though much closer in ideology to the former than the latter, W. J. Cash was more ambivalent than either about leisure. Conceding that the South's "ancient leisureliness—the assumption that the first end of life is living itself . . . is surely one of its greatest virtues," he thought that "all the elaborately built-up pattern of leisure and hedonistic *drift;* all the slow, cool, gracious and graceful gesturing of movement . . . was plainly marked out for abandonment as incompatible with success" and the ethic of the new industrial order. This was not to be written off as pure loss. The lot of the poor white had been a "void of pointless leisure," and for that matter, "in every rank men lolled much on their verandas or under their oaks, sat much on fences, dreaming." Leisure easily degenerated into laziness. Both leisure and laziness perpetuated frontier conditions and neither produced cities or a real sense of community. Cash leaned to the Northern view that culture and community are largely developed in towns, "and usually in great towns."[3]

When one gets down to modern economists and the theory of under-developed countries and regions like the South, ambivalence about leisure and laziness tends to disappear. The two become almost indistinguishable and equally reprehensible. In the opinion of one Southern economist, leisure becomes "a cover-up for lack of enterprise and even sheer laziness among Southerners." For the mass of them, in fact, "leisure was probably from early days a virtue by necessity rather than by choice. If they were small landowners they lacked sufficient resources to keep them busy more than half the year. If they were slaves or sharecroppers the near impossibility of advancing themselves by their own efforts bred inefficiency, lassitude, and improvidence." The phenomenon of television aerials over rural slums "may clearly make (through its positive effect on incentives) its own substantial contribution to regional economic progress." But the tradition of leisure has been a major cause of underdevelopment.[4]

[2] Twelve Southerners, *I'll Take My Stand: The South and the Agrarian Tradition* (New York, 1930), 12–14.

[3] W. J. Cash, *The Mind of the South* (New York, 1941), 384, 150, 50, 95.

[4] William H. Nicholls, *Southern Tradition and Regional Progress* (Chapel Hill, 1960), 34–39.

I

New light on this ancient dispute comes from a number of sources—
new works on moral, intellectual, economic, and slavery history—and a
reconsideration of the debate would seem to be in order. One of these
new sources is a work by David Bertelson, whose preference between the
Janus faces is clearly announced by the title of his book, *The Lazy South*.
The informality of the title might suggest to some that this is another
light-hearted and genial essay on regional foibles. Nothing could be
further from the author's intentions. He is fully conscious of the "strong
volitional and moral connotations" of the word "laziness" and never
flinches in his employment of it. This presumes to be the history of a
failure, the moral failure of a whole society.

Mr. Bertelson is not one to borrow support casually from conventional
assumptions and traditional explanations. Much has been written of
geographical determinants of Southern history. "But geography did not
create the South," he writes. Pennsylvania, with its waterways and its soil,
was as easily adaptable to a tobacco staple culture as Virginia. Nor will
he seek an out in economic determinism: rather he asks what determined
the economy. He scarcely pauses over the old climatic and ethnic chestnuts.
As for the uses of the Peculiar Institution, he is simply not in the market.
"Negro servitude did not make the southern colonies different from New
England and Pennsylvania. They were different first. That is why slavery
became so widespread there. The presence of a small number of slaves
in the northern colonies did not change the essential conditions of life
in these either. That is why the number remained so small." He has little
space for the familiar biological determinants—pellagra, malaria, hookworm, and the rest. They were the accompaniments of poverty and laziness,
not their causes. Laziness afflicted the affluent as often as the parasites
afflicted the indigent.[5]

What then does account for this distinctive trait of the South? "The
difference lay not in the land but in the people," we are told, "and that
difference was ultimately due to the different attitudes and assumptions
which they brought with them and their descendants perpetuated." The
attitudes and assumptions derive ultimately from values, in other words
morals, ethics. "To get at what lies behind poverty, slavery, staple crops,
and stressing personal enjoyment one must consider historically the
meaning of work in the South." It all boils down to an analysis of the
Southern Ethic—though that is not a term the author uses.[6]

Virginia existed first in the minds of Englishmen as an answer to the

[5] David Bertelson, *The Lazy South* (New York, 1967), 244, 104.
[6] *Ibid.*, 244, viii.

problem of idleness in England. The cure for idleness, it was thought, lay in the allurements of material gain in the New World which would induce men to work without the necessity of violating their freedom. Spokesmen of Virginia were sometimes vague about personal responsibility to society and a sense of community. Puritans, on the other hand, "thought of themselves as small societies before they established communities."[7] Authoritarians failed in Virginia, and no prophet of a godly community prevailed, no Chesapeake Zion appeared. The same was true of Maryland, the Carolinas, and after abortive experiments, Georgia.

Without coercion and community, Southern colonists established societies based on the exploitation of natural resources. The motive force was individual aggrandizement, we are told, not social purpose or community aims. They established plantations, not cities, and cultivated staples, not trade. The result was dispersion, fragmentation, and chaotic self-aggrandizement. The meaning of work in the Southern colonies thus came to have no social dimension or content. Work there *was*, hard work, but it produced idleness with plenty and was intermittent according to seasonal necessities.

"The problem then is," it seems to Mr. Bertelson, "to explain why most men in the southern colonies *seemed* to lead idle lives while in actuality they were often very busy. The answer lies in the fact that they were not busy all of the time." When crops were laid by they tended to go fishing. Max Weber, to whom the author attributes the conception of his study, associated with "the spirit of capitalism" a pattern of industry and diligence that was not based on economic considerations. This pattern is found to be conspicuously absent in the South, along with "the intellectual climate to favor diligence." As a figure of contrast the author pictures "young Benjamin Franklin trudging the streets of Philadelphia in the early morning and his remark that he took care not only to be industrious but to appear industrious." It is conceded that the South was "not without examples of industrious people like Franklin, but ... most of them were recently arrived foreign Protestants." Your genuine Southerner did not even bother to *appear* industrious.[8]

Yet we are told that the Southerners were deeply troubled with guilt about laziness and took extreme measures to overcome an oppressive sense of purposelessness with sheer "busyness." Thus William Byrd, for all his pre-dawn vigils with Hebrew, Greek, and Latin, was desperately driven by the specter of laziness and futility. Even that model of methodical industriousness Thomas Jefferson, in advising his daughter about work

[7] *Ibid.*, 40–41.
[8] *Ibid.*, 75–77.

habits, "was advocating simply keeping busy rather than purposefulness." Anyway, Jefferson and James Madison "expressed very little of the South" in the way, presumably, that Cotton Mather expressed New England and Benjamin Franklin, New England and Pennsylvania. As for George Washington, he proves to have had very rational and Yankeefied notions about work (though the evidence offered is not very persuasive), notions shared by Patrick Henry and Richard Henry Lee. Apart from these unrepresentative deviants, the pattern of Virginia prevailed among Southerners generally. James Winthrop, a Massachusetts Federalist, is quoted as distinguishing sharply between the "idle and dissolute inhabitants of the South" and "the sober and active people of the North."[9]

The trouble with the South, one of the many troubles perceived, was its total inability to conceptualize social unity in terms other than personal relationships, to achieve any real sense of community, or to define industry in social terms. The plantation as community is written off as "imaginary." Southerners, it seems, proved unable to derive social unity "from a community of belief in God and love for one another as it had been for early Puritans."[10] Their efforts to define community in terms of home, personal affections, and local loyalties, the very essence of patriarchal community in the South, are summarily dismissed as futile. Southerners are also said to have been incapable of any real sense of loyalty. Unlike charity, loyalty does not appear to begin at home.[11] "While many Southerners doubtless had great affection for family and friends," he concedes, "and for the localities in which they lived, this did not involve any larger social unity nor any sense of loyalty to the South as a whole—but rather a pervasive particularism."[12]

Personalism and persistent local attachments have been offered by David M. Potter as evidence of the survival of an authentic folk culture in the South long after it had disappeared in urban culture elsewhere.[13] While Mr. Bertelson concedes that "at times in the past or in certain

[9] *Ibid.*, 166, 161.

[10] *Ibid.*, 65.

[11] In a strongly contrasting analysis of the roots of loyalty, David M. Potter writes, "The strength of the whole is not enhanced by destroying the parts, but is made up of the sum of the parts. The only citizens who are capable of strong national loyalty are those who are capable of strong group loyalty, and such people are likely to express this capacity in their devotion to their religion, their community, and their families, as well as in their love of country." "The Historian's Use of Nationalism and Vice Versa," *American Historical Review,* LXVII (1961–1962), 932.

[12] Bertelson, *The Lazy South,* 210.

[13] David M. Potter, "The Enigma of the South," *Yale Review,* LI (1961–1962), 150–151.

limited areas of the South people's lives did attain relatedness and meaning," in the region as a whole disruptive economic forces, pursuit of gain,
and chaotic mobility have made impossible "the kind of stability which
one usually associates with folk culture." Far from constituting evidence
of a sense of community, "courtesy, hospitality, graciousness—is simply
a series of devices for minimizing friction only to create the appearance of
intimacy or affection."[14] If these particular myths *are* indeed Janus-faced,
one face would seem to be effectively veiled from the author's vision.

The emphasis throughout is on the want of any meaningful sense of
community in the South. The essence of community is tacitly assumed to
be urban, something associated with cities—preferably built on a hill or in
a wilderness. "Both the Quakers and to an even greater degree the Puritans
in New England founded societies based on communities of consent and
common goals. Imbued with a sense of community and social purposefulness, these people were truly able to build cities in the wilderness."[15] It is
perhaps inevitable and even appropriate that the myths of an urban society
should attach symbolic significance to cities, and it is understandable that
these symbols should retain their appeal long after the metropolis has
become something less than the ideal embodiment of community, has
become in fact the symbol of anti-community. What is surprising is the
total unconsciousness of the mythic quality of these symbols and the faith
that they embody.

Harry Levin has commented on the "mythoclastic rigors" of the early
Christians. "Myths were pagan," he writes, "and therefore false in the light
of true belief—albeit that true belief might today be considered merely
another variety of mythopoeic faith. Here is where the game of debunking
starts in the denunciation of myth as falsehood from the vantage point
of a rival myth."[16]

Mr. Bertelson erects at least one guard against the charge of drawing a
geographical line between virtue and vice. He concedes that "Northern
society only imperfectly exemplified a sense of community," and that
personal aggrandizement, anarchic individualism, and maybe Old Adam
himself have been known to break out at times above the Potomac. "The
South," he nevertheless maintains, "represents the logical extreme of this
tendency. To the degree that America has meant economic opportunity
without social obligations or limitations, Southerners are Americans
and Americans are Southerners."[17] Some comfort is gratefully derived

[14] Bertelson, *The Lazy South,* 242–243.
[15] *Ibid.,* 244.
[16] Harry Levin, "Some Meanings of Myth," *Daedalus,* LXXXVIII (1959), 225.
[17] Bertelson, *The Lazy South,* 245.

from this remarkable concession, even if it is the comfort the poor white derives in Southern myth as repository of the less fortunate traits: at least he belongs.

II

It is, however, just on this score of Southern distinctiveness that a vulnerable spot occurs in the thesis. In a recent analysis of what he calls "the Puritan Ethic," Edmund S. Morgan addresses himself to many of the traditional values that Mr. Bertelson denies the South.[18] Yet in Mr. Morgan's analysis these were "the values that all Americans held," even though the claim upon them varied in authenticity, and adherence to them differed in consistency and tenacity. And in spite of the name assigned to the ethic, he disavows any proprietary regional exclusiveness about it and holds that "it prevailed widely among Americans of different times and places," and that "most Americans made adherence to the Puritan ethic an article of faith."[19] Indeed, leaders of North and South found "room for agreement in the shared values of the Puritan Ethic" until the break over slavery. Thomas Jefferson was "devoted to the values of the Puritan Ethic," and Mr. Morgan quotes the identical letters containing Jefferson's advice to his daughter that Mr. Bertelson presents as evidence of the Southern syndrome about idleness and remarks that they "sound as though they were written by Cotton Mather."[20] In a mood of generosity he makes honorary Puritans of numerous Southerners: Richard Henry Lee of Virginia was "a New Englander manqué," Henry Laurens of South Carolina had characteristics that made him "sound like a Puritan," Hugh Williamson of North Carolina was forever "drawing upon another precept of the Puritan Ethic," and the thousands of Southerners who poured into Kentucky and Tennessee in the 1780's "carried the values of the Puritan Ethic with them," whence they presumably suffused the Cotton Belt.[21]

These references are undoubtedly of generous intent, and there are rules about looking a gift horse in the mouth. Mr. Morgan is careful to say that " 'The Puritan Ethic' is used here simply as an appropriate short-hand term" to designate widely held American ideas and attitudes. And perhaps he is right that "it matters little by what name we call them or where they came from."[22] What's in a name? Yet there is *something* about

[18] Edmund S. Morgan, "The Puritan Ethic and the American Revolution," *William and Mary Quarterly,* 3d Ser., XXIV (1967), 3–43.
[19] *Ibid.,* 7, 23, 24, 33, 42.
[20] *Ibid.,* 7, 24, 42.
[21] *Ibid.,* 21–22, 28–29, 38.
[22] *Ibid.,* 6.

the name that does raise questions. One cannot help wondering at times how some of those Southern mavericks, sinners that they were, might have reacted to being branded with the Puritan iron. It might have brought out the recalcitrance, or laziness, or orneriness in them—or whatever it was that was Southern and not Puritan. There are in fact, as will later appear, certain limits to the indiscriminate applicability of the Puritan Ethic down South.

By whatever name, however, Mr. Morgan's insights provide needed help in understanding the polemical uses of regional myth and the study of regional character. And he does have a point that in sectional disputes, each side often tended to appeal to the same values. He notes that in the sectional conflict between East and West that followed the Revolution and was accompanied by talk of secession of the lower Mississippi and Ohio Valley, "each side tended to see the other as deficient in the same virtues": "To westerners the eastern-dominated governments seemed to be in the grip of speculators and merchants determined to satisfy their own avarice by sacrificing the interests of the industrious farmers of the West. To eastern- ers, or at least to some easterners, the West seemed to be filled up with shiftless adventurers, as lazy and lawless and unconcerned with the values of the Puritan Ethic as were the native Indians." In this confrontation of East and West the tendency of each to accuse the other of deficiencies in the same virtues and delinquencies in the same code, Mr. Morgan holds that "the role of the Puritan Ethic in the situation was characteristic."[23]

This sectional encounter of the 1780's recalls another one a century later when the Populists were the spokesmen of Southern (and Western) grievances against the East. The Populist Ethic—perhaps I had better say myth—the Populist Myth had much in common with this Puritan Ethic. According to Populist doctrine, labor was the source of all values, and work to be productive had to have social meaning. Productive labor was the index to the health of a society. Populists swore by producer values. Farmers and laborers were "producers." Merchants were the favored symbol of non-productive labor. They were "middle men" who merely moved things around. With them were classified bankers and "monopolists" and "speculators." Their work was not socially useful and served only selfish ends. They exploited the industrious farmers and laborers of the South and West. They deprived men of the just fruits of their labors and removed one of the main motives of industry and frugality. Their gains were ill-gotten, and they could be justly deprived of such gains by the state for the welfare of the community, for their profits were not the fruit of virtuous industry and frugality.

Populists were by and large an inner-directed lot, geared to austerity by

[23] *Ibid.,* 20.

necessity, suspicious of affluence, and fearful of prosperity. They were the children of a life-long depression. They looked with baleful eye upon the city as productive of idleness, luxury, extravagance, and avarice. If the city was an appropriate symbol of community for the Puritan Myth, it was just as naturally a symbol of anti-community for the Populist Myth. Cities were full of non-producers—merchants, bankers, usurers, monopolists. Merchants and cities were concentrated in the East and particularly in New England. A great deal of Populist animus therefore had a regional target.

The Populists believed they had a direct line of inspiration and continuity from the American Revolution, that Thomas Jefferson was its true spokesman, and that their creed of agrarian radicalism was authentically blessed. They harked back continually to the Revolutionary period for fundamental principles and lamented with traditional jeremiads the expiring of republican virtue. It was their historic mission, they believed, to restore virtue and ideals and drive out those who had fouled the temple.[24]

True to tradition, spokesmen of the urban East in the 1890's replied in kind. They pronounced the Populists deficient in virtue and wholly given over to shiftlessness, laziness, and greed. It was the Populists who had defected from the code, not the Eastern capitalist. It was their own deficiencies and lapses from virtue and not exploitation by the East or hostile policies of the government that had brought the farmers to their unhappy plight. Populist resort to government aid and monetary manipulation for relief instead of reliance on frugality and the sweat of their brows was further evidence of shiftlessness and moral delinquency.

Sectional confrontation between the South and other parts of the country in the 1960's has hinged more on moral than on economic issues, but these encounters nevertheless have called forth many familiar recriminations and echoes of the traditional rhetoric of sectional polemics, including those of the 1860's, and their deep moral cleavages. Once again, each side has tended to view the other as deficient in similar virtues while proclaiming its own undeviating adherence. It is, however, perhaps the first instance in the annals of sectional recrimination (not even excepting the 1860's) in which one region has been seriously denied any allegiance to a common ethic, in which historic violations have been treated not as defections but as the promptings of an alien code. For in this instance the delinquencies have been attributed not to some institutional peculiarity that could be eradicated at a cost, nor to some impersonal force of nature or economics for which allowance might be made, but to indigenous,

---

[24] For examples from Populist literature see Norman Pollack, ed., *The Populist Mind* (Indianapolis, 1967), 51, 66–69, 211–221, 501–519, and *passim*.

ineradicable attitudes of a whole people "which they brought with them and their descendants perpetuated." This introduces a modern use for an ancient concept resembling the tragic flaw that cursed families in Greek tragedy, something inexorable and fatefully ineluctable.

III

Nothing in this vein of critical evaluation, however, is intended as endorsement of the concept of an undifferentiated national ethic, whether it is called Puritan, Protestant, or by any other name. To be sure, there do exist deep ethical commitments that override barriers of section, class, religion, or race. Otherwise there is no accounting for such limited success as the country has enjoyed in achieving national unity. Mr. Morgan and other historians have served their calling well in bringing these commitments to light. But there still remain sectional differences to be accounted for, and the distinctiveness of the South in this respect is especially unavoidable. The evidence of this distinctiveness, however unsatisfactory the explanations for it may be, is too massive to deny. Where there is so much smoke—whether the superficial stereotypes of the Leisure-Laziness sort, or the bulky literature of lamentation, denial, or celebration that runs back to the seventeenth century, or the analytical monographs of the present day—there must be fire. It remains to find a satisfactory explanation for this aspect of Southern distinctiveness.

Before exploring some explanatory approaches to this problem it would be well to start with an underpinning of agreement, if possible. First there is the question of the foundations of settlement and what the settlers brought with them. Perhaps we could do no better for this purpose than to quote the views of Perry Miller. He pointed out that "however much Virginia and New England differed in ecclesiastical politics, they were both recruited from the same type of Englishmen, pious, hard-working, middle-class, accepting literally and solemnly the tenets of Puritanism—original sin, predestination, and election—who could conceive of the society they were erecting in America only within a religious framework." It is true, he went on to say, that even before Massachusetts was settled, "Virginia had already gone through the cycle of exploration, religious dedication, disillusionment, and then reconciliation to a world in which making a living was the ultimate reality." But even after "the glorious mission of Virginia came down to growing a weed," and even though there were never any Winthrop-type "saints" hanging around Jamestown, the religious underpinnings remained.[25]

[25] Perry Miller, *Errand into the Wilderness* (Cambridge, Mass., 1956), 108, 138, 139.

In her exhaustive study of Puritanism in the Southern colonies, Babette M. Levy avoids estimates of percentage, but her investigation suggests that a majority of the original settlers were Puritans or Calvinists of some persuasion. Of Virginia she writes that "their presence was felt throughout the colony," and that it was felt extensively in the other Southern colonies as well.[26] Southern colonies sustained two further infusions of Puritans, the Huguenots in the seventeenth century and the Scotch-Irish in the eighteenth. They were assimilated in the evolving Southern Ethic, but not without leaving their mark. Then there were the Methodists. Quoting John Wesley to the effect that "the Methodists in every place grow diligent and frugal," Max Weber comments that "the idea of duty in one's calling prowls about in our lives like the ghost of dead religious beliefs."[27] Even after the Enlightenment and the cotton gin those ghosts continued to prowl under the magnolias and, perhaps more wanly, even in the Spanish-moss and cabbage-palm latitudes. Doubtless they were less at home under the palm than under the pine, but their presence was felt nonetheless.

Yet it is Weber who points out "the difference between the Puritan North, where, on account of the ascetic compulsion to save, capital in search of investment was always available" and "the condition in the South," where such compulsions were inoperative and such capital was not forthcoming.[28] He goes further to compare religio-cultural contrasts in England with those in America. "Through the whole of English society in the time since the seventeenth century," he writes, "goes the conflict between the squirearchy . . . and the Puritan circles of widely varying social influence. . . . Similarly, the early history of the North American Colonies is dominated by the sharp contrast of the adventurers, who wanted to set up plantations with the labour of indentured servants, and live as feudal lords, and the specifically middle-class outlook of the Puritans."[29] Weber was conscious of the paradox that the New England colonies, founded in the interest of religion, became a seedbed of the capitalist spirit, while the Southern colonies, developed in the interest of business, generated a climate uncongenial to that spirit.

This is not the place to enter the "scholarly meleé"[30] over the validity of Max Weber's thesis regarding the influence of the Protestant Ethic in the

[26] Babette M. Levy, "Early Puritanism in the Southern and Island Colonies," in American Antiquarian Society, *Proceedings*, LXX (1960), Pt. i, 60–348, esp. 86, 119, 308.

[27] Max Weber, *The Protestant Ethic and the Spirit of Capitalism*, trans. Talcott Parsons (London, 1930), 175, 182.

[28] *Ibid.*, 278n. But see Gabriel Kolko, "Max Weber on America: Theory and Evidence," *History and Theory*, I (1960–1961), 243–260.

[29] Weber, *The Protestant Ethic*, trans. Parsons, 173–174.

[30] For examples see Robert W. Green, ed., *Protestantism and Capitalism: The Weber Thesis and Its Critics* (Boston, 1959), *passim*.

development of modern capitalism. But here is Weber's delineation of the Puritan Ethic based on his gloss of Richard Baxter's *Saints' Everlasting Rest* (London, 1650) and *Christian Directory* (London, 1673), which he describes as "the most complete compendium of Puritan ethics":

> Not leisure and enjoyment, but only activity serves to increase the glory of God, according to the definite manifestations of His will.
>
> Waste of time is thus the first and in principle the deadliest of sins. The span of human life is infinitely short and precious to make sure of one's own election. Loss of time through sociability, idle talk, luxury, even more sleep than is necessary for health, six to at most eight hours, is worthy of absolute moral condemnation. It does not yet hold, with Franklin, that time is money, but the proposition is true in a certain spiritual sense. It is infinitely valuable because every hour lost is lost to labour for the glory of God. Thus inactive contemplation is also valueless, or even directly reprehensible if it is at the expense of one's daily work.[31]

With regard to "the Puritan aversion to sport," unless it "served a rational purpose" or was "necessary for physical efficiency," Weber observes that "impulsive enjoyment of life, which leads away both from work in a calling and from religion, was as such the enemy of rational asceticism, whether in the form of seigneurial sports, or the enjoyment of the dance-hall or the public-house of the common man."[32]

The precise relation of Puritan asceticism to the "spirit of capitalism" is disputed, but in his characterization of the latter, Weber's friend Ernst Troeltsch makes apparent the affinity between the two:

> For this spirit displays an untiring activity, a boundlessness of grasp, quite contrary to the natural impulse to enjoyment and ease, and contentment with the mere necessaries of existence; it makes work and gain an end in themselves, and makes men the slaves of work for work's sake; it brings the whole of life and action within the sphere of an absolutely rationalised and systematic calculation, combines all means to its end, uses every minute to the full, employs every kind of force, and in the alliance with scientific technology and the calculus which unites all these things together, gives to life a clear calculability and abstract exactness.[33]

[31] Weber, *The Protestant Ethic,* trans. Parsons, 157–158.

[32] *Ibid.,* 167–168.

[33] Ernst Troeltsch, *Protestantism and Progress, A Historical Study of the Relation of Protestantism to the Modern World,* trans. W. Montgomery (Boston, 1958), 133–134.

Commenting upon the influence of the Puritan Ethic on "the development of a capitalistic way of life," Weber adds that "this asceticism turned with all its force against one thing: the spontaneous enjoyment of life and all it had to offer."[34]

With all deference to Weber's reputation, this would seem to be an excessively harsh characterization of the Puritan Ethic. He does remind us that "Puritanism included a world of contradictions."[35] Surely the code must have been honored in the breach as well as in the observance, and even Puritans in good standing must have had occasional moments of "the spontaneous enjoyment of life." One would hope so, and one is comforted by assurances of modern authorities on the subject that they in fact occasionally did. If not, then it is obvious that "a capitalistic way of life," even with a couple of industrial revolutions thrown in for good measure, came at much too high a cost.

The views of Max Weber, nevertheless, still carry weight.[36] And if his delineation of the Puritan Ethic bears any resemblance to the real thing, then it is abundantly clear that no appreciable number of Southerners came up to scratch. There are to be found, of course, authentic instances of Puritan-like behavior in various periods down South. And no doubt a genuine deviant occasionally appeared, some "New Englander manqué," just as a Southerner manqué might, more rarely, turn up in the valleys of Vermont or even on State Street. By and large, however, the great majority of Southerners, including those concerned about their "election," shamelessly and notoriously stole time for sociability and idle talk, and the few who could afford it stole time, and sometimes more than time, for luxury. It is likely that a statistically significant number of them of a given Sunday morning stole more than their allotted eight hours of sleep. It is extremely unlikely that a sports event—horse race, fox hunt, cock fight, or gander pulling anywhere from the Tidewater to the Delta—was typically preceded by a prayerful debate over whether it "served a rational purpose" or was "necessary for physical efficiency." It was more likely to be contaminated with "the spontaneous expression of undisciplined impulses." Such "inactive contemplation" as went on below the Potomac does not appear to have altered the mainstream of western civilization, but the temptation to indulge the impulse would rarely have struck the inactive contemplator as morally reprehensible.

A regional propensity for living it up had tangible manifestations of more practical consequence than habits of sociability, sleeping, and sports.

[34] Weber, *The Protestant Ethic,* trans. Parsons, 166.

[35] *Ibid.,* 169.

[36] For a spirited and persuasive defense of Weber from a recent critic, see Edmund S. Morgan's review of Kurt Samuelsson, *Religion and Economic Action* (New York, 1961), in *Wm. and Mary Qtly.,* 3d Ser., XX (1963), 135–140.

Modern economists have often sought to explain why a region of such abundant natural and human resources as the South should have remained economically underdeveloped in a nation of highly developed regional economies—some with poorer natural resources—and suffered the attendant penalties of strikingly lower levels of per capita wealth and income. The Southern scene as of 1930 could be described as "an almost classic picture of an underdeveloped society."[37] Many explanations are offered and no one alone is adequate, but of prime importance in modern theory on the subject is the factor of capital formation. Apart from sheer productivity, the ability to produce more than enough to support the population, the key variable in the rate of capital growth is the willingness to save, or the other side of the coin, the propensity to consume. "Any difference among regions," one economist writes, "in their tendency to consume rather than to save will probably be reflected in their respective rates of capital formation."[38]

Economic and social historians have long remarked on distinctive spending habits, not to say extravagance, of Southerners—the Populist Myth to the contrary notwithstanding. Most often such habits have been attributed to antebellum planters and their tastes for fast horses, fine furniture, and expensive houses. The flaunting of wealth in an aristocratic society was, according to Weber, a weapon in the struggle for power. These generalizations of historians about extravagance in the South have been based on more or less well-founded impressions and random samples. The only comprehensive statistical study of regional spending habits of which I am aware is one made by several agencies of the federal government covering the years 1935 and 1936 and embracing thousands of families analyzed by population segments and income groups. The limited samples studied indicate that "people in the South did spend, in given income classes, a larger amount for consumption than did residents of other regions"; that in small-city samples low-income groups saved less in the South than in other parts of the country; that at higher income levels in this urban sector "southerners showed a tendency towards higher levels of consumption and less saving"; and that among high farm-income groups in the South "the proportion spent for consumption was significantly higher than that for the same farm income levels elsewhere."[39]

Thus the differences between the Puritan North and the Southern

[37] Douglas F. Dowd, "A Comparative Analysis of Economic Development in the American West and South," *Journal of Economic History*, XVI (1956), 563, and *passim*.

[38] W. H. Baughn, "Capital Formation and Entrepreneurship in the South," *Southern Economic Journal*, XVI (1949–1950), 162.

[39] *Ibid.*, 165–166. Since no allowance was made in these computations for the lower living costs in the South, according to Mr. Baughn, they tend to understate the extent of Southern spending.

colonies over "the ascetic compulsion to save" that Weber saw operating to influence the availability of capital for investment in the 1600's appeared to be still operative in the 1930's. If the ascetic compulsion is rightly attributed to the Puritan Ethic, then the absence or remission of that compulsion might be another indication of a distinctive Southern Ethic.

IV

The real question then is not whether Southerners fell under the discipline of the Puritan Ethic, but rather—given their heritage and the extent of their exposure—how it was they managed to escape it, in so far as they did. To attribute their deliverance to attitudes they brought with them to America seems rather unhelpful in view of the fact that they brought so many of the same attitudes the New Englanders brought and that these were reinforced by massive transfusions of Puritan blood in later years. Their escape would seem to be more plausibly derived from something that happened to them after they arrived. An acceptable explanation would probably turn out to be plural rather than singular, complex rather than simple, and rather more "environmental" than ideological. To explore and test all the reasonably eligible hypotheses would be the work of elaborate researches and much *active* contemplation. Here it is only possible to suggest a few hypotheses that would appear worth such attention.

Slavery would not come first in any chronological ordering of causal determinants of Southern attitudes toward work, but it hardly seems wise to brush it off entirely into the category of consequences. Granting that some distinctive Southern attitudes on work appeared before slavery attained very much importance in the economy, and conceding that these attitudes played a certain part in the spread of the institution, it would be willful blindness to deny the influence it had, once entrenched, in the evolution of the Southern Ethic. The causes of slavery are another subject—a very large one. But once the system became rooted in the land in the seventeenth century, its influence was all-pervasive, and the impact it had on the status of important categories of necessary work and on white and black attitudes toward them was profound and lasting. For not only were these types of work associated firmly with a degraded status, but also fatefully linked with a despised race that continued to perform the same types of work, with no appreciable improvement in racial status, long after slavery disappeared. The testimony of white Southerners themselves, ranging in authority and prestige from Thomas Jefferson to Hinton Rowan Helper, is impressive on the effect that slavery had upon the honor and esteem accorded work in the South. Statistical analysis of the comparative figures on employment might be effectively used in testing these impressions.

Regional variations in the nature of work might also deserve attention as determinants of the Southern Ethic. Much of the work required of men in all parts of early America was crude and hard, and little of it anywhere could honestly be characterized as stimulating, creative, or inherently enjoyable. Those who wrote of its joys and rewards probably had a larger share of work that could be so characterized than those who failed to record their impressions. Perhaps it was somewhat easier to surround the labors of shop, countinghouse, and trade with the aura of honor and glamor. That type of work was in short supply in the South.

The agrarian myth of yeoman farmers as "the chosen people of God" certainly did bestow honor and a literary aura of dignity, even glamor, upon a way of making a living, but not necessarily on work itself. No other class of Americans was so persistently and assiduously flattered. The qualities for which the hero of the myth was admired, however, were his independence, his republican virtues, his purifying communion with nature. It was the political and public qualities of the yeomanry that Jefferson had in mind when he wrote that "the small land holders are the most precious part of the state." Work itself was not the essential thing, and certainly not the religion-driven, compulsive, ascetic work of the Puritan Ethic. In fact, neither the hired man nor the slave who did the same work (and probably more of it) shared the dignity and honor conferred by the myth on the yeoman, while the employer or owner of such labor might do little work by himself and yet enjoy the blessings of the myth. In its full flower in the late eighteenth century the agrarian myth, in fact, stressed escape from the bustle of the world and celebrated pastoral contentment and ease, the blandishments and pleasures of the simple life—the very "impulsive enjoyment of life" held up by Puritan divines as "the deadliest of sins." Never did the agrarian myth regard yeomen as "slaves of work for work's sake." The myth of the happy yeoman was much more congenial to the Southern Ethic than it was to the Puritan Ethic.[40]

As for the black slaves, their very existence did violence to the Puritan Ethic. No one could have a "calling"—in Weber's sense of the term—to be a slave. Since slaves were denied the fruits of their labor, they were deprived of the basic motive for industry and frugality. Circumstance made laziness the virtue and frugality the vice of slaves. Work was a necessary evil to be avoided as ingeniously as possible. Such work as was required of slaves—as well as of those who did work slaves typically performed—was rather difficult to associate with the glory of God or many of the finer aspirations of man. Could such work have been endowed with the mystique of a "calling" or a conviction of divine purpose, it might have

[40] Henry Nash Smith, *Virgin Land: The American West as Symbol and Myth* (New York, 1957), 138–150.

rested more lightly on the shoulders of those of whom it was required and on the conscience of those who required it. That seems to have been the way it worked with onerous non-slave work elsewhere. There appears, however, to have been less stomach for such theological exercises—indeed more need for stomach—in the South than in some other parts. Few sermons to slaves indulged in them. Work therefore lacked the sort of sanctification it might have derived from this source. The attitude of the slave toward work, like many of his attitudes and ways, found secure lodgement in the Southern Ethic.

Turning from the slave to the slave holder and the plantation system for a look at their influence on the evolution of the Southern Ethic, we move into more troubled waters. Genuine and important differences of opinion about the fundamental nature of the slave economy exist among experts in the field. Members of one school, the most distinguished of whom was Lewis C. Gray, think of the slave holder as a "planter-capitalist." According to Gray, the plantation system was a "capitalist type of agricultural organization in which a considerable number of unfree laborers were employed under a unified direction and control in the production of a staple crop."[41] The crop was produced for a remote market in response to standard laws of supply and demand by the use of capital sometimes obtained from banks or factors that was invested in land and in slaves. The whole operation was "rational," in the peculiar way economists use that remarkable word—that is, it operated single-mindedly to maximize profits on investment. A contrasting view was that of Ulrich B. Phillips, who believed that the plantation system was not nearly that simple, that it was a complicated "way of life," a social as well as an economic system. It contained numerous "irrational" elements, goals unrelated or antithetical to the profit motive. It was something of an anachronism, a pre-capitalist economy existing in a capitalist world.[42]

It makes a great deal of difference for the implications of the plantation system in accounting for the distinctiveness of the Southern Ethic as to which of these schools is "sound on the goose." For if Gray and his school are right, then there is relatively little to be learned from the political economy of slavery about the distinctiveness of the South from the rest of a uniformly capitalist America. If Phillips is on the right track, however, there might be a great deal to learn. It may be a long time before a consensus on the slave economy is reached among scholars, and certainly no attempt is made to settle the dispute here.

It is instructive to note, however, a convergence between the old-school

[41] Lewis C. Gray, *History of Agriculture in the Southern United States to 1860,* I (Washington, 1933), 302.

[42] Ulrich B. Phillips, *American Negro Slavery: A Survey of the Supply, Employment and Control of Negro Labor as Determined by the Plantation Régime* (Baton Rouge, 1966), *passim.*

views of Phillips and a new-school view developed by the investigations of Eugene D. Genovese.[43] In the findings of the latter, the plantation economy was shot through with "irrationality" (in the market-place sense) and given to wild deviations from the capitalistic norm. "The planters were not mere capitalists," he writes. "They were pre-capitalist, quasi-aristocratic landowners who had to adjust their economy and ways of thinking to a capitalist world market. Their society, in its spirit and fundamental direction, represented the antithesis of capitalism, however many compromises it had to make." He elaborates on the antithesis as follows:

The planters commanded Southern politics and set the tone of social life. Theirs was an aristocratic, antibourgeois spirit with values and mores emphasizing family and status, a strong code of honor, and aspirations to luxury, ease, and accomplishment. In the planters' community, paternalism provided the standard of human relationships, and politics and statecraft were the duties and responsibilities of gentlemen. The gentleman lived for politics, not, like the bourgeois politician, off politics.

The planter typically recoiled at the notions that profit should be the goal of life; that the approach to production and exchange should be internally rational and uncomplicated by social values; that thrift and hard work should be the great virtues; and that the test of the wholesomeness of a community should be the vigor with which its citizens expand the economy. The planter was no less acquisitive than the bourgeois, but an acquisitive spirit is compatible with values antithetical to capitalism. The aristocratic spirit of the planters absorbed acquisitiveness and directed it into channels that were socially desirable to a slave society: the accumulation of slaves and land and the achievement of military and political honors. Whereas in the North people followed the lure of business and money for their own sake, in the South specific forms of property carried the badges of honor, prestige, and power.[44]

He goes on to observe that "at their best, Southern ideals constituted a rejection of the crass, vulgar, inhumane elements of capitalist society. The slaveholders simply could not accept the idea that the cash nexus offered a permissible basis for human relations." The planters reinforced their paternalism toward their slaves by a semipaternalism toward their neighbors and "grew into the closest thing to feudal lords imaginable in a nineteenth-century bourgeois republic."[45]

[43] See for example Genovese's "Foreword" to the 1966 edition of Phillips, *American Negro Slavery* cited above.

[44] Eugene D. Genovese, *The Political Economy of Slavery: Studies in the Economy and Society of the Slave South* (New York, 1965), 23, 28.

[45] *Ibid.*, 30, 31.

Mr. Genovese has greatly complicated and enhanced the fascination of the game of ethic identification. One shrinks at the prospect of encouraging studies of "feudal" and "aristocratic" themes in Southern history, and even more at anticipated glances from colleagues in European history. It would be well to emphasize the prefix *quasi* that Mr. Genovese judiciously attaches to these terms. With these precautions (and misgivings) and with no disposition to prejudge the outcome of the revived and flourishing controversy over the political economy of American slavery, one might at least say that this interpretation of the slave South contains a number of suggestive hypotheses relating to the distinctiveness of the Southern Ethic.

On the themes of pre-capitalist economies the work of Max Weber again becomes relevant. He strongly emphasized the "irrational" characteristics of slave economies, particularly in master-slave relationships, consumer behavior, and politics. At the risk of reviving the Waverly-novel approach, the following characterization of the aristocratic ethic by Weber is offered as summarized by his biographer:

> In feudal ideology the most important relations in life are pervaded by personalized ties, in contrast to all factual and impersonal relationships. . . . From this standpoint luxury is not a superfluous frill but a means of self-assertion and a weapon in the struggle for power. This antiutilitarian attitude toward consumption was of a piece with the equally antiutilitarian orientation toward one's life. Aristocratic strata specifically rejected any idea of a 'mission in life,' any suggestion that a man should have a purpose or seek to realize an ideal; the value of aristocratic existence was self-contained. . . . Aristocrats deliberately cultivated a nonchalance that stemmed from the conventions of chivalry, pride of status, and a sense of honor.[46]

Social role-playing is a broad mark for satire, but all societies engage in it consciously or unconsciously. The sharpest ridicule is reserved for the unfortunate society that is caught at the height of collective posturing, brought low with humiliating exposure of its pretenses, and forced to acknowledge them—or live with them. The Old South has had its share of exposure along this particular line, and more at this juncture has rather low priority among the pressing tasks of historiography. More needful are analytical appraisals of the social content of the patriarchal, paternalistic, and aristocratic values and the remarkable qualities of leadership they developed. A comparative approach could be helpful, but the traditional moralistic comparison with the contemporary society to the north might profitably be ex-

[46] Reinhard Bendix, *Max Weber: An Intellectual Portrait* (New York, 1962), 364–365.

changed for comparisons with English and Latin slave societies to the south that shared more of the South's traditions, institutions, and values.

An abhorrence of slavery and an identification with abolitionists on the part of both liberal and radical historians have skewed and clouded their interpretation of the Old South. In a critique of Marxian and liberal historiography of slavery, Mr. Genovese holds that the main problem "arises from the duality inherent in a class approach to morality" and contends that both liberals and Marxists have made the mistake of judging the ruling class of Southern planters "by the standards of bourgeois society or by the standards of a projected socialist society." With reference to rulers of the Old Regime, he continues:

> These men were class conscious, socially responsible, and personally honorable; they selflessly fulfilled their duties and did what their class and society required of them. It is rather hard to assert that class responsibility is the highest test of morality and then to condemn as immoral those who behave responsibly toward their class instead of someone else's. There is no reason, unless we count as reason the indignation flowing from a passionate hatred for oppression, to withhold from such people full respect and even admiration; nor is there any reason to permit such respect and admiration to prevent their being treated harshly if the liberation of oppressed peoples demands it. The issue transcends considerations of abstract justice or a desire to be fair to one's enemies; it involves political judgment. If we blind ourselves to everything noble, virtuous, honorable, decent, and selfless in a ruling class, how do we account for its hegemony? . . . Such hegemony could never be maintained without some leaders whose individual qualities are intrinsically admirable.[47]

Also needed are discerning assessments of the skill, conviction, and zest which other players brought to the colorful variety of roles assigned them by the Old Regime. That of "Sambo" has been subjected to appreciative analysis of late, with commendable efforts to illuminate the personality and values of his descendants. The roles of his master and mistress, Lord and Lady Bountiful, as well as those of the lesser gentry, the squirearchy, the yeomanry, and the poor whites deserve comparable study. It is possible that a majority of the players identified completely with their roles as "real life" —as completely perhaps as the saints, prophets, and come-outers in other quarters found identity in their roles. At least the cast for the Old South

[47] Eugene D. Genovese, "Marxian Interpretations of the Slave South," in Barton J. Bernstein, ed., *Toward a New Past: Dissenting Essays in American History* (New York, 1968), 114.

drama, slaves included, often acted as if they did, and sometimes they put on rather magnificent performances. Study of the institutional setting in which they performed—the patriarchal tradition, the caste system, the martial spirit, the racial etiquette, the familial charisma—all deserve attention from the historian of the Southern Ethic.

V

After the curtain fell on the Old South in 1865, the same cast of characters had to be taught strange roles and learn new lines. For a people who had been schooled so long in the traditional roles, and especially for those who played them for "real life," this was not an easy assignment. The social dislocations and traumas of Reconstruction and the period that followed can be seen as drastic experiments from two sides: the conservative side trying to preserve the Southern Ethic, and the radical side trying to destroy it. As we shall see, neither of these experiments was destined wholly to succeed.

To convert the ex-slaves miraculously into "slaves of work for work's sake" in the classic model of Weber's "spirit of capitalism" was clearly beyond the reasonable expectations of either side. Given the freedman's age-long indoctrination in a work ethic appropriate to his enslavement, and given the necessity of his now doing the same kinds of work without the old compulsions, the question was whether he could be induced to do any work beyond what would provide him a bare subsistence, if that. Planter conservatives were convinced that the only answer was force in some guise, and in lieu of bondage they put forward schemes of apprenticeship and vagrancy laws embodied in "Black Codes." In effect they offered the old allegiance of paternalistic responsibility for abject dependents while tacitly retaining the sanction of the whip.

Ruling these schemes illegal and a travesty on freedom, Northern agencies, including the Freedmen's Bureau, missionaries, and private speculators, confidently maintained that "normal" economic incentives were the solution: wages, profits, and assurance of the fruits of one's labor. Northern agencies and employers launched their program with a campaign of indoctrination laced with the rhetoric of diligence, frugality, and the sanctity of contracts—staples of the Puritan Ethic. Needless to say, the Puritan Ethic had acquired its own Janus face over the centuries, and it was the face of Yankee acquisitiveness that was presented to the South. Along with this went the promise of free land held out to the freedmen by Congress and the Freedmen's Bureau. But that promise ran afoul of two conflicting principles of their own: the sanctity of property and the doctrine of equal rewards for equal labor. The first blocked the confiscation of planters' property to provide the free land, and the second inhibited the granting of special privilege unearned by honest labor. The North reneged on the promise of free land,

and the freedmen sulked. The "normal" incentives were not operating. Northern business joined Southern planters in demanding that the Freedmen's Bureau get the Negro back to the cotton fields. When General O. O. Howard, head of the bureau, received "authentic complaints of idleness for which no remedy seemed to exist," he ordered enforcement and extension of state vagrancy laws. His assistants withheld relief, compelled freedmen to accept labor contracts, and enforced their harsh terms with penalties of forfeited wages and withheld rations. Gradually the North withdrew and left the freedmen to make what terms they could with planters.[48]

In the meantime the campaign to convert Southern white men went forward briskly and at first hopefully. "It is intended," declared Thaddeus Stevens, "to revolutionize their principles and feelings," to "work a radical reorganization in Southern institutions, habits, and manners."[49] The difficulties of the undertaking were acknowledged. "The conversion of the Southern whites to the ways and ideas of what is called the industrial stage in social progress," wrote Edwin L. Godkin, was a "formidable task." He believed that "the South, in the structure of its society, in its manners and social traditions, differs nearly as much from the North as Ireland does, or Hungary, or Turkey."[50] But the revolutionizing process would go forward, promised Horatio Seymour, "until their ideas of business, industry, money making, spindles and looms were in accord with those of Massachusetts."[51] The Southern whites, like the Negroes, were subjected to indoctrination in diligence, austerity, frugality, and the gospel of work. They were advised to put behind them the "irrationality" of the Old Order, outmoded notions of honor, chivalry, paternalism, pride of status, and noblesse oblige, together with all associated habits of indolence, extravagance, idle sports, and postures of leisure and enjoyment. In the name of "rationality" they were adjured to get in there like proper Americans and maximize profits.

The verbal response from the South, after a refractory interlude and apart from a continued undertone of muttered dissent, must have been gratifying. The antebellum business community, long inhibited by ties to the Old Order, burst into effusions of assent and hosannas of delivery. "We have sowed towns and cities in the place of theories and put business above politics," announced Henry W. Grady to the cheering members of the New

---

[48] Willie Lee Rose, *Rehearsal for Reconstruction: The Port Royal Experiment* (Indianapolis, 1964), 212–216, 308–310; George R. Bentley, *A History of the Freedmen's Bureau* (Philadelphia, 1955), 79–86; for a revisionary estimate of the bureau see a forthcoming work of William McFeely, *Yankee Stepfather: General O. O. Howard and the Freedmen's Bureau* (New Haven, 1968).

[49] Quoted in Howard K. Beale, *The Critical Year: A Study of Andrew Johnson and Reconstruction* (New York, 1930), 149.

[50] *Nation*, XXXI (1880), 126.

[51] *Herald* (New York), Oct. 31, 1866.

England Society of New York. "We have fallen in love with work."[52] And Richard H. Edmunds of the *Manufacturers' Record,* invoking the spirit of Franklin, announced, "The South has learned that 'time is money.' "[53] A Richmond editor rejoiced that "the almighty dollar is fast becoming a power here, and he who commands the most money holds the strongest hand. We no longer condemn the filthy lucre."[54] The range of New South rhetoric left unsounded no maxim of the self-made man, no crassness of the booster, no vulgarity of the shopkeeper, no philistinism of the profit maximizer. For egregious accommodation and willing compliance the capitulation was to all appearances complete.

But appearances were deceptive, and the North was in some measure taken in by them. The New South orators and businessmen-politicians who took over the old planter states gained consent to speak for the region only on their promise that Southerners could have their cake and eat it too. That was one of the meanings of the Compromise of 1877. The South could retain its old ways, the semblance or outer shell at any rate, and at the same time have an "industrial revolution"—of a sort, and at a price. White supremacy was assured anyway, but home rule and states' rights meant further that the South was left to make its own arrangements regarding the plantation system, the accommodation of the freedman and his work ethic, and his status as well as that of white labor in the new economy and polity. The price of the "industrial revolution" and the reason for the distorted and truncated shape it took was an agreement that the North furnish the bulk of investment capital and entrepreneurship, while the New South managers smoothed the way by a "cooperative spirit" that assured generous tax exemptions, franchises, land grants, and most important of all an abundant supply of cheap, docile, and unorganized labor.

The South got its railroads and mines, its Birmingham heavy industry and its Piedmont factories. That is, they were located in the South. But they were largely owned elsewhere and they were operated in the interest of their owners. They were of one general type: low-wage, low value-creating industries that processed roughly the region's agricultural and mineral products but left the more profitable functions of finishing, transporting, distributing, and financing to the imperial Northeast. The South remained essentially a raw-material economy organized and run as a colonial dependency. On the agricultural side a sort of plantation system survived along with the one-crop staple culture, but the absentee owners dropped the wage contracts, substituted debt slavery for chattel slavery, and organized the

[52] Raymond B. Nixon, *Henry W. Grady: Spokesman of the New South* (New York, 1943), 345.

[53] *Manufacturers' Record* (Baltimore), Nov. 3, 1888.

[54] *Whig and Advertiser* (Richmond), Apr. 4, 1876.

labor force, now more white than black, as share croppers or tenants bound by an iron crop lien into virtual peonage. The cropper-tenants rarely handled any money, subsisted on fatback, cornbread, and molasses, and constituted a mass market for Southern manufacturers of chewing tobacco, moonshine whiskey, and very little else. They were in fact a non-market.

The New South neither preserved the Southern Ethic intact nor abandoned the allegiance entirely. It substituted a compromise that retained a semblance at the expense of the essence. The substitute was more defiantly proclaimed, articulately defended, and punctiliously observed than the genuine article had been. The cult of the Lost Cause covered the compromise with a mantle of romantic dignity and heroism. Surviving heroes in gray became Tennysonian knights. The Plantation Legend took on a splendor that shamed antebellum efforts. There was a place in the new cast —with important exceptions to be noted—for all players of the old roles as well as for newcomers with only imaginary identification with them, and there was a gratuitous upgrading of status all around. Great energy went into the performance. Spectators were impressed with the graciousness and hospitality, the leisurely elegance and quaint courtliness at upper levels, and with a pervasive kindliness, a familial warmth, and a deferential courtesy that prevailed generally.

There were even those who affected the patriarchal and paternalistic roles. Right here, however, came the sad falling off, the point at which the sacrificed essence—aristocratic obligations of noblesse oblige, responsibilities of leadership, solicitude for dependents and subordinates, and an antibourgeois disdain for the main chance and the fast buck—gave way to the bourgeois surrogate. For the children of the new patriarchs and the dependents of the new paternalists were the mass of forlorn croppers and tenants, black and white, in their miserable rural slums, undefended victims of ruinous interest rates, mined-out soil, outmoded techniques, debt slavery, and peonage—these and the first-generation industrial proletariat, white and black, in their urban or company-town slums, victims of the lowest wages, longest hours, and deadliest working conditions in the country.

The oppressed were not so docile as to submit without show of resistance. As the nineties came on, Negroes and white labor under the leadership of desperate farmers combined in the Populist Revolt to mount the most serious indigenous political rebellion an established order ever faced in the South. In their panic over the rebellion, the New South leaders relinquished their last claim to responsibility derived from the Old Order. Abandoning their commitment to moderation in racial policy, they turned politics over to racists. In the name of white solidarity and one-party loyalty, they disfranchised the Negro and many lower-class whites and unleashed the fanatics and lynchers. In their banks and businesses, in their clubs and social life, as well as in their inner political councils, they moved over to make room for increasing delegations of Snopeses. In place of the old sense of community based on an ordered if flexible hierarchy, they substituted a mystique of kinship, or clanship, that extended the familial ambit spuriously to all whites—and to such Negroes as had mastered and sedulously practiced the Sambo role to perfection.

There have been lamentations for the passing of the Southern Ethic all down the years and periodic jeremiads for its demise. Referring to the Puritan Ethic, Edmund Morgan writes that "it has continued to be in the process of expiring," that it has "always been known by its epitaphs," and that "perhaps it is not quite dead yet."[55] The future of either of these two historic relics in an affluent, consumer-oriented society of the short work week, early retirement, and talk of a guaranteed income looks rather dubious, though in a giant supermarket world the ethic of the grasshopper would seem to have somewhat more relevance than that of the ant. And puritanical condemnations of leisure already seem a bit quaint. Whether the Southern Ethic is dead or not, the lamentations and jeremiads show no sign of languishing. In fact, the works of William Faulkner constitute the most impressive contribution to that branch of literature yet. If epitaphs are indeed a sign of life in this paradoxical field of ethical history, then the lamentations here, too, may be premature.

[55] Morgan, "The Puritan Ethic," 42–43.

5

The First South

John Richard Alden

A definite consensus persists among students of the southern past that the distinct regional identification, so long a hallmark of southernism, was first articulated and defined via the sectional controversies of the pre–Civil War decades. Such consensus has concluded that The South did not function as a consistent regional entity, nor did it have a particularly graphic perception of itself as distinct from the North, at least not until the decade of the 1820s. John Richard Alden, Professor of History at Duke University, Durham, North Carolina, challenges this standard interpretation, taking notable exception to these "classic" explanations of southern regional consciousness. Lying beyond the historical horizon of the familiar Old South, Alden contends, lies an earlier South—a First South if you will. Though geographically distinct from its later counterpart, the First South was of kindred spirit in terms of climate, people, economy, and social order. In short, the land to the south of the Susquehanna "behaved as a section before 1789." Focusing on the Revolutionary War period, Professor Alden notes that perceptions of a constitutional, economic, and racial nature were already surfacing which foreshadowed an eventual southern Confederacy. It would be for later generations to reinforce and firmly establish these sectional feelings.

We Americans who are not too familiar with our history harbor a haunting memory of an Old South—an Old South of broad plantations; of their gracious masters and charming mistresses; of humble, cheerful, and loyal

From John R. Alden, *The First South*. Baton Rouge, Louisiana State University Press, 1961. Reprinted by permission of the publisher.

slaves who rose occasionally in ferocious revolt; of poor whites fearing naught but the wrath of Heaven; of cotton, magnolias, and Spanish moss— an Old South menaced and at last overwhelmed and demolished by Northern masses and machinery. We see through a glass doubtfully, and it is surely true that every general idea we have of that Old South is subject to exception and fuller description. The thousands of earnest historians who have delved into its remains must and do tell us that it was not as we are accustomed to think it was. Herein it is not intended to try to correct and clarify your vision, erroneous as it may be, of that familiar Old South, but to limn as truthfully as talents and energies will permit an even older South, which shall be named for convenience the First South.

This First South existed during the years 1775–1789. It appeared with the American nation; it was christened as early as 1778; and it clashed ever more sharply with a First North during and immediately after the War of Independence. This First South did not hasten under the Federal Roof with swift and certain steps, but haltingly and uncertainly. Many of her people feared that the Federal cover would offer greater protection north of the Susquehanna than it would south of that river. It should not be said that their alarm was without cause, that they saw troubles which the future did not bring. They feared lest they become a minority in an American union dominated by a Northern majority, lest they suffer in consequence. Whatever may be the merits of measures since imposed upon the South by the North—and the West—it will not be denied that the South has felt the power of external American forces, especially since the middle of the nineteenth century.

Now this First South, the Revolutionary South, the South of Patrick Henry, Light-Horse Harry Lee, and John Rutledge, was not the Old South of John C. Calhoun nor that of Jefferson Davis. In essence, nevertheless, they were the same, for they were alike in land, climate, people, economy, and social order. Even with respect to political structure and relations with the North, they were not so different as historians have commonly conceived. The Old South sought to leave the Union and to form a new nation; the First South—and for similar reasons—was not at all sure in the years 1787–1789 that it was wise to become part of that Union. Indeed, surprising as it may be, there were those in South Carolina, especially William Henry Drayton, who feared that South Carolina might suffer from the tyranny of Congress by giving consent to the Articles of Confederation. To be sure, the doubts of the First South were set aside, and it ultimately endorsed the Constitution of 1787, while the doubts of the Old South regarding the Union became so great that it denounced and sought to leave the Union. Here we have, however, an important difference in degree, not opposites absolutely.

There may be captious scholars—are not scholars by definition captious?

—who will go so far as to deny that there was a South in the Revolutionary time.[1] One may be tempted to find importance in the fact that the First South and the Old South were geographically not the same. Obviously enough, the First South was definitely limited by the Mississippi, while the Old South stretched westward into the empire of Texas; the First South was principally on the Atlantic seaboard, while the Old South contained both that seaboard and the lower half of the valley of the Mississippi. No matter, for the limits of a section, unless they be remarkably narrow, do not determine whether or not it exists.

More seriously, it may be asserted that the First South cannot have been because it lacked unity. It has been well said by Carl Bridenbaugh that there were actually three or four societies in the states from Maryland to Georgia at the beginning of the Revolution: an aristocratic order on the shores of the Chesapeake; another in the Carolina Low Country; a frontier society in the Old West; and possibly a fourth society not easily described in central North Carolina. But if there were three, or even four, societies below the Mason-Dixon line, it must be remembered that these were not three or four permanent societies completely distinct from each other. Those of the Chesapeake and the Low Country actually had much in common, including well-established American aristocracies and very large bodies of Negro slaves; and that of the Old West was actually only a passing phenomenon, since it would vanish with the frontier. Nor did central North Carolina possess one which could easily and positively be distinguished from those of the Chesapeake and the Low Country. The social differences to be discerned in the First South were hardly more impressive than were those in the Old South, the existence of which is not frequently or forcefully denied. The First South was not monolithic; neither was the Old South. Again, during the period 1775–1789, as afterward, heat, geography, racial and national composition, economic pursuits, social order, and even political structure, were ties of unity rather than sources of discord below the Susquehanna. That such was so is proven by events, for the First South frequently behaved as a section before 1789. It may be added that it was increasingly taken for granted by political men of the Revolutionary generation that the South was a distinct area with special and common interests that could not be ignored in the affairs of the nation.

All of which is not to say that there was such a region generally or even frequently referred to in 1775 or 1789 as the South. That name was used on a few interesting occasions, but the region was usually described between those years as the "Southern states." It follows, then, that there was

---

[1] The writer indicated briefly in his *The South in the Revolution, 1763–1789* (Baton Rouge, 1957) that there was such a South. So far as he is aware, none of the reviewers of that volume expressed dissent.

a South even before the name came into common use, a fact which hardly surprises, since the infant should precede the christening. Before the War of Independence the colonies were often divided by observers into "Eastern" and "Southern," the term "Eastern" covering New England, the word "Southern" including all the colonies from New York to Georgia. Sometimes "Northern" was used as a synonym for "Eastern." Thus in 1767, when advising General Thomas Gage to establish a military base at or near Manhattan, General Guy Carleton pointed out that such a fortified place would not only provide security for military stores but would also "separate the Northern from the Southern colonies." The division between "Eastern" and "Southern" endured through the early years of the war, a usage which has confused some historians, who have occasionally and forgivably assumed that no one could think of Pennsylvania or New Jersey as Southern. It is nevertheless true that a quarrel between men of the Delaware valley and New England troops in 1776 was referred to as one between Southerners and Easterners. Even at that time, however, the word Southern was acquiring a more restrictive meaning, the phrase "Middle states" being used more and more to describe New York, New Jersey, Pennsylvania, and Delaware. These "Middle states" with the "Eastern states" were increasingly put together as the "Northern states," another usage which long endured.

Quickly shorn of the Middle states, the Southern states became a South and a section. The limits of that section were, of course, only gradually established in the minds of men; indeed, they cannot now be firmly laid down between it and the Middle states. There was disagreement about its northern boundaries at the time, although no one doubted that the Carolinas and Georgia were part of it.

Strange to say, none other than George Washington, until the adoption of the Constitution, was reluctant to include Virginia within the First South. In 1787 and again in 1788 he refers in his correspondence to the Carolinas and Georgia as the "Southern states." In 1786 he invited Don Diego de Gardoqui, the official emissary of Spain to the United States, to pay a visit to Mount Vernon "if you should ever feel an inclination to make an excursion into the middle states." It is apparent that Washington, a stout nationalist even before the close of the War of Independence, wished to minimize the South and its special interests. But he was forced to recognize that they existed, and he too began to refer to the region between Pennsylvania and the Floridas as the "Southern states." Not until his first term as president did he fully realize the vitality of a Southern section that included Virginia. Becoming genuinely and even gravely alarmed, he urged his countrymen, in his Farewell Address, to soften their sectional antagonisms.

Except for Washington, I have found no Revolutionary worthy who would have drawn a line between Virginia and the South. And I have discovered only one other Founding Father who did not include Maryland in the "Southern states." That person was William Henry Drayton of South Carolina, who declared most emphatically in the winter of 1777–1778 that Virginia, the Carolinas, and Georgia formed "the body of the southern interest." Almost invariably, men in public life perplexed by North-South contests said or assumed that Maryland belonged to the Southern connection. Frequently politicians referred to difficulties between the eight Northern states and the five Southern ones. Others indicated that the North and the South were set apart by the Susquehanna River. The prevailing view was put flatly in 1787 by Charles Pinckney of South Carolina, who declared, "When I say Southern, I mean Maryland, and the states to the southward of her."

However Maryland may be classified—Southern, border, or Northern—in the nineteenth and twentieth centuries, it is appropriate to place her with the South in the Revolutionary time. It is true that central Maryland and western Maryland, even then, were countries of farms rather than plantations; of corn, wheat, and livestock instead of tobacco; of yeoman farmers rather than white masters and black slaves. But it should be remembered that only eastern Maryland, a plantation region, was then fully settled. It is also true that Maryland was slightly more commercial and a trifle more urban than Virginia. Nevertheless, in the days of the Revolution, the two states above and below the Potomac were fundamentally identical both economically and socially. Maryland at that time belonged with Virginia, and both with the South.

It was assumed soon after the close of the War of Independence that the northern limits of the South were on the Ohio as well as the Mason-Dixon line. Before the end of that conflict Virginia abandoned her claim to the Old Northwest; and Southerners generally sanctioned the Northwest Ordinance, which effectively placed the region between the Ohio, the Mississippi, and the Great Lakes outside the South. There was, however, agreement among politicians Northern and Southern, that the new settlements of Kentucky and Tennessee were Southern. As parts of Virginia and North Carolina until after the adoption of the Constitution, it could hardly be doubted at the time that they were parts of the South. Nor should we doubt it, even though we may not share the alarm then felt by leaders of New England because they saw the occupation of Kentucky and Tennessee as evidence that the South was expanding at the cost of the North. The Revolutionary South included the settlements of Boonesborough and Nashville as well as Annapolis and Savannah.

Proportionally to the remainder of the Union, the Revolutionary South was the largest South, both in size and in people. In fact, the Southern population in the first Federal census of 1790 was only a trifle smaller than that of the rest of the nation, there being then counted about 1,900,000 persons below the Mason-Dixon line, slightly more than 2,000,000 above it. At that time Virginia was by far the most populous state, and North Carolina ranked fourth, behind Massachusetts and Pennsylvania. Had not Maine been a part of Massachusetts, North Carolina would have been the third state in numbers. Moreover, there were Southerners who believed that population was increasing more rapidly in the South than elsewhere. These facts had influence upon the decision of the Southern states to ratify the Constitution, for it could be asserted with some show of reason that the South would soon surpass the remainder of the Union in numbers. It was not fully realized, perhaps, that the three-fifths provision of the Constitution respecting the slaves would place the South in a minority position in the national House of Representatives, even in the composition of the first Congress based on the census. Besides, as it turned out, the appearance of more rapid growth in the Southern population was illusory—the gap between North and South soon widened rather than diminished, as the census of 1800 indicated.

Hitherto it has been asserted rather than shown that there was a Revolutionary South. Nor will all the proof that such was the case be marshalled in detail at this point. Much of the best sort of proof, consisting of sectional quarrels, will be offered later. Nevertheless, it may be well to bring forth at this point certain fundamental reasons why the First South was crudely a unit with interests and views opposed to those of the rest of the Union.

Nature herself certainly set apart the South, giving to the South tropical summers, long growing seasons, and mild winters. Nature also gave soils and waters suitable for growing vast quantities of tobacco and rice, products which could be consumed only in small part in the South, which were much desired by foreign peoples, especially Europeans. In the Chesapeake region tobacco growing long seemed to be the best road to wealth, although it obviously was a road marred by ruts and mudholes; in the Carolina Low Country after the middle of the eighteenth century rice growing, together with the production of indigo, offered a surer and smoother highway to affluence. In consequence, the South had become before the Revolution a country of general farming and also of highly specialized farming that sent forth exports in great quantity and value. Meanwhile, the people of the Northern colony-states, with their colder climates, continued to engage in general farming, fishing, and lumbering, but turned increasingly toward internal trade, shipbuilding, sea-borne commerce, and manufacturing. Thus the economic pursuits of South and North became not only different, but often seemingly opposed. Instances enough of clashes over economic issues in the Revolutionary time will be offered later.

The special farming of the South was also the chief cause for a profound racial divergence between the sections, since the raising of tobacco and rice led to the importation into the South of large numbers of Negroes. In the Northern states, except for Delaware, at the time of the Revolution, the Negroes formed only small minorities. Below the Mason-Dixon line it was otherwise, for in the South 35 of every 100 persons were Negroes. They made up a full 30 per cent of the populations of Maryland and North Carolina, 40 per cent of that of Virginia, and more than half of that of South Carolina. The Negroes, burgeoning in numbers because of the special farming of the South, in turn helped to perpetuate such farming. The Southerners could think of few occupations for them beyond toil in tobacco rows, care of rice plants, weeding of corn, and other field tasks. Moreover, the presence of the Negro, together with the Southern economy and climate, tended to discourage white immigration, a fact which was noted by and which alarmed some astute Southern observers even before 1775, a fact which census returns afterward made evident to all who would bother to read such reports.

Economic and racial divergences between South and North brought with them serious social variation. Negro slavery was quite fixed upon the South, while it had few and weak roots above the Susquehanna. Slavery and special farming widened social cleavage among the Southern whites, giving added strength to the principle of aristocracy below the Mason-Dixon line. At the day of the Revolution there were admittedly socially superior persons in the Northern colony-states, chiefly country magnates and wealthy merchants. They were fewer and less powerful in New England than they were in the Middle states; and they were more conspicuous and more influential on the Chesapeake and in the Carolina Low Country than they were on the Hudson or the Delaware. Even North Carolina had its Tidewater aristocracy. The tobacco and rice lords often could not see eye-to-eye with the dominant middle-class men of the North. John Adams did not feel unmixed respect and liking for the "nabobs" of South Carolina whom he met in Congress after 1774; nor did the aristocratic-minded Southern delegates feel unadulterated admiration for the Yankees with whom they considered men and measures in New York and Philadelphia.

There were indeed important differences between the Northerners and the Southern whites as a whole in the Revolutionary time, as Thomas Jefferson pointed out in a letter to the Marquis de Chastellux in 1785. He said:

In the North they are cool, sober, laborious, independent, jealous of their own liberties, and just to those of others, interested, chicaning, superstitious and hypocritical in their religion. In the South they are fiery, voluptuary, indolent, unsteady, zealous for their own liberties, but trampling on those of others, generous, candid, without attachment or pretentions to any religion but that of the heart.

"These characteristics," asserted the thoughtful Virginian, became "weaker and weaker by gradation from North to South and South to North, insomuch that an observing traveller, without the aid of the quadrant may always know his latitude by the character of the people among whom he finds himself. It is in Pennsylvania that the two characters seem to meet and blend and to form a people free from the extremes both of vice and virtue." We need not accept precisely the opinion of Jefferson regarding either Northerners or Southerners, and we may also doubt that the Golden Mean existed in Pennsylvania, but there is obvious merit in his analysis. Assuredly, it is significant that he saw contrasts, even mistakenly, and that he thought them important enough to relate to his French friend.

Since colonial federation, though occasionally talked about and even planned, never was undertaken, serious clash between North and South did not appear before 1775. There were many contests between colony and colony, but none in which the one region was challenged by the other. It is true that jealousies of a sectional nature arose because some Southern colonists fancied that their Northern brethren were too hasty and too forward in asserting American rights against Britain during the decade before Lexington and Concord. Conversely, Northern defenders of American rights sometimes felt that the Southerners moved too slowly and too uncertainly. When the program of general nonimportation of British goods was rather hastily abandoned in the Northern ports after the repeal of most of the Townshend duties in 1770, just as nonimportation was being effectively put into force in South Carolina, there was genuine resentment in Charleston.[2] But here we have passing irritations rather than enduring troubles. Actually the struggles of the Americans against Britain before 1775, and the War of Independence especially, served to bring the Americans together by supplying them with a common, dangerous, and detested enemy.

Indeed, let us not forget that there were many and powerful forces pushing the Americans together in both the colonial and Revolutionary epochs. Too much may be made of economic and social antagonisms between North and South; too little heed may be given to unifying vigors. It should be recalled that almost all the Americans, save the Negroes, had a common background in the British Isles and that part of the European continent west of the Elbe River; that nearly all of them spoke English—English with perhaps fewer differences between North and South than afterward; and that they shared the benefits and evils of an English cultural and political heritage. Moreover, the Americans had felt alike the influence of similar elements in their New World environment. At the opening of the Revolutionary time they were aware of their oneness, a fact indicated by their ever-increasing use of the term American as descriptive of all the inhabitants of the Thirteen Colonies—a usage which also became dominant in

[2] Yankee Josiah Quincy, Jr., found in Charleston in 1773, "a general doubt of the firmness and integrity of the Northern colonies."

Britain after 1763. The beginning of the Revolutionary contest with Britain near the end of the French and Indian War added, as has been suggested, a new dynamic toward unity, Britain the foe of America as a whole. Northerners and Southerners had a common political enemy before 1775; even more important, they were faced by a common military antagonist between 1775 and 1783; after the close of the War of Independence, they continued to share fears of British and European aggressions. Those who fear the same menaces, those who fight the same foes, tend to feel that they are one.

Above all, the War of Independence aroused an American emotion. Virginians served at Boston and Quebec, Carolinians at Brandywine and Germantown, Yankees at Trenton and Yorktown. The "hard core" of the Revolutionary forces was the Continental army; and "Continental" was, or rather soon became, a synonym for "American." Few of the men who served in it could afterward be easily convinced that they fought only for their home state, or for a South, or for a North.[3] For the Continental veteran, officer and man, and doubtless almost to a man, America was his country. None were more devoted to the nation than were Virginia soldiers George Washington, Light-Horse Harry Lee, Daniel Morgan, and John Marshall. If one had suggested to a Southern veteran that he had not found Connecticut or New Jersey troops remarkably congenial, he would almost surely have responded that such was sometimes the case, but that they had been, when all was said and done, true and worthy comrades in a great cause.[4] And that cause could hardly be the creation of a string of small independent countries along the Atlantic coast; or of two or three nations; or even of one confederacy so feeble at its heart that it would be absurd to describe it as an American union.

American nationalism during the Revolutionary era should not be considered minor, nor were the forces creating and supporting it meager or temporary. The same should be said for the divisive tendencies of sectionalism. In that era nationalism was to triumph.

The contest between South and North began even before the Declaration of Independence. In the first general American assembly—in the First Continental Congress in 1774—came the first quarrel. It was, as were most of such struggles before 1789, economic in nature. When that body con-

---

[3] A Virginia newspaper reported in June, 1780 that "Captain Lieutenant Richard Coleman of Spotsylvania county, fell in the defense of his country on the 29th day of May . . . in South Carolina."

[4] In early acquaintance Southerners often disliked New Englanders, whose worst qualities were only too evident, whose finer ones required time to discover. Even in the long run the Yankees were more likely to inspire respect rather than fondness in the Southerner. James Fallon of South Carolina offered an early impression of them in 1779: "The inhabitants hereabouts [Fishkill, N.Y.] are all Yankees. I mean not to reflect *nationally;* but their manners are, to me, abhorrent. I long to leave and get clear of their oddities. They are, for the most part, a *damned* generation."

sidered measures to compel Parliament and Crown to change their course to American wishes, it decided to use a weapon which had become familiar, a boycott of British goods. There was no sectional disagreement regarding the use of this boycott, even though the importation of Negro slaves was also forbidden. Nor was there any difficulty between North and South because the Congress decreed nonconsumption of British goods, this measure being calculated to prevent merchants from pulling profits out of scarcities. It was otherwise when the delegates decided to use the club of nonexportation to Britain and the British West Indies, in case of need, the date for cessation being set at September 10, 1775. The delegates from South Carolina, except for Christopher Gadsden, asked that rice and indigo be excepted from the embargo, and so raised a controversy.

In this clash varying economic interests were basic. On the surface, the South Carolina men in the Congress were asking a special favor for the Low Country; from their point of view they were merely requesting equal sacrifice from all sections. Because of British law and other circumstances rice and indigo markets in England and the British West Indies were very important to South Carolina. Were exportation of those products to those markets forbidden, the Low Country planters, almost utterly dependent upon sales of rice and dye stuffs, must suffer grievously. The Northern colonies would be able to sell outside Britain and the islands, as they had in the past; and even the Chesapeake colonies, their tobacco going largely to London, Bristol, and Liverpool because of Parliamentary law, could escape the worst effects of the self-inflicted punishment of embargo by turning to wheat-growing. Even so, the attitude of the South Carolina delegation was not generous, especially with respect to their fellow planters of the Chesapeake; and Gadsden was prepared to offer a total sacrifice. When Northerners in Congress cried favoritism, the dominant Carolinians withdrew their request for excepting indigo; and for the sake of creating a solid front against Britain, the free sending of South Carolina's rice to sea was permitted. Thus the quarrel was resolved by concession on the part of the others to the Low Country planters. It has been suggested that Gadsden's colleagues should not be judged too harshly; it is worthy of mention that the news of the arrangement did not create great joy in Charleston. Early in 1775 the South Carolina Provincial Congress, considering the situation, and perhaps feeling some pangs of conscience, defeated a motion to ban rice exportation by the narrow margin of 87 to 75.

Early in the Second Continental Congress another issue threatened sectional trouble, and was settled in such fashion that nationalism won a victory of vast consequences. When that body decided to form a Continental army, it was immediately faced by a momentous question: who should be its commander in chief? It is now well known that George Washington had many merits and that these were not entirely unfamiliar in Philadelphia.

However, New Englanders were inclined to favor the appointment of a Yankee, Israel Putnam or some other hero of the lands east of the Hudson. Aware that unity would be secured by choosing a Southerner and that Washington was otherwise suitable, John and Samuel Adams consented to the appointment of the Virginia colonel. The decision did allay sectional feeling at the time.[5] Far more important, the personal fortunes of Washington became entwined with those of a national army. He felt the adverse effects of particularism and sectionalism in the war effort as could no other person. It may even be said that Washington's fame came to depend in part upon the creation of a permanent American union. Were his military achievements to lead to the making of a number of small American nations, he could hardly be the mighty figure he became. Whether the commander in chief was fully conscious that his glory was inextricably linked with that of the United States is a question of no importance. Such was the fact; and there was no more sturdy, no more steady nationalist in the South than the great Virginian at the end of the war. As he said farewell to his army, he begged that his comrades give their support to a solid union; and he was to be more responsible than any other man for putting the Constitution into force. We are all accustomed to praising the man of Mount Vernon for his military merits, and there have been those who have contended—I think, without full cause—that his services as president were even more remarkable than those he offered in his campaigns and battles. Let it not be forgotten that he was also the man above all others responsible for the general adoption of the Constitution. Many a great American of his time and later ones was to be first a nationalist and later a regionalist, or a sectionalist and then a nationalist—the names of John C. Calhoun and Daniel Webster come to mind. Not so with Washington, who stoutly and firmly fought against sectional prejudice in the Continental army, in the struggle over the Constitution, and in the presidency. Even now we perhaps do not value

---

[5] Long afterward, the Reverend Jonathan Boucher, whose acquaintance with Washington was hardly intimate, said the Southern colonists feared in 1775 that they would be dominated by a Northern army after independence had been achieved and that Washington's acceptance of the supreme command was dictated, "more than anything else," by a desire to prevent such a horrid outcome. At the time, Governor Jonathan Trumbull of Connecticut expressed a hope that the selection of Washington would "cement the union between the Northern & Southern colonies— & remove any jealousies of a N England army (if they should prove successfull) being formidable to the other provinces." In the summer of 1776 General Persifor Frazer of Pennsylvania also commented from Fort Ticonderoga upon fear of New England. "No man was ever more disappointed in his expectations respecting New Englanders than I have been. They are a set of low, dirty, griping, cowardly, lying rascals. There are some few exceptions and very few.... You may inform all your acquaintance not to be afraid that they will ever conquer the other provinces (which you know was much talked of), 10,000 Pennsylvanians would I think be sufficient for ten times that number out of their own country. All the Southern troops live in great harmony."

fully his devotion to the nation. First in war, first in peace, first in the hearts of his countrymen, he was also first in his allegiance and contribution to American unity.

Although the appointment of Washington as commander in chief was a triumph for nationalism, sectionalism also had its victories during that part of the Revolutionary War which preceded the Declaration of Independence. It will be recalled that the movement toward complete separation from Britain during the first fifteen months of the Revolutionary War was accompanied by a movement toward an American union. Thus when Richard Henry Lee of Virginia introduced in Congress on June 7, 1776, his famous resolution declaring that "These United Colonies are and of right ought to be free and independent states," he also called for the making of an American federation. By most public men in Congress and out, independence and political union were considered as virtually inseparable. Indeed, there were Patriot leaders in the spring of 1776, including Patrick Henry, who asserted that the Americans should marry each other before they declared themselves divorced from the British. These claimed that independence would be easier to achieve if union were secured before issuing a formal announcement that America had left the empire. As early as the fall of 1775 the Revolutionary legislature of North Carolina indicated its disapproval of the famous plan of confederation submitted by Benjamin Franklin because it gave New England larger representation in the federal legislature than the North Carolina men were willing to concede to it. This was much to the satisfaction of Josiah Martin, the last royal governor of North Carolina, who claimed that Franklin's arrangements would enable the North "to give law" to the South and who gleefully asserted that the North would use its power, since there was in New England a "lust of domination."

Any argument which might serve to sow dissension among the Patriots was welcomed by Josiah Martin, and also by James Anderson, another supporter of the Crown, who sought to frighten the South to the advantage of Britain. In a pamphlet published at Edinburgh in 1776 Anderson predicted that an independent American union would be disastrous for the Southerners. They would form a minority in an American legislature, and their economic interests would be injured to the benefit of those of the Northerners. Time would bring so great exasperation at the South that the Southerners would seek to form a new nation. They would not be permitted to leave the union peacefully; and, fewer in numbers and enervated by heat, they would be defeated in war. Thereafter they would live in a state of inferiority and subjection to the North. It turned out that there was basic truth coupled with error in Anderson's calculations and predictions. And his reputation as a prophet must also suffer because he foresaw what he wished to foresee, that parting from England would not bring such sweet tomorrows to the Americans.

Josiah Martin and James Anderson, not friends to American freedom, told the Southerners they should not join an American union. Other men not hostile to independence said such a union could not be formed because of the contrarieties which existed in the Thirteen. In the middle of the 1780's it was frequently suggested by Americans not seeking to return to the British empire that two or even three confederacies would rise along the Atlantic coast. One of these would be Southern, including Maryland and the states to her southward. There might be two confederations north of the Mason-Dixon line, one in New England and another composed of the Middle states; or New England and the Middle states might form one union. As late as 1788 Patrick Henry was accused, and not entirely without reason, of seeking to create a Southern confederacy. There were even Southern public men of the Revolutionary period who believed, because of the power of local loyalties, that the Thirteen States must go their separate ways. So Thomas Burke of North Carolina asserted in 1778 that an American union was a "chimerical project." So William Blount of the same state in July, 1787, declared, "I still think we shall ultimately and not many years ... be separated and distinct governments perfectly independent of each other." To be sure, both Burke and Blount afterward changed their minds.

Because of the difficulty of assessing the conflicting forces which supported state loyalties, regional confederacies, and general union, no one could assuredly predict during the twelve years after the Declaration of Independence what political form or forms the Americans would adopt. It may be guessed that personalities, and even chance, affected the outcome, despite the conviction of George Bancroft that the course of events was personally and intimately directed by the Deity.

It could be safely predicted, however, that troubles must arise between South and North in a union with a central government possessing substantial powers. Sectional conflicts continued throughout the war. When Washington's army was undergoing its ordeal at Valley Forge in the winter of 1777–1778, Virginians and South Carolinians were voicing alarm lest Congress under the Articles of Confederation possess too great authority, to the detriment of Southern interests. That body during the years 1781–1787 was often riven by strife between South and North. Southern fears of Northern domination appeared in the Philadelphia Convention of 1787, and were frequently and forcefully asserted in the contests over ratification of the Constitution which took place below the Mason-Dixon line. Those fears were often based in part upon acute reasoning; indeed, in view of later occurrences, few will say they were without some solid foundation.

6

Of Time and Frontiers: The Myth of "Cavalier" Confederate Leadership

Wilbur J. Cash

Of those myths peculiar to the pre–Civil War South, none has
proved more enduring than the belief in a historically continuous
southern aristocracy. According to the romantic myth of the Old
South, country gentlemen of courtliness and stately hospitality pre-
sided over southern society during the antebellum period. The late
Wilbur Cash, freelance writer and former Associate Editor of the
Charlotte (North Carolina) *News,* seeks to counter this image by
forwarding arguments against such a legendary sociology. In pur-
suing the social reality of the antebellum South, Mr. Cash notes
that two critical factors were perpetually at odds with the idea of
an all-pervasive cavalier society—the element of time and the ever
present frontier environment. In addition, the proven incidence of
social mobility among earlier southerners scarcely suggests the existence of a full-blown, closed aristocracy in the making. To the
degree that subtle notions of class did begin to manifest themselves
in the Old South, such social distinctions were linked, as is invariably the case in most Western societies, not to lineage but rather to
property ownership. The southern "aristocracy" of the Old Regime
was at best one of rank rather than caste—a creation of the mind
of the South.

Though . . . nobody any longer holds to the Cavalier thesis in its overt
form, it remains true that the popular mind still clings to it in essence. Explicit or implicit in most considerations of the land, and despite a gathering

tendency on the part of the more advanced among the professional historians, and lately even on the part of popular writers, to cast doubt on it, the assumption persists that the great South of the first half of the nineteenth century—the South which fought the Civil War—was the home of a genuine and fully realized aristocracy, coextensive and identical with the ruling class, the planters; and sharply set apart from the common people, still pretty often lumped indiscriminately together as the poor whites, not only by economic condition but also by the far vaster gulf of a different blood and a different (and long and solidly established) heritage.

To suppose this, however, is to ignore the frontier and that *sine qua non* of aristocracy everywhere—the dimension of time. And to ignore the frontier and time in setting up a conception of the social state of the Old South is to abandon reality. For the history of this South throughout a very great part of the period from the opening of the nineteenth century to the Civil War (in the South beyond the Mississippi until long after that war) is mainly the history of the roll of frontier upon frontier—and on to the frontier beyond.

Prior to the close of the Revolutionary period the great South, as such, has little history. Two hundred years had run since John Smith had saved Jamestown, but the land which was to become the cotton kingdom was still more wilderness than not. In Virginia—in the Northern Neck, all along the tidewater, spreading inland along the banks of the James, the York, the Rappahannock, flinging thinly across the redlands to the valley of the Shenandoah, echoing remotely about the dangerous water of Albemarle—in South Carolina and Georgia—along a sliver of swamp country running from Charleston to Georgetown and Savannah—and in and around Hispano-Gallic New Orleans, there was something which could be called effective settlement and societal organization.

Here, indeed, there was a genuine, if small, aristocracy. Here was all that in aftertime was to give color to the legend of the Old South. Here were silver and carriages and courtliness and manner. Here were great houses—not as great as we are sometimes told, but still great houses: the Shirleys, the Westovers, the Stratfords. Here were the names that were some time to flash with swords and grow tall in thunder—the Lees, the Stuarts, and the Beauregards. Charleston, called the most brilliant of American cities by Crèvecoeur, played a miniature London, with overtones of La Rochelle, to a small squirarchy of the rice plantations. In Virginia great earls played at Lord Bountiful, dispensing stately hospitality to every passer-by—to the barge captain on his way down the river, to the slaver who had this morning put into the inlet with a cargo of likely Fulah boys, to the wandering Yankee peddling his platitudinous wooden nutmeg, and to other great earls, who came, with their ladies, in canopied boats or in coach and six with liveried outriders. New Orleans was a pageant of dandies and coxcombs, and all the swamplands could show a social life of a considerable pretension.

It is well, however, to remember a thing or two about even these Virginians. (For brevity's sake, I shall treat only of the typical case of the Virginians, and shall hereafter generally apply the term as embracing all these little clumps of colonial aristocracy in the lowlands.) It is well to remember not only that they were not generally Cavaliers in their origin but also that they did not spring up to be aristocrats in a day. The two hundred years since Jamestown must not be forgotten. It is necessary to conceive Virginia as beginning very much as New England began—as emerging by slow stages from a primitive backwoods community, made up primarily of farmers and laborers. Undoubtedly there was a sprinkling of gentlemen of a sort—minor squires, younger sons of minor squires, or adventurers who had got themselves a crest, a fine coat, and title to huge slices of the country. And probably some considerable part of the aristocrats at the end of the Revolution are to be explained as stemming from these bright-plumed birds. It is certain that the great body of them cannot be so explained.

The odds were heavy against such gentlemen—against any gentlemen at all, for that matter. The land had to be wrested from the forest and the intractable red man. It was a harsh and bloody task, wholly unsuited to the talents which won applause in the neighborhood of Rotten Row and Covent Garden, or even in Hants or the West Riding. Leadership, for the great part, passed inevitably to rough and ready hands. While milord tarried at dice or languidly directed his even more languid workmen, his horny-palmed neighbors increasingly wrung profits from the earth, got themselves into position to extend their holdings, to send to England for redemptioners and convict servants in order to extend them still further, rose steadily toward equality with him, attained it, passed him, were presently buying up his bankrupt remains.

The very redemptioners and convict servants were apt to fare better than the gentleman. These are the people, of course, who are commonly said to explain the poor whites of the Old South, and so of our own time. It is generally held of them that they were uniformly shiftless or criminal, and that these characters, being inherent in the germ plasm, were handed on to their progeny, with the result that the whole body of them continually sank lower and lower in the social scale. The notion has the support of practically all the standard histories of the United States, as for example those of John Bach McMaster and James Ford Rhodes. But, as Professor G. W. Dyer, of Vanderbilt University, has pointed out in his monograph, *Democracy in the South before the Civil War,* it has little support in the known facts.

In the first place, there is no convincing evidence that, as a body, they came of congenitally inferior stock. If some of the convicts were thieves or cutthroats or prostitutes, then some of them were also mere political prisoners, and so, ironically, may very well have represented as good blood as there was in Virginia. Perhaps the majority were simply debtors. As for the redemptioners, the greater number of them seem to have been mere children or adolescents, lured from home by professional crimps or outright kidnapped. It is likely enough, to be sure, that most of them were still to be classed as laborers or the children of laborers; but it is an open question whether this involves any actual inferiority, and certainly it involved no practical inferiority in this frontier society.

On the contrary. Most of them were freed while still in their twenties. Every freeman was entitled to a headright of fifty acres. Unclaimed lands remained plentiful in even the earliest-settled areas until long after the importation of bound servants had died out before slavery. And to cap it all, tobacco prices rose steadily. Thus, given precisely those qualities of physical energy and dogged application which, in the absence of degeneracy, are pre-eminently the heritage of the laborer, the former redemptioner (or convict, for that matter) was very likely to do what so many other men of his same general stamp were doing all about him: steadily to build up his capital and become a man of substance and respect. There is abundant evidence that the thing did so happen. Adam Thoroughgood, who got to be the greatest planter in Norfolk, entered the colony as an indentured servant. Dozens of others who began in the same status are known to have become justices of the peace, vestrymen, and officers of the militia—positions reserved, of course, for gentlemen. And more than one established instance bears out *Moll Flanders.*

In sum, it is clear that distinctions were immensely supple, and that the test of a gentleman in seventeenth-century Virginia was what the test of a gentleman is likely to be in any rough young society—the possession of a sufficient property.

Aristocracy in any real sense did not develop until after the passage of a hundred years—until after 1700. From the foundations carefully built up by his father and grandfather, a Carter, a Page, a Shirley began to tower decisively above the ruck of farmers, pyramided his holdings in land and slaves, squeezed out his smaller neighbors and relegated them to the remote Shenandoah, abandoned his story-and-a-half house for his new "hall," sent his sons to William and Mary and afterward to the English universities or the law schools in London. These sons brought back the manners of the Georges and more developed and subtle notions of class. And the sons of these in turn began to think of themselves as true aristocrats and to be accepted as such by those about them—to set themselves consciously to the elaboration and propagation of a tradition.

But even here the matter must not be conceived too rigidly, or as having taken place very extensively. The number of those who had moved the whole way into aristocracy even by the time of the Revolution was small.

Most of the Virginians who counted themselves gentlemen were still, in reality, hardly more than superior farmers. Many great property-holders were still almost, if not quite, illiterate. Life in the greater part of the country was still more crude than not. The frontier still lent its tang to the manners of even the most advanced, all the young men who were presently to rule the Republic having been more or less shaped by it. And, as the emergence of Jeffersonian democracy from exactly this milieu testifies, rank had not generally hardened into caste.

But this Virginia was not the great South. By paradox, it was not even all of Virginia. It was a narrow world, confined to the areas where tobacco, rice, and indigo could profitably be grown on a large scale—to a relatively negligible fraction, that is, of the Southern country. All the rest, at the close of the Revolution, was still in the frontier or semi-frontier stage. Here were no baronies, no plantations, and no manors. And here was no aristocracy nor any fully established distinction save that eternal one between man and man.

In the vast backcountry of the seaboard states, there lived unchanged the pioneer breed—the unsuccessful and the restless from the older regions; the homespun Scotch-Irish, dogged out of Pennsylvania and Maryland by poverty and the love of freedom; pious Moravian brothers, as poor as they were pious; stolid Lutheran peasants from northern Germany; ragged, throat-slitting Highlanders, lusting for elbow-room and still singing hotly of Bonnie Prince Charlie; all that generally unpretentious and often hard-bitten crew which, from about 1740, had been slowly filling up the region. Houses, almost without exception, were cabins of logs. Farms were clearings, on which was grown enough corn to meet the grower's needs, and perhaps a little tobacco which once a year was "rolled" down to a landing on a navigable stream. Roads and trade hardly yet existed. Life had but ceased to be a business of Indian fighting. It was still largely a matter of coon-hunting, of "painter" tales and hard drinking.

Westward, Boone had barely yesterday blazed his trail. Kentucky and Tennessee were just opening up. And southward of the Nashville basin, the great Mississippi Valley, all that country which was to be Alabama, Mississippi, western Georgia, and northern Louisiana, was still mainly a wasteland, given over to the noble savage and peripatetic traders with an itch for adventure and a taste for squaw seraglios.

Then the Yankee, Eli Whitney, interested himself in the problem of extracting the seed from a recalcitrant fiber, and cotton was on its way to be king. The despised backcountry was coming into its own—but slowly at first. Cotton would release the plantation from the narrow confines of the coastlands and the tobacco belt, and stamp it as the reigning pattern on all the country. Cotton would end stagnation, beat back the wilderness, mow the forest, pour black men and plows and mules along the Yazoo and the

Arkansas, spin out the railroad, freight the yellow waters of the Mississippi with panting stern-wheelers—in brief, create the great South. But not in a day. It was necessary to wait until the gin could be proved a success, until experience had shown that the uplands of Carolina and Georgia were pregnant with wealth, until the rumor was abroad in the world that the blacklands of the valley constituted a new El Dorado.

It was 1800 before the advance of the plantation was really under way, and even then the pace was not too swift. The physical difficulties to be overcome were enormous. And beyond the mountains the first American was still a dismaying problem. It was necessary to wait until Andrew Jackson and the men of Tennessee could finally crush him. 1810 came and went, the battle of New Orleans was fought and won, and it was actually 1820 before the plantation was fully on the march, striding over the hills of Carolina to Mississippi—1820 before the tide of immigration was in full sweep about the base of the Appalachians.

From 1820 to 1860 is but forty years—a little more than the span of a single generation. The whole period from the invention of the cotton gin to the outbreak of the Civil War is less than seventy years—the lifetime of a single man. Yet it was wholly within the longer of these periods, and mainly within the shorter, that the development and growth of the great South took place. Men who, as children, had heard the war-whoop of the Cherokee in the Carolina backwoods lived to hear the guns at Vicksburg. And thousands of other men who had looked upon Alabama when it was still a wilderness and upon Mississippi when it was still a stubborn jungle, lived to fight—and to fight well, too—in the ranks of the Confederate armies.

The inference is plain. It is impossible to conceive the great South as being, on the whole, more than a few steps removed from the frontier stage at the beginning of the Civil War. It is imperative, indeed, to conceive it as having remained more or less fully in the frontier stage for a great part— maybe the greater part—of its antebellum history. However rapidly the plantation might advance, however much the slave might smooth the way, it is obvious that the mere physical process of subduing the vast territory which was involved, the essential frontier process of wresting a stable foothold from a hostile environment, must have consumed most of the years down to 1840. . . .

How account for the ruling class, then? Manifestly, for the great part, by the strong, the pushing, the ambitious, among the old coon-hunting population of the backcountry. The frontier was their predestined inheritance. They possessed precisely the qualities necessary to the taming of the land and the building of the cotton kingdom. The process of their rise to power was simplicity itself. Take a concrete case.

A stout young Irishman brought his bride into the Carolina up-country about 1800. He cleared a bit of land, built a log cabin of two rooms, and sat down to the pioneer life. One winter, with several of his neighbors, he loaded a boat with whisky and the coarse woolen cloth woven by the women and drifted down to Charleston to trade. There, remembering the fondness of his woman for a bit of beauty, he bought a handful of cotton seed, which she planted about the cabin with the wild rose and the honeysuckle—as a flower. Afterward she learned, under the tutelage of a new neighbor, to pick the seed from the fiber with her fingers and to spin it into yarn. Another winter the man drifted down the river, this time to find the halfway station of Columbia in a strange ferment. There was a new wonder in the world—the cotton gin—and the forest which had lined the banks of the stream for a thousand centuries was beginning to go down. Fires flared red and portentous in the night— to set off and answering fire in the breast of the Irishman.

Land in his neighborhood was to be had for fifty cents an acre. With twenty dollars, the savings of his lifetime, he bought forty acres and set himself to clear it. Rising long before day, he toiled deep into the night, with his wife holding a pine torch for him to see by. Aided by his neighbors, he piled the trunks of the trees into great heaps and burned them, grubbed up the stumps, hacked away the tangle of underbrush and vine, stamped out the poison ivy and the snakes. A wandering trader sold him a horse, bony and half-starved, for a knife, a dollar, and a gallon of whisky. Every day now—Sundays not excepted—when the heavens allowed, and every night that the moon came, he drove the plow into the earth, with uptorn roots bruising his shanks at every step. Behind him came his wife with a hoe. In a few years the land was beginning to yield cotton—richly, for the soil was fecund with the accumulated mold of centuries. Another trip down the river, and he brought home a mangy black slave—an old and lazy fellow reckoned of no account in the ricelands, but with plenty of life in him still if you knew how to get it out. Next year the Irishman bought fifty acres more, and the year after another black. Five years more and he had two hundred acres and ten Negroes. Cotton prices swung up and down sharply, but always, whatever the return, it was almost pure velvet. For the fertility of the soil seemed inexhaustible.

When he was forty-five, he quit work, abandoned the log house, which had grown to six rooms, and built himself a wide-spreading frame cottage. When he was fifty, he became a magistrate, acquired a carriage, and built a cotton gin and a third house—a "big house" this time. It was not, to be truthful, a very grand house really. Built of lumber sawn on the place, it was a little crude and had not cost above a thousand dollars, even when the marble mantel was counted in. Essentially, it was just a box, with four rooms, bisected by a hallway, set on four more rooms bisected by another hallway, and a detached kitchen at the back. Wind-swept in winter, it was difficult to keep clean of vermin in summer. But it was huge, it had great columns in front, and it was eventually painted white, and so, in this land of wide fields and pinewoods it seemed very imposing.

Meantime the country around had been growing up. Other "big houses" had been built. There was a county seat now, a cluster of frame houses, stores, and "doggeries" about a red brick courthouse. A Presbyterian parson had drifted in and started an academy, as Presbyterian parsons had a habit of doing everywhere in the South—and Pompeys and Caesars and Ciceros and Platos were multiplying both among the pickaninnies in the slave quarters and among the white children of the "big houses." The Irishman had a piano in his house, on which his daughters, taught by a vagabond German, played as well as young ladies could be expected to. One of the Irishman's sons went to the College of South Carolina, came back to grow into the chief lawyer in the county, got to be a judge, and would have been Governor if he had not died at the head of his regiment at Chancellorsville.

As a crown on his career, the old man went to the Legislature, where he was accepted by the Charleston gentlemen tolerantly and with genuine liking. He grew extremely mellow in age and liked to pass his time in company, arguing about predestination and infant damnation, proving conclusively that cotton was king and that the damyankee didn't dare do anything about it, and developing a notable taste in the local liquors. Tall and well made, he grew whiskers after the Galway fashion—the well-kept whiteness of which contrasted very agreeably with the brick red of his complexion—donned the long-tailed coat, stove-pipe hat, and string tie of the statesmen of his period, waxed innocently pompous, and, in short, became a really striking figure of a man.

Once, going down to Columbia for the inauguration of a new Governor, he took his youngest daughter along. There she met a Charleston gentleman who was pestering her father for a loan. Her manner, formed by the Presbyterian parson, was plain but not bad, and she was very pretty. Moreover, the Charleston gentleman was decidedly in hard lines. So he married her.

When the old man finally died in 1854, he left two thousand acres, a hundred and fourteen slaves, and four cotton gins. The little newspaper which had recently set up in the county seat spoke of him as "a gentleman of the old school" and "a noble specimen of the chivalry at its best"; the Charleston papers each gave him a column; and a lordly Legaré introduced resolutions of respect into the Legislature. His wife outlived him by ten years—by her portrait a beautifully fragile old woman, and, as I have heard it said, with lovely hands, knotted and twisted just enough to give them character, and a finely transparent skin through which the blue veins showed most aristocratically.

7

American Slavery

Gerald N. Grob and George Athan Billias

A great measure of the South's mythology not only results from the undeniable strength of the region's collective beliefs, social codes, and cultural rituals but eminates from its racially based mythology as well. Compounding the matter still further, the peculiar nature of the institution of slavery has generated significant points of debate and interpretation—a contributing influence in its own right to the ambiguities that plague one's clear understanding of the region. Drawing special attention to the historiography of slavery—the perpetual interplay of historical facts and the theoretical frames of interpretation historians have drawn in an attempt to explain an elusive past—Gerald N. Grob of Rutgers and George Athan Billias of Clark University dramatize the point that the usual image of slavery as rather exclusively a southern phenomenon must itself be adjusted in favor of a national perspective. The patterns of "American slavery" not only implicitly obliterate what has been called the "myth of the Mason-Dixon Line"—the guilt-relieving assumption most often made by northerners that their responsibility in relation to slavery was peripheral at best—but also emphasize the many points of theoretical and practical debate with which historians have and still do contend. The "politics of interpretation," the manner in which set assumptions as to the nature and meaning of slavery most always reflects contemporary preoccupations, itself is a contributing influence to the creation of myth. Moreover, the black experience must be seen as central to the southern experience—blacks, if you will, are southerners too. Resting solidly at the center, for those

> seeking to explain the black experience in some detail, are recurring questions regarding slavery's morality, legitimacy, profitability, its relationship to paternalism and capitalism, and its effects upon black culture, identity, community, and social institutions.

Although Americans of the mid-nineteenth century were prone to glorify their nation and its institutions, they were also aware that millions of blacks remained enslaved and possessed none of the legal rights and privileges promised to citizens by the Declaration of Independence. Paradoxically, a people who prided themselves on having created one of the freest societies in the world also sanctioned slavery—an institution that many other nations less free had long since abolished.

The existence of the "peculiar institution," of course, played a crucial role in American history. In the Constitutional Convention of 1787 the founding fathers were forced to deal with its presence. Despite subsequent efforts at suppression the slavery controversy would not remain quiescent. The presumed compromise settlements of 1820 and 1850 proved transitory. Ultimately it took a long and bloody civil war to end the legal existence of the "peculiar institution." Even after that war the problems posed by the presence of a black minority in a predominantly white society continued to plague generations of Americans from the Civil War to the present.

Just as northerners and southerners debated the morality and legitimacy of slavery in antebellum decades, so too have later historians disagreed over the nature of the "peculiar institution." Controversy rather than consensus characterizes the debates among historians. Scholars cannot agree on the origins of slavery; they debate why it was that only blacks were enslaved and Indians and indentured servants were not. They disagree as to whether racism preceded slavery or if racial prejudice developed as a rationalization of an already established institution.[1] Similarly, historians continue to debate the nature of slavery and its immediate and enduring impact upon black Americans.

The framework for the historical debate over slavery was first established by the participants in the controversy in the decades preceding the

---

[1] Cf. Oscar and Mary F. Handlin, "Origins of the Southern Labor System," *William and Mary Quarterly,* 3d ser. 7 (1950): 199–222; Winthrop D. Jordan, *White over Black: American Attitudes toward the Negro, 1550–1812* (Chapel Hill, 1968); and Edmund S. Morgan, *American Slavery, American Freedom: The Ordeal of Colonial Virginia* (New York, 1975).

Civil War. Northerners bent on making a strong case against slavery were prone to seek out those facts that buttressed their positions. Southerners, on the other hand, were equally determined to show the beneficence of their "peculiar institution." Similarly, the large number of eyewitness accounts of travelers in the South tended to reflect personal views regarding the morality or immorality of slavery. From the very beginning, therefore, questions about the nature of slavery tended to be discussed within a predominantly moral framework.

The first serious scholarly effort to delineate the nature of slavery came from a group of historians who came to the fore in the 1880s and 1890s. Being a generation removed from the Civil War they were less involved emotionally in the issue. These scholars tended to view the end of slavery as a blessing to both North and South. The Civil War, once and for all, had sealed the bonds of unity in blood and had created a single nation rather than a collection of sovereign states. Nationalistic in their orientation, these historians developed an interpretation of slavery similar in many respects to the one held by some prewar antislavery partisans.

James Ford Rhodes, a businessman turned historian who published a major multivolume history of the United States covering the period from 1850 to 1877, was perhaps typical of this nationalist school of scholars. His first volume began with an unequivocal statement of his position: slavery was an immoral institution. Rhodes's treatment of slavery was little more than a restatement of Henry Clay's famous dictum that "slavery is a curse to the master and a wrong to the slave." He cited evidence that blacks were often overworked and underfed. The institution was brutalizing; the slave and slave family lacked any legal right to afford a measure of protection against the arbitrary and often cruel behavior by white masters. Pointing to the sexual exploitation of black women, Rhodes insisted that slavery had debased the entire nation.[2] His study established the pattern for much of the subsequent treatment of American slavery by historians.

Surprisingly enough Rhodes's work gained general acceptance not only among northern historians but among southern scholars as well. Southerners were willing to condemn slavery as a reactionary institution that inhibited the economic development of their section. They now welcomed its abolition and looked forward to a new era of prosperity in which the South would share in the nation's industrial progress. Rhodes's hostility toward the Radical Reconstruction program after 1865 and his willingness to acquiesce in the right of southern whites to deal with the

[2] James Ford Rhodes, *History of the United States from the Compromise of 1850 to the Final Restoration of Home Rule in the South in 1877*, 7 vols. (New York, 1893–1906), 1.

race question as they saw fit made his views acceptable in that part of the country.

For nearly a quarter of a century, the historical view of slavery followed the pattern set forth by Rhodes and other nationalist scholars. In 1918, however, Ulrich Bonnell Phillips—undoubtedly the most important historian of the antebellum South—published his *American Negro Slavery*. From that moment the debate over slavery assumed a somewhat different form. Subsequent historians, whatever their views, had to take Phillips's work into account. Indeed, it may not be too much to claim that the vitality of the historiographical debate over slavery was due in large measure to Phillips's pioneering contributions.

Born in Georgia in 1877, Phillips attended the state university and then went on to receive his doctorate at Columbia University. Rather than return to the South he accepted an offer from the University of Wisconsin, then a center of American Progressivism. Phillips adopted many of the tenets of Progressivism; as a scholar he attempted to break with the emphasis on political and legal events and to study the underlying social and economic factors responsible for shaping the nation's history. Aside from his commitment to much of the ideology of Progressivism, Phillips was an indefatigable researcher; his work was marked by deep and intensive study of original sources drawn from plantation records.

Phillips's view of slavery grew out of his general interpretation of antebellum Southern society. Focusing on the plantation system he sought to demonstrate that it was more than a system of landholding or of racial exploitation. The plantation was rather a complete social system in which paternalism and capitalism went hand in hand. Indeed, his commentaries on the new postwar South tended to be highly critical because he believed that industrial capitalism without any redeeming humane and paternalistic features was cruel and harsh. His sympathetic portrayal of the Old South, as Eugene Genovese remarked, was "an appeal for the incorporation of the more humane and rational values of pre-bourgeois culture into modern industrial life."

Slavery, according to Phillips, was above all a system of education. Sharing the racial views held by many southerners and northerners (particularly those who believed in the Progressive ideology), Phillips viewed blacks as a docile, childlike people who required the care and guidance of paternalistic whites. In this sense he rejected another stereotype held by many of his contemporaries who feared and hated blacks. Bringing together massive evidence from original sources Phillips painted a subtle and complex portrait of slavery that repudiated the older allegations that the system was inhumane and cruel. Indeed, he emphasized over and over again the profound human relationship that existed between paternal white masters and faithful and childlike black slaves. Yet Phillips, despite the sharp differences in interpretation, owed a significant debt to earlier scholars like Rhodes, for his categories in studying slavery—labor, food, clothing, shelter, care, and the profitability of the system—were precisely the same as those of his predecessor. *American Negro Slavery*, then, was both a sympathetic portrait of the past and commentary on a harsh and impersonal present.[3] For nearly a generation Phillips's view of slavery remained the dominant one. Scholars who followed in his footsteps made a few revisions, but none altered the general picture he had so skillfully sketched. One of the few exceptions was Herbert Aptheker's study of slave revolts in 1943. Aptheker challenged Phillips's portrait of docile slaves and insisted that "discontent and rebelliousness" was more characteristic.[4]

At the same time that Phillips's interpretation of slavery was becoming dominant, a reaction began setting in against the prevailing theories of race. The work of figures like Franz Boas and others had begun to undermine racial interpretations of culture; an emphasis on environment slowly began to replace the earlier belief in the primacy of race. The experiences of the 1930s and 1940s further discredited racist theories, particularly after the ramifications of this doctrine were revealed by events in Nazi Germany. The political ideologies of these decades, moreover, involved a rejection of race theory on both scientific and philosophical grounds. In view of these developments, it was not surprising that the interpretation espoused by Phillips began to be challenged by critics who did not share his historical, racial, or political ideas.

The attack on Phillips and the efforts to discredit *American Negro Slavery*, oddly enough, did not alter the framework within which the debate over slavery took place. Indeed, critics accepted the same categories of analysis employed by Phillips and his predecessors. Their differences with him were largely moral in character. Where Phillips painted a portrait of a harmonious, interdependent, and humane system, his detractors emphasized the cruel and arbitrary nature of slavery, its economic and sexual exploitation, and the degree to which blacks resisted the abominations practiced by their masters. Moreover, Phillips's research methodology came under careful scrutiny. Richard Hofstadter, in an article published in 1944, argued that *American Negro*

[3] For sympathetic evaluations of Phillips's achievements see Eugene D. Genovese, "Race and Class in Southern History: An Appraisal of the Work of Ulrich Bonnell Phillips," *Agricultural History* 41 (October 1967): 345–358; and Daniel J. Singal, "Ulrich Bonnell Phillips: The Old South as the New," *Journal of American History* 63 (March 1977): 871–891.

[4] Herbert Aptheker, *American Negro Slave Revolts* (New York, 1943).

Slavery was flawed because its thesis rested on a faulty sampling of plantation records. Most slaves lived on smaller plantations or farms, Hofstadter noted, whereas Phillips used records of large plantations.[5]

The attack on Phillips culminated in 1956 when Kenneth M. Stampp published *The Peculiar Institution*. Stampp, some years earlier, had become convinced that the time was ripe for a complete reappraisal of the subject. Besides the problems of a biased sample of plantation records and a reluctance to use unfavorable contemporary travel accounts, Stampp charged, Phillips had accepted without question assumptions about the supposed inferiority of blacks.[6] *The Peculiar Institution*, then, was written specifically to revise *American Negro Slavery*. In place of a harmonious antebellum South, Stampp pictured a system of labor that rested upon the simple element of force. In a chapter entitled "To Make Them Stand in Fear," he argued that, without the power to punish, the system of bondage could not have been sustained.

Yet Stampp was unable to break out of the mold within which the debate over slavery had taken place; his analytical categories were virtually identical to those of Rhodes and Phillips. The difference— which was by no means insignificant—was that Stampp's view of slavery was quite similar to that held by northern abolitionists.

The Peculiar Institution summed up nearly a century of historical controversy. Its author, as a matter of fact, was forced by his own evidence to qualify any sweeping generalization about slavery. He conceded that the "only generalization that can be made with relative confidence is that some masters were harsh and frugal, others were mild and generous, and the rest ran the whole gamut in between." Moreover, Stampp's egalitarian commitment led him to see slavery not through the eyes of slaves (an admittedly difficult task) but through the eyes of whites. "Negroes," he wrote in his introduction, "*are,* after all, only white men with black skins, nothing more, nothing less."[7]

Shortly after Stampp published his book the debate over slavery took a new shape. There were a number of reasons for this transformation. No doubt the diminishing returns within the traditional conceptual framework played a role. More important, historians and social scientists were beginning to raise certain kinds of issues about the nature of the black

[5] Richard Hofstadter, "U.B. Phillips and the Plantation Legend," *Journal of Negro History* 29 (April 1944): 109–124. The criticisms of Phillips can be followed in the pages of the *Journal of Negro History*.

[6] Kenneth M. Stampp, "The Historian and Southern Negro Slavery," *American Historical Review* 57 (April 1952): 613–624.

[7] Kenneth M. Stampp, *The Peculiar Institution: Slavery in the Ante-Bellum South* (New York, 1956), pp. vii, 616.

experience in America that resulted in some radical rethinking about slavery. Computer technology also make it possible for the first time to use data in ways that were previously impracticable. But perhaps the most significant factor was the changes in the intellectual milieu of the late 1950s and the period thereafter. During the civil rights movement, blacks and whites alike challenged the prevailing patterns of social and economic relations between the races. The ensuing reorientation of social and political thought quickly influenced the writing of American history. Slavery became one of the most vital and controversial subjects in American history, and the evidence is strong that the subject will continue to be of great interest to future scholars.

The first major challenge to traditional historiography came in 1959 when Stanley Elkins published a brief study entitled *Slavery: A Problem in American Institutional and Intellectual Life*. Elkins's book was not based on new data. Indeed, when compared with Stampp's *The Peculiar Institution*, it was evident that *Slavery* was written without significant research in existing primary sources. What Elkins did—and herein lay the significance of his work—was to pose a series of questions that moved the debate over the nature of slavery to a totally new plane.

Elkins began his study by noting that the abolition of slavery in Latin America had not left the severe race problem faced by the United States. Intrigued by this observation, Elkins concluded that it was the absence of countervailing institutions in the United States such as a strong national church that permitted slavery to develop without any obstructions that might mitigate its power. Second, Elkins stressed the harshness of American slavery and argued that it had a devastating impact on the black personality. He insisted that the Black Sambo stereotype—the shuffling, happy-go-lucky, not very intelligent black—had a basis in fact. Elkins used the analogy of the Nazi concentration camps to demonstrate that total, or totalitarian, institutions could reduce their inmates to perpetual childlike dependency. Hence the all-encompassing institution of slavery had given rise to the Sambo personality type. Implicit in Elkins's work was the belief that slavery victimized blacks by stripping them of their African heritage, making them dependent on whites, and preventing them from forming any cohesive family structure.

Elkins's thesis seemed acceptable to historians and other Americans, at first, partly because it undermined still further a racial ideology that had assumed the innate inferiority of blacks. By stressing that blacks were victims of slavery, Elkins repudiated the more benign view of that institution and even made Stampp's unflattering description far less potent. Moreover, Elkins appeared to provide intellectual support for compensatory social and economic programs in the 1960s designed to help blacks overcome residual effects of slavery. Elkins implicitly placed the responsibility for the nation's racial dilemmas squarely upon whites by picturing blacks as unwilling victims of white transgressions.

Elkins's book had (and still has) a profound influence. First, it raised questions heretofore neglected, such as the relationship between slavery and subsequent racial conflict. Second, it inspired a group of scholars to undertake studies of comparative slave systems in order to answer some questions posed by Elkins. Third, it placed the slavery debate within a new conceptual framework, for Elkins had focused less on slavery as an institution and more upon blacks themselves. Finally, Elkins—more than his colleagues—had linked history with other social science disciplines.[8]

Yet within a few years after the appearance of his book, Elkins found himself under attack from both within and outside his discipline. Some historians were concerned about the book's facile use of hypotheses taken from the other social sciences and its relative neglect of data from primary sources. Others felt that Elkins had made too much of the Sambo stereotype; evidence of slave resistance seemed to disprove the thesis that blacks had been reduced to childlike dependency. Still others, though not explicitly contradicting Elkins, produced studies that demonstrated that slavery was a far more complex institution than Elkins implied. Richard C. Wade's study of urban slavery, for example, showed that there were behavioral differences between urban black slaves and those who labored on plantations and farms. Conceding that urban slavery was in a state of decline before the Civil War because of the difficulties in maintaining social control, Wade's portrait of urban slaves was not always in agreement with Elkins's Sambo stereotype.[9]

The major assault on Elkins, however, came from outside the ranks of historians. By the mid-1960s a number of ideologies had emerged within the black community. Although integration was still the dominant goal for most blacks, a significant number of them turned inward and articulated black nationalist or other separatist points of view. Bitter at continued white resistance to black demands for full equality, they rejected the goal of integration and assimilation as inappropriate and unattainable. To such spokesmen Elkins's Sambo stereotype undermined

[8] See Ann. J. Lane, ed., *The Debate over Slavery: Stanley Elkins and His Critics* (Urbana, Ill. 1971); and Kenneth M. Stampp, "Rebels and Sambos: The Search for the Negro's Personality in Slavery," *Journal of Southern History* 27 (August 1971): 367–392. For examples of the recent concern with comparative slave systems see Herbert S. Klein, *Slavery in the Americas: A Comparative Study of Cuba and Virginia* (Chicago, 1967); Carl N. Degler, *Neither Black nor White: Slavery and Race Relations in Brazil and the United States* (New York, 1971); and David Brion Davis, *The Problem of Slavery in Western Culture* (Ithaca, 1966), and *The Problem of Slavery in the Age of Revolution* (Ithaca, 1975).

[9] Richard C. Wade, *Slavery in the Cities: The South 1820–1860* (New York, 1964).

the search for a usable past that emphasized instead black achievement and black pride in the face of unremitting white oppression. Moreover, some blacks (and whites) did not care for a thesis that emphasized deprivation. They felt it was simply a sophisticated restatement of racism because it placed part of the responsibility or blame upon the deprived group. Finally, some radicals were hostile to the Sambo image. They posited the idea of perpetual conflict between the oppressors and oppressed, and acceptance of the concept of a docile and nonresisting slave would contradict their own ideological position.

Disagreement with Elkins's view of slave personality and his emphasis on the absence of resistance to white pressure soon led some scholars to study anew the actual life of slaves on plantations. Previous scholarship dealing with slavery, of course, was largely dependent on predominantly *white* sources, including plantation records, newspapers, manuscripts, court records, and travel accounts. The newer scholarship, however, was based on hitherto neglected sources, including a significant number of slave narratives published both before and after the Civil War. During the depression of the 1930s, moreover, the Federal Writers' Project of the Work Projects Administration had subsidized an oral history project in which more than two thousand ex-slaves who were still alive were interviewed. Using these and other sources, historians began to raise some new questions. If, for example, the control of whites was so complete, why did some slaves run away and others engage in all kinds of covert resistance? What kind of institutional structures developed within the slave community? To what degree were these black institutions partly or fully autonomous? Influenced by the "new social history," scholars began to study slave society not as one created by whites but as one that represented to some degree the hopes, aspirations, and thoughts of blacks.

Indicative of the newer approach was the publication in 1972 of two works. The first, *From Sundown to Sunup: The Making of the Black Community,* was based upon the interviews with ex-slaves during the 1930s. Its author, George P. Rawick, also edited eighteen additional volumes printing the text of the interviews. Rawick emphasized that slaves were not passive; he ir   life showed considerable interaction between w   oved from
Africa, blacks created a way   ritage with
the "social forms and behavic   he slave personality, Rawick emphasized   slaves were
submissive and accepted th   a slave. On
the other hand they demor   served as a
protection against infantili   , concluded

Rawick, "developed an independent community and culture which molded the slave personality" and permitted a measure of autonomy.[10]

In a similar vein, John Blassingame's *The Slave Community: Plantation Life in the Ante-Bellum South* described a social setting in which slaves employed a variety of means to circumscribe and inhibit white authority. Family ties among slaves persisted, thus creating a partial protective shield. Blacks also developed and retained religious and mythological beliefs that enabled them to maintain a high degree of autonomy. Slowly but surely the focus of the debate over slavery began a shift of emphasis away from white slaveowners and toward the slaves themselves.[11]

The works of Rawick and Blassingame were received without fanfare or extended debate. Although some criticisms were raised, their contributions were relatively noncontroversial. The same was not true of a book by Robert Fogel and Stanley L. Engerman, *Time on the Cross: The Economics of American Negro Slavery,* which appeared in 1974. Based on quantified data, computer-based analysis, and modern economic theory, Fogel and Engerman presented an interpretation of slavery that set off a fierce and heated debate. Purportedly rejecting virtually every previous work on slavery, the two "new economic historians" presented what seemed to be a series of novel findings about the institution.

Slavery, the two authors emphasized, was not an economically backward system kept in existence by plantation owners unaware of their true interest. On the contrary, southern slave agriculture was highly efficient on the eve of the Civil War. "Economies of large-scale operation, effective management, and intensive utilization of labor and capital made southern slave agriculture 35 percent more efficient than the northern system of family farming." Nor were slaves Sambo-like caricatures; they were hardworking individuals who within the limitations of bondage were able to pursue their own self-interest precisely because they internalized the capitalist values of their masters. Slaveowners encouraged stable black families, rejected the idea of indiscriminate force, did not sexually abuse black women, and provided—by the standards of that era—adequate food, clothing, and shelter. Slavery, therefore, was a model of capitalist efficiency. Within its framework blacks learned and accepted the tenets of the "Protestant ethic" of work. They received, in return, incentives in the form of material rewards,

---

[10] George P. Rawick, *From Sundown to Sunup: The Making of the Black Community* (Westport, 1972), and *The American Slave: A Composite Autobiography,* 18 vols. (Westport, Conn., 1972).

[11] John W. Blassingame, *The Slave Community: Plantation Life in the Ante-Bellum South* (New York, 1972).

opportunities for upward mobility within the plantation hierarchy, and a chance to create their own stable families. Although Fogel and Engerman in no way diminished the moral evil of slavery, they claimed their goal was "to strike down the view that black Americans were without culture, without achievement, and without development for their first two hundred and fifty years on American soil." A major corollary to their view of slavery was their conclusion that in the century following its abolition white Americans systematically attacked and degraded black citizens. Whites drove freed blacks out of skilled occupations, paid them minimal wages, limited their access to education, and imposed a rigid system of segregation that deprived them of many of the opportunities available to whites.[12]

Time on the Cross immediately became the object of an acrimonious debate. Some condemned the hypothesis that slaves willingly accepted white-imposed values. Others attacked the way in which the two authors used historical data to reach flawed conclusions. Still others were unwilling to accept many of the underlying assumptions of the two authors. Indeed, within a short period of time the literature criticizing *Time on the Cross* was enormous.[13]

At precisely the same time that *Time on the Cross* appeared Eugene D. Genovese published *Roll, Jordan, Roll: The World the Slaves Made*. Genovese, who had already written some distinguished works on the antebellum South, denied in his book that slavery was to be understood within the context of modern capitalism. The key to an understanding of the peculiar institution, he insisted, was to be found in the crucial concept of *paternalism*. The destinies of masters and slaves were linked by a set of mutual duties and responsibilities comparable in many ways to the arrangements between lords and serfs under the feudal system. Whites exploited and controlled the labor of socially inferior blacks and, in return, provided them with the basic necessities of life. To blacks slavery meant a recognition of their basic humanity, and this gave them a claim upon their masters. This claim could be manipulated by slaves who accepted the concessions offered to them by their masters and molded them to suit themselves. Within the limitations of the legal system of bondage, therefore, blacks were able to create their own culture. Genovese particularly emphasized slave religion because its affirmation of life served as a weapon for "personal and community

[12] Robert W. Fogel and Stanley L. Engerman, *Time on the Cross: The Economics of American Slavery*, 2 vols. (Boston, 1974). The second volume was subtitled *Evidence and Methods*.

[13] See Herbert G. Gutman, *Slavery and the Numbers Game: A Critique of Time on the Cross* (Urbana, Ill., 1975); and Paul A. David *et al.*, *Reckoning with Slavery: A Critical Study in the Quantitative History of American Negro Slavery* (New York, 1976).

survival." The price the blacks paid for this partial autonomy was the development of a nonrevolutionary and prepolitical consciousness.[14]

In keeping with the newer focus upon the autonomy of slave society as contrasted with the earlier emphasis on dependency, Herbert G. Gutman in 1976 published his study of the black family. Gutman had been one of the most severe critics of *Time on the Cross,* and he wrote a book-length critique which attacked Fogel and Engerman precisely because of their claims of "black achievement under adversity." In *The Black Family in Slavery and Freedom, 1750–1925,* Gutman offered his own views, which, surprisingly enough, were not at all at variance with Fogel and Engerman or, for that matter, with Rawick, Blassingame, or Genovese.

Like many recent "new social historians" Gutman stressed the ability of blacks to adapt themselves to oppression in their own unique ways. In this respect he rejected the claims of Elkins and others about the debilitating impact of slavery upon its unwilling victims. Yet Gutman at the some time denied that plantation capitalism (Fogel and Engerman) and paternalism (Genovese) were necessary components in the process of adaptation. Slaves were able to create their own society, not by reacting to white offers of rewards or by molding the concessions granted them by their masters, but rather by developing a sophisticated family and kinship network that transmitted the Afro-American heritage from generation to generation. The black family, in effect, served to cushion the shock of being uprooted from Africa. If parents were separated from their children by being sold, other relatives became surrogate parents to the remaining children. The stability of the black family rested upon a closely knit nuclear arrangement. Adultery after wedlock, for example, was infrequent. These family values were not imposed by white masters, according to Gutman, for they were rooted in the African cultural inheritance. Blacks were more loyal to each other than were whites, moreover, because the community was the basic means of survival.[15]

The debate over the nature of slavery took a somewhat different turn with the publication in 1977 of Lawrence Levine's *Black Culture and Black Consciousness: Afro-American Folk Thought from Slavery to Freedom.* Rather than utilizing standard plantation and demographic records, Levine uncovered and studied thousands of black songs, folk-

---

[14] Genovese's major works include *The Political Economy of Slavery: Studies in the Economy & Society of the Slave South* (New York, 1965), *The World the Slaveholders Made: Two Essays in Interpretation* (New York, 1969), and *Roll, Jordan, Roll: The World the Slaves Made* (New York, 1974).

[15] Herbert G. Gutman, *The Black Family in Slavery and Freedom, 1750–1925* (New York, 1976).

tales, jokes, and games in an effort to penetrate the minds and personalities of individuals who left few written records. Levine emphatically
rejected Elkins's claim that slavery destroyed black culture and thus
helped to create a dependent childlike individual. On the contrary,
Levine insisted the evidence suggested that blacks preserved communal
values amid the harsh restrictions of a slave environment.

The newer emphasis on slave society and culture has had several
curious results. One has been the subtle transformation of slavery from
an ugly and malignant system to an institution that is somewhat more
benign in its character. This is not to imply that scholars like Fogel,
Engerman, Genovese, and Gutman are in any way sympathetic to
slavery, for all of them concede without reservation its immorality. But
by focusing on the ability of black slaves to create a partially autonomous culture and society they implicitly diminish the authority of
dominant white masters whose control was less than complete. Ironically, the emphasis on an indigenous black culture moved contemporary
scholarship closer to Ulrich Bonnell Phillips, who had emphasized the
contentment of blacks under slavery. Recent scholars, of course, take a
quite different approach, but there is a distinct implication in their work
that whites did not control many major elements in the lives of their
slaves, who exercised considerable authority in determining their personal and familial relations. Compared with the Stampp and Elkins
interpretation of slavery, these more recent works diminish, in part, the
tragic view of slavery as an institution.

There is little doubt also that the parameters of the lively debate over
the nature of slavery has been defined by a strong intellectual current
that emphasizes the autonomy rather than the dependence of the American black experience. White scholars have been extremely sensitive to
charges (particularly by blacks) that they have made the history of
blacks a mere appendage of white actions and behavior. Consequently
the emphasis on a unique and separate black identity and culture has had
the effect of diminishing the importance of the white man's oppression as
a major determinant in black history. By way of contrast, the Stampp-
Elkins approach emphasized white responsibility for black problems.[16]

Virtually all of the interpretations of slavery since the 1950s tended to
treat the "peculiar institution" as a single unit; with only an occasional
exception historians did not distinguish between time and place. In 1980,
however, Ira Berlin threw down an explicit challenge to his colleagues. In

[16] For some recent discussions of this point see Stanley M. Elkins, *Slavery: A
Problem in American Institutional and Intellectual Life* (3rd ed., Chicago, 1976), pp.
223–302; and George M. Fredrickson, "The Gutman Report," *New York Review of
Books* 23 (September 30, 1976): 18–23.

a significant article in the *American Historical Review* he noted that "time and space" — the "traditional boundaries of historical inquiry" — had been largely ignored by American historians, most of whom had produced a "static vision of slave culture." In a detailed examination of seventeenth- and eighteenth-century slavery Berlin went on to identify three distinct slave systems: a northern nonplantation system; and two southern plantation systems, one in the Chesapeake Bay region and the other in the Carolina and Georgia low country. In each of these areas slavery developed in a unique manner; the differences had important consequences for black culture and society.

In the North, according to Berlin, acculturation incorporated blacks into American society while at the same time making them acutely conscious of their African past. Whites, who outnumbered blacks by a wide margin, allowed their slaves considerable autonomy. In the Southern low country, on the other hand, blacks were deeply divided; urban blacks pressed for incorporation into white society while plantation blacks remained physically separated and estranged from the Anglo-American world and closer to their African roots. In the Chesapeake region a single unified Afro-American culture emerged. Because of the impress of white paternalism, Afro-American culture paralleled Anglo-American culture; the African heritage was submerged. Berlin's analysis constituted an explicit and clear challenge to the parameters of the debate over slavery from the 1950s through the 1970s. "If slave society during the colonial era can be comprehended only through a careful delineation of temporal and spatial differences among Northern, Chesapeake, and low-country colonies," Berlin observed, "a similar division will be necessary for a full understanding of black life in nineteenth-century America. The actions of black people during the American Revolution, the Civil War, and the long years of bondage between these two cataclysmic events cannot be understood merely as a function of the dynamics of slavery or the possibilities of liberty, but must be viewed within the specific social circumstances and cultural traditions of black people. These varied from time to time and from place to place. Thus no matter how complete recent studies of black life appear, they are limited to the extent that they provide a static and singular vision of dynamic and complex society."[17]

In evaluating the competing interpretations of American slavery it is important to understand that more than historical considerations are involved. Any judgment upon the nature of slavery implicitly offers a judgment of the present and a prescription for the future. To emphasize

---

[17] Ira Berlin, "Time, Space, and the Evolution of Afro-American Society on British Mainland North America," *American Historical Review* 85 (February 1980): 44–78.

the harshness of slavery and the dependence of its victims is to maximize the white man's responsibility. On the other hand to downplay the effectiveness of white authority is to move toward a position that concedes black autonomy and hence accepts the view that responsibility for post–Civil War developments rests in part with blacks.

Which of the various viewpoints of slavery are correct? Were slaves contented or discontented under slavery? In what ways were they successful in resisting the efforts of their masters to make them totally dependent human beings? To what degree did an autonomous black culture and social order develop during slavery? Was slavery a pre-bourgeois feudal system or a modern version of rational capitalism? What was the nature of the master-slave relationship? Is it possible to generalize about the lives of several millions of individuals under slavery? Must historians begin to distinguish between the common and the unique elements of the institution of slavery in terms of time and space? The answers to these questions undoubtedly will rest upon the continued analysis of surviving sources. But to a considerable degree they will rest also upon the attitudes and values of historians, whose own personal commitments play a role in shaping their perceptions of the past and their view of the present and future.

8

Women in the Land of Cotton

Catherine Clinton

The plantation legend, that most cherished, sunny "stage piece" of the nineteenth century—the allegedly gentlemanly massa, the supposedly sinister overseer, the happy darkie, the general romantic ambiance of the plantation itself—in all of its details has come fundamentally to be reexamined and the former image significantly refashioned. Perhaps no greater readjustment to this once fashionable historical imagery has come of late than to the place of women—both black and white—in what was once regarded, at least in memory, as an enviable, romantic, and stylized antebellum southern world. Catherine Clinton, of Harvard University, is one historian critically responsible for revising the former, highly ceremonial image; for stripping the romance from women's life on the plantation. Neither the portrait of a pampered life for white ladies in Tara-style elegance nor the good-humored world of the lovable, loyal mammy is any longer considered in keeping with the findings of historical research. Based on correspondence, journals, memoirs, household accounts, physician's accounts, and diaries, Professor Clinton finds, beyond the plantation's mythic pillared porticos, a less decorous world of physical, mental, and emotional hardship spent in house, garden, field, storehouse, and cattle shed. Southern women were far more than prime, asexual, exalted angels in the "big house" (the image of preference for white women) or duty-bound female Sambos or promiscuous, sensual black wenches (the contrary images attributed to black women). The truthful

history of southern women, in multiple ways, transcends these
stereotypes. They performed essential and complex functions within
the marketplace conditions of the cotton economy as well as in the
ideological world of the planter. Though "hemmed in by the ideal of
the 'lady'," or tyrannized by racial mythology, southern women in a
plantation setting gave significant and unique shape to a world of
their own.

The pageantry of days gone by—chivalrous cavaliers and belles in hoop
skirts—lives in memory for many southerners. The popular celebration
of plantation legend, the Lost Cause, and the romance of Confederate
lore (boy generals and seductive Rebel spies) spin a web of wonder, even
today. This reverence for the Old South reveals an ironic obsession with
glory as well as history. Southerners are as concerned with what might
have been as with what was. The canvas of the southern past is liberally
splashed with folklore, embellished by exaggeration, highlighted with
pomp and spectacle. By redrawing history, in fact, the vanquished South
defies defeat. Repeated and loving resurrection of the Old South's glory
renovates the plantation past to a splendor that far outshines its foundation in reality. . . .

    In 1620 ninety maids landed in Virginia, a gift from the proprietors to
the colony. They were intended as brides for members of the planter
class; only freemen could wed these available women upon payment of
120 pounds of leaf tobacco to defray transportation costs. Colonial
authorities encouraged marriage by granting a freeholder an increased
lot of land if he had a wife. English gentlemen who supported these
tactics argued that "the plantation can never flourish till families be
planted and the respect of wives and children fix the people on the soil."[1]
The ploy was successful. Virginia shortly received two other shipments
of fifty women each from the colony's sponsors. Thirty-eight more
potential brides were supplied by private entrepreneurs, who raised the
price per wife to 150 pounds of tobacco. By 1622 all these maids had
married.
    Women were an economic commodity. Much like slaves, these early
women settlers were plucked from the Old World and deposited in the

---

[1] Julia Cherry Spruill, *Women's Life and Work in the Southern Colonies* (1938: reprint
ed., New York: W. W. Norton & Co., 1972), p. 9.

New. Shipped across the ocean like stock, they were sold off into marriage with little regard for their human status and dignity. This high "value" but chattel treatment put women in a complex position within plantation society. Under Colonial law, females found their political and economic situation somewhat better than it had been in England but substantially worse than that of male colonists. And as in the Old World, women were locked into their dependent status. The Maryland Assembly, for example, passed a "seven year" provision for women: females were required to marry or remarry within seven years of landholding. Daughters were subject to their fathers' will, and a married female was by law wholly under her husband's control.[2] Despite this inferior status, females in early America were highly valued by the male authorities. Much like another disadvantaged group, African slaves, women immeasurably boosted prospects of success for these southern colonies. As the Virginia House of Burgesses had declared in 1619, "in a newer plantation it is not knowen whether man or woman be the most necessary."[3]

After the Revolution, tobacco was no longer a boom crop for the southern planters. Erosion and soil exhaustion combined to disfigure the tidewater countryside, and with arable land in disrepair, Virginia estates were overstocked with slaves. Land depletion was not, however, as great a problem along the Carolina-Georgia coast, where planters still prospered.

Some historians have argued that slavery was a dying institution during the third quarter of the eighteenth century, kept alive only by the development of the cotton gin in the century's last decade. But the slave population was dramatically increased during the 1780s and 1790s by slave imports. Despite any temporary short-term setbacks (panics and drops in cotton prices), slaveholders retained confidence in the cotton plantation system. Although their buoyancy might have been as misplaced as Scarlett O'Hara's — in the scene from *Gone with the Wind* when, at war's end, she remarks that "cotton will go sky high" — planters were optimistic and greedy for hard cash. They believed that cotton was a profitable crop and slave labor the most economical means to cultivate it. To expand both their "Cotton Kingdom" and the productivity of cotton plantations, planters pushed southwestward. This geographical expansion, the increase in slaveholdings, and the demand for cotton combined to accelerate settlement of the New South regions: western Georgia, Alabama, Mississippi, northern Florida and Louisiana, Arkansas, and Texas.

[2] The status of women in the American colonies is still a subject of debate. See Mary Beth Norton, "The Myth of the Golden Age," in Carol Berkin and Mary Beth Norton, *Women and America: A History* (Boston: Houghton Mifflin Co., 1979).

[3] Spruill, *Women's Life and Work,* p. 9.

From the Colonial era onward, southern settlement patterns had diverged from those of the North, and in the antebellum era these differentials increased. While the political center in New England remained the town, plantation society revolved around the county unit. Urbanization and industrialization, which made such inroads into northern society, had little impact upon the plantation South. European immigrants avoided the region; the planters discouraged any influx of foreigners, from a xenophobic impulse to preserve their own homogeneity; and the recent arrivals shunned competition with slave labor. The economic differential between the two regions increased in these decades with the growth of manufacturing in New England and the boom in cotton in the Gulf states. Planter arrogance centered on the agricultural pre-eminence of the South; in 1858 South Carolina Senator James Hammond boasted: "What would happen if no cotton was furnished for three years. . . . England would topple headlong and carry the civilized world with her save the South. No, you dare not make war on cotton. No power on earth dares to make war on it. Cotton is King."[4]

Political economy was not the only area in which North and South diverged. The cultures that had sprung from these two regions differed radically. Both Yankee and planter accepted these incompatibilities, each arguing for his own superiority. Thomas Jefferson articulated this line of thought in his catalog of differences between northerners— "cool, sober, laborious, persevering, independent, jealous of their own liberties, chicaning, superstitious and hypocritical in their religion"— and southerners—"fiery, voluptuary, indolent, unsteady, independent, zealous of their own liberties but trampling on those of others, generous, candid and without attachments or pretentions of any religion but that of the heart."[5] By the outbreak of the Civil War, Dixie ideologues had refined their racist doctrine, identifying Yankees as well as blacks as inferior. In 1861 the *Southern Literary Messenger* published an article the title of which proclaimed "The True Question: A Contest for the Supremacy of Race, as between the Saxon Puritan of the North and the Norman of the South."[6]

In the great mass of evidence demonstrating the split between the antebellum North and South, one significant aspect has been repeatedly overlooked by historical scholarship: the role of women. Although the southern lady remains a staple of plantation legend, indeed an icon of the

[4] Clement Eaton, *The Growth of Southern Civilization, 1790–1860* (New York: Harper & Row, 1961), p. 25.

[5] Carl Degler, *Place over Time: The Continuity of Southern Distinctiveness* (Baton Rouge: Louisiana State University Press, 1977), pp. 29–30.

[6] *Southern Literary Messenger,* 33 (no. 1, July 1861).

Old South, her symbolic impact seems to have overshadowed and indeed substituted for any assessment of her substantial contributions, much in the way the roles of blacks were ignored until recent scholarship.

That slavery provided for the exalted position of whites within society is a truism of southern history. What remains to be explored is how this system contributed to a parallel oppression of women, both white and black—for slavery and the plantation system imposed handicaps on the women of the owner class. The challenge in evaluating this oppression is to assess the impact of slavery on the preexisting patriarchal structure, not in the least unique to southern society.

The term "family" comes from the Latin word meaning all those included in a household—slaves, women, and children—who were subject to the master's supreme will. Each huge southern household conferred proportionate authority on the "father" of the vast plantation family. These dependents, moreover, formed a solid base of power that extended into the apparatus of the state. The more dependents, the more power; and the more power, the larger the share of influence within the state apparatus. Thus slavery, while it did not alone create women's oppression, did accentuate sex roles and perpetuated women's subordinate status.

A free woman's status within slave society was an extension of her family role; indeed, her status emphasized her dependency and inferiority. Without the oppression of *all* women, the planter class could not be assured of absolute authority. In a biracial slave society where "racial purity" was a defining characteristic of the master class, total control of the reproductive females was of paramount concern for elite males. Patriarchy was the bedrock upon which the slave society was founded, and slavery exaggerated the pattern of subjugation that patriarchy had established.

Women's lives were also affected by plantation agriculture itself. Although northern society was slowly transformed by modernization (industrialization, urbanization, the growth of a market economy, and consumerism), southern society remained rural, provincial, and dependent upon staple-crop production. The household, not the marketplace, was the central focus of the southern economy.

When families on farms were the basic economic unit of society, the female portion of the population participated equally in domestic labor. Women, however, did not share equal credit for their work. Within agricultural production, chores were sex-differentiated. Women might do men's work when the male was absent, and, conversely, men might fill in for women, but farm labor was ordinarily divided along gender lines. Despite this partnership, only male work was highly rewarded with economic compensation, political recognition, and social esteem.

Relatively little is actually known of women's work in the antebellum South. This leads to a fundamentally distorted view of the operation of the plantation economy. Slaves supplied the field labor, but wives generally provided the domestic labor force for southern household management. Women administered food production, purchase, and distribution not only in the planter's home but for the whole plantation. While their husbands supervised the raising of the cash crops, women managed the dairy, the garden, and the smokehouse. Although the overseer might have given some assistance in the barnyard, the critical food-production spheres were clearly those of "women's work." The plantation mistress held the keys as the symbol of her domain.

During the early national era, rhetoric celebrated the importance of republican motherhood: the virtue and vitality of patriotic women who reared future statesmen. These lavish notions of their essential role in the building of a nation and of the nobility of their sacrifice socialized American women. New emphasis on the significance of feminine influence considerably reshaped popular ideology. Continuing in the tone of Revolutionary propaganda, men wanted women's participation to take private rather than public forms. Politicians promised status and esteem to women but delivered only marginal improvements in women's position. At the same time, a bourgeois notion of the division of spheres — male and female as well as public and private — flourished in response to the growth of a market economy. The rise of industrial capitalism in the North stimulated this ideological split between "life" and "work" which placed household labor outside the realm of "the economy."[7]

Sexual reproduction has always been a woman's religious and cultural duty, but maternity became a patriotic obligation in the new republic. In the South, populating the frontier with whites was among the most urgent of political necessities. This ideology sought to bind a woman's self-concept completely with her "biological destiny." A woman's primary duty to her husband was to provide him with heirs, and her primary duty to her country was to produce citizens. When one southerner wrote to his sister that she should serve the nation and get married, she wryly responded: "You say you think it is time I was doing something for my country, but I think it is time enough to enter such business as I am not so very fond of domestic affairs and brawling affairs of children."[8]

Women over all took their new tasks with patriotic seriousness, however, and transformations followed. This era ushered in the acad-

[7] Eli Zaretsky, *Capitalism, the Family, and Personal Life* (New York: Harper & Row, 1976).

[8] Elizabeth Hampton to Edmund Bryan, 25 January 1836, Bryan-Leventhorpe Papers, SHC.

emy, to educate girls for republican motherhood. Virtue and piety were equally important for the northern maiden and for the southern belle. Domesticity was the realm of all American women, and in both the urbanizing, industrializing North and the primarily agricultural South, the exercise of any measure of political control in the public domain became less and less possible for them. In plantation society, this rule of female exclusion was universally observed.

The same phenomena of restriction and oppression appeared in both North and South but often took markedly different forms. For example, in the plantation South, women were firmly tied to the household, with chaperonage limiting their mobility. In New England and Middle Atlantic farming communities, women were equally subject to restrictions, but because of the relative proximity of households to each other, these women did not suffer the isolation of their southern counterparts. Chaperonage was a matter of propriety in both regions, but this "protection" of women carried more handicaps for plantation females. Planter wives constantly complained about their lack of female companionship and about their inability to travel for want of chaperones. The irony of this plight appears even more bitter when one realizes that many women were left alone by their absent husbands to manage large estates and numerous slaves—sometimes without an overseer—yet forbidden to travel because of the "dangers" involved. When a husband returned, he might arrange an excursion for his wife, but most often the devoted helpmate was expected to remain at home with her spouse. Thus even—or especially—when acting as surrogate for the master, the plantation mistress became a prisoner of circumstance.

The biracial character of American slavery played no small part in this imprisonment. Each plantation was essentially a protectorate, a small fiefdom ruled by the planter. The lady of the manor was guaranteed safety so long as she remained within the limits of proper behavior, in the abstract, and, concretely, within the boundaries of the plantation. "Off the land" a lady was afforded no such protection. The South pictured itself as a country fraught with danger and challenge. Most threatening were runaway slaves, together with roughnecks and ruffians; farther west, even Indians lurked in the imagination, if not the woods. Poor roads and the difficulties of negotiating the backwoods presented even more intractable obstacles to female travel. The exhilaration of independence and mobility was severely tempered for southern women, who spent most of their lives in sidesaddle, hemmed in by the ideal of the "lady."

The North provided women with a much more realistic model: the "notable housewife," the ideological granddaughter of Cotton Mather's "daughters of Zion." This virtuous housewife, the standard by which northern women lived their lives, was easily transformed into the "true woman" Barbara Welter discusses in her collection of essays, *Dimity Convictions,* or the "sentimental conspicuous consumer" described in Ann Douglas's *Feminization of American Culture.* New England women, especially, found their roles more tolerable during the transformations of the post-Revolutionary North.[9] Accomplished women met the demands of housewifery with a growing sense of importance within the domestic realm. They strove for attainable goals and were assured of social recognition as their reward. No such luxury was afforded on the plantation.

Northern women during this era were busily building their own community. All across New England and the Middle Atlantic states, females transformed the liability of segregation into the asset of collective identity. This movement was so widespread and important that historian Nancy Cott has called her study of New England women from 1780 to 1835 *The Bonds of Womanhood.* The title was taken, ironically enough, from the correspondence of a southern woman, Angelina Grimké, who signed herself "thine in the bonds of womanhood." Of course, the Grimké sisters had exiled themselves from the South; their philosophical and political bent made them pariahs within slaveowning culture. But the spirit and sorority of the North beckoned them. Within northern society, women were able to create a successful counterculture that undermined patriarchal oppression.

The roots of this counterculture were deeply imbedded in the very impulse to separate male and female spheres that patriarchy had spawned and nourished. As early as the post-Revolutionary era, American men were rightly concerned that women might attempt to translate the egalitarian rhetoric and ideology of the rebellion into their own bid for liberty. Indeed, Abigail Adams warned of such a revolt in her correspondence with her husband John: "I desire you would Remember the Ladies, and be more generous and favourable to them than your ancestors. Do not put such unlimited power into the hands of the Husbands. Remember all Men would be tyrants if they could. If perticular care and attention is not paid to the Ladies we are determined to foment a Rebellion, and will not hold ourselves bound by any Laws in which we have no voice, or Representation."[10] Although Adams's quotation is perhaps overused, there was no lack of similar sentiment among women of her class and level of education. American historians have, during the past decade,

[9] Nancy Cott, *The Bonds of Womanhood: Woman's Sphere in New England* (New Haven, Conn.: Yale University Press, 1978).

[10] L. H. Butterfield, Marc Friedlander, and Mary Jo Kline, eds., *The Book of Abigail and John* (Cambridge, Mass.: Harvard University Press, 1975), p. 121.

introduced us to a wide array of accomplished and challenging women of the late eighteenth and early nineteenth centuries: Judith Sargent Murray, Susannah Rowson, Hannah Webster Foster, Mercy Otis Warren, Grace Galloway, Sarah Livingston Jay, Catherine Livingston, Esther De Berdt Reed, Sarah Franklin Bache, Eliza Lucas Pinckney, Theodosia Burr, and Elizabeth Drinker, among others. They all testify to the vigor and complexity of the debate over women's position and political responsibilities in American society.

During the early years of the Republic, national and regional changes were transforming the lives of women both North and South. The shift from "hearthside" to "marketplace" economies created a vacuum allegedly filled by women's role as "republican mothers." But perhaps more crucial was the growth and influence of a bourgeois consumer consciousness.[11]

Women's sudden preoccupation with finding "values" (bargains) as well as preserving "values" (mores) created a new American domestic model, celebrated in the tons of feminine literature churned out during the antebellum era. Between 1784 and 1860 almost one hundred magazines concentrating on "women's interests" were published. Also during this era, a class of women novelists sprang up to meet the demand for popular fiction. Their themes and scenarios featured both sharp and sentimental renderings of domestic life.[12]

Besides this explosion of prescription and analysis, northern women created their own female culture. This stemmed partly from young women's dynamic and disproportionate role in the Second Great Awakening during the opening decades of the nineteenth century. Designated as the active stewards of religion within the culture, women were given a moral crusade during the antebellum era; their roles were culturally exalted. Ministers turned their attention toward these newly significant members of dwindling congregations, as church attendance plummeted during the period following the Revolution. Religious fervor began to manifest itself outside formal denominational activities. Women throughout the country began to organize benevolent societies and reform organizations,[13] most abundant in the cities, but supported even in rural New England.

[11] Ann Douglas, *The Feminization of American Culture* (New York: Alfred A. Knopf, 1977).

[12] Carl Degler, *At Odds: Women and the Family in America from the Revolution to the Present* (New York: Oxford University Press, 1980), pp. 377, 378–379.

[13] See Keith Melder, "Ladies Bountiful: Organized Women's Benevolence in Early 19th Century America," *New York History* 58 (1967): 231–54; Carroll Smith-Rosenberg, "Beauty, the Beast and the Militant Woman: A Case Study in Sex Roles and Social Stress in Jacksonian America," *American Quarterly* 23 (October 1971): 562–84.

Similar reform in the South, however, definitely lacked the size and scope of the movement in northern communities. This was a consequence both of the physical isolation of southern women and of the needs of plantation society itself. Although southern planters urged their women to do good works and promote benevolence, this effort was to extend itself no farther than the boundaries of the plantation. If women's attention wandered from the welfare of their families and their husbands' slaves and other property, it might stray to a critical attack on society. Many antebellum evangelicals, especially northerners, identified slavery as one of America's greatest ills. If plantation mistresses came under the influence of such propaganda, planters feared for their way of life.

Slaveowners often discouraged their wives openly from such agitation-prone activity. Virginia planter David Campbell had a close and affectionate relationship with his wife, Maria. The couple were childless, and although they adopted nieces and nephews, they relied heavily upon each other. While Campbell spent much of his career in Richmond, leaving his wife alone on their remote estate in western Virginia, he encouraged her to participate in entertainments that would make her less melancholy in his absence. But the usually indulgent Campbell became testy over the issue of his wife's interest in camp meetings. His protests cite numerous drawbacks but fail to specify what must have been his greatest objection: that his wife might be influenced by these "fanatics." He sent her a letter of disapproval in 1823: "You mention that you had intended going to a Methodist class meeting. . . . Have you not often seen my anxiety about you at those places, and why would you be willing to go to them and run the hazard of being jostled about in a crowd of fanatics without my protecting arm?—Indeed, why go there at all? A person of your good sense must be satisfied that he who gave us being cannot delight in such worship. . . ."[14]

The female academy movement swept the South as well as the North after the Revolution, creating a more critical intellectual perspective for upper-class women. Such a perspective sometimes led women to speak out against the evils of their society, and slavery became a target. Many females in the South were unable to voice their criticisms, but some attempted to enact their ideas in individual protests. The never-married Mary Telfair of Savannah hoped, with her confidante, Mary Few, to start a conversation circle like that of their idols, the British bluestockings. Soon after, Mary Telfair resolved to free herself from the toils of slavery: "I have abandoned the old fashion of having a waiting maid, the first step towards a reform. Alexander [her brother] seems to think I will be too independent for a Lady, but I already experience the salutary effects of

[14] David Campbell to Maria Campbell, 3 January 1823, Campbell Collection, DU.

9

There Was Another South

Carl N. Degler

As a student of both individual and social behavior, the historian must constantly seek to establish the tenuous line between the truth of the particular and that of the general. Since the profiles of history have generally been drawn either in terms of its "great men" or in terms of its general "movements," the historian's problem is to find generalizations that neither distort nor violate the truth, while at the same time allowing for the fascinating aspects of nuance, complexity, and irony. Such a balance is offered here by Carl N. Degler, of Stanford University, as he treats the subjects of secession and slavery in the antebellum South—two of the largest and most historically distorted generalizations (myths) concerning that region. If the South seceded based on states' rights theory and the right to own slaves, then all southerners, it would seem to follow, must have been secessionists and proslavery. As Degler suggests, contrary to these easy and thus popular generalizations, the South before the Civil War did not display a monolithic point of view on these issues. On the subject of secession he offers the pro-Union views of such disparate individuals as James Madison, Andrew Jackson, and Henry Clay. Whig party political strength throughout the South until 1854, particularly among large planters, attests to the viability of Unionism, as that party's philosophy was strongly nationalist. Even after the demise of the Whig party, Unionism remained vital in the South, represented by the nationalist views of the Constitutional Union party, widespread antisecession sentiment, and southern pro-Union activity during the war itself. In the postwar period Degler notes payments by the Southern Claims Commission and the continuance of nationalism in the form of southern allegiance to the Republican party, in a large sense a continuance of prewar Whig nationalism. As for the proslavery myth, Degler offers the writings and activities of Cassius Marcellus Clay and Hinton Rowan Helper to expose antislave—though certainly not pro-Negro—views. Also, the issue of emancipation surfaced dramatically during the great 1832 debate in the Virginia state legislature. Although difficult to assess accurately, Degler further notes countless southern individuals who rofor personal, Christian, or humanitarian reasons abhorred slavery and no doubt rejoiced at its demise. Too, there were the national back-to-Africa efforts of the American Colonization Society which, although ultimately a failure, did involve many southerners who helped send six thousand blacks to Liberia. Clearly, in the prewar South, there was a scarcity neither of Unionists nor abolitionists.

The stereotype of the South is as tenacious as it is familiar: a traditionally rebellious region which has made a dogma of states' rights and a religious order of the Democratic party. Here indeed is a monotonous and unchanging tapestry, with a pattern of magnolia blossoms, Spanish moss, and the inevitable old plantations running ceaselessly from border to border. To this depiction of almost willful backwardness, add the dark motif of the Negro problem, a few threads of poor white, and the picture is complete.

Such is the mythical image, and a highly inaccurate one it is, for the South is a region of immense variety. Its sprawling landscape ranges from the startlingly red soil of Virginia and North Carolina to the black, sticky clay of the Delta; from the wild and primitive mountain forests of eastern Kentucky to the lush, junglelike swamps of southern Louisiana; from the high, dry, wind-swept plains of the Texas Panhandle to the humid tidelands of the South Carolina coast. An environment so diverse can be expected to produce social and political differences to match, and in fact, it always has.

Today, with the South in ferment, we have come to recognize increasingly the wide variety of attitudes that exist in the region. But this denial of the southern stereotype is a relatively new development, even among historians. For too long the history of the region has been regarded as a kind of unbroken plain of uniform opinion. This is especially true of what has been written about the years before the Civil War; a belief in states' rights, the legality of secession, and the rightfulness of slavery has been accepted almost without question as typical of southern thought. In a sense, such catch phrases do represent what many southerners have believed; but at the same time there were many others who both denied the legality of secession and denounced slavery. It is time this "other South" was better known.

Let us begin with the story of those southerners who so cherished the Union that they refused to accept the doctrine of nullification and secession. They included not only humble farmers and remote mountain men but some of the greatest names in the history of the South; their devotion to the Union was tested in several bitter clashes with states' righters during the antebellum decades. The first of these contests came over the question of the high protective tariffs which many southerners felt would hurt the cotton trade; the arguments advanced at the beginning set forth the basic lines of debate that were followed thereafter. South Carolina's *Exposition and Protest of 1828,* which John C. Calhoun wrote secretly in opposition to the tariff passed that year, embodied the classic defense of state sovereignty. In the *Exposition,* Calhoun contended that nullification of federal legislation by a state and even secession were constitutional—a doctrine rejected by many prominent southerners in 1828 and after.

Foremost among them was former president James Madison, the reputed "father of the Constitution." As a Jeffersonian in politics and a Virginian by birth and heritage, Madison was no friend of the protective tariff and certainly not of the monstrous one of 1828, which had been promulgated by the Jacksonian faction in Congress in an effort to discredit the Adams administration. But he could not accept even that politically inspired tariff as sufficient reason for nullification. Indeed, he could not accept the constitutional doctrine of nullification on any grounds. It is worthwhile to consider briefly Madison's views on nullification because virtually all subsequent southern defenses of the Union followed his line of thought; at the time, no man in the South carried more authority on the meaning and interpretation of the Constitution that the venerable Virginian, who celebrated his eightieth birthday in 1830 and was the last surviving signer of that document.

Many political leaders sought his views all through the tariff crisis of 1828–33, and to all of them Madison reiterated the same conclusions. The United States was a "mixed government" in which the states were supreme in some areas and the federal government in others. In the event of conflict between them, the Supreme Court was the intended arbiter under the Constitution; the Court, Madison wrote, was "so constituted as to be impartial as it could be made by the mode of appointment and responsibility of the judges."

If confidence were lacking in the objectivity of the judges, Madison continued, then there were further remedies: the impeachment of offending officials, election of a new government, or amendments to the Constitution. But neither nullification nor secession was legal, he tirelessly pointed out. Of course, if tyrannized sufficiently, a state could invoke its natural right to overthrow its oppressor; but that was a right of revolution and not a constitutional right as Calhoun and his followers maintained.

As a southern Unionist, Madison did not stand alone, either at the time of the nullification crisis or later. In Calhoun's own state, in fact, the Unionists were a powerful and eloquent minority. Hugh S. Legare (pronounced Legree, curiously enough), Charleston aristocrat, intellectual, and one-time editor of the *Southern Review,* distinguished himself in defense of the Union, vigorously opposing Calhoun during the heated debates in Charleston in 1832. (Eleven years later, as United States attorney general, Legare again differed with the majority of southerners when he offered the official opinion that free Negroes in the United States enjoyed the same civil rights as white men.)

James Petigru and Joel Poinsett (who, as minister to Mexico, gave his name to the Poinsettia) were two other prominent Charlestonians who would not accept the doctrine that a state could constitutionally withdraw from the Union. Unlike Legare and Poinsett, Petigru lived long enough to fight nullification and secession in South Carolina until that state left the Union. (When asked by a stranger in December 1860 where the insane asylum was, he contemptuously pointed to the building where the secession convention was meeting.)

Andrew Jackson is often ignored by those who conceive of the South as a monolith of states' rights and secession. A Carolinian by birth and Tennessean by choice, Jackson acted as an outspoken advocate of the Union when he threatened South Carolina with overwhelming force in the crisis of 1832–33. Jackson's fervently nationalistic proclamation to the people of the dissident state was at once a closely reasoned restatement of the Madisonian view that the United States was a "mixed government" and a highly emotional panegyric to the Union. Though there can be no question of Jackson's wholehearted acceptance of every patriotic syllable in that proclamation, it comes as no surprise to those acquainted with the limited literary abilities of Old Hickory that its composition was the work of an adviser. That adviser, it is worth noting, was a southerner, Secretary of State Edward Livingston of Louisiana.

There were few things on which Henry Clay of Kentucky and Andrew

Jackson could agree, but the indissolubility of the Union was one of them. Clay never concurred with those southern leaders who accepted Calhoun's position that a state could nullify national legislation or secede from the Union. As a matter of fact, Henry Clay's Whig party was probably the most important stronghold of pro-Union sentiment in the antebellum South. Unlike the Democratic party, the Whigs never succumbed, in defending slavery, to the all-encompassing states' rights doctrine. Instead, they identified themselves with the national bank, internal improvements, the tariff, and opposition to the "tyranny" of Andrew Jackson. Despite the "unsouthern" sound of these principles to modern ears, the Whig party was both powerful and popular, capable of winning elections in any southern state. In the heyday of the Whigs, a solidly Democratic South was still unimaginable.

In 1846, the attempt of antislavery forces to prohibit slavery in the vast areas about to be acquired as a result of the Mexican War precipitated another bitter sectional struggle. But as much as they might support the "peculiar institution," the southern Whigs stood firm against Calhoun's efforts to commit the whole South to a states' rights position that once more threatened the existence of the Union. When, in 1849, Calhoun invited southern congressmen to join his Southern Rights movement in order to strengthen resistance against northern demands, forty of the eighty-eight he approached refused to sign the call. Almost all of them were Whigs.

Throughout the Deep South in the state elections of 1851, Unionist Democrats and Whigs combined to stop the incipient secessionist movement in its tracks. In Georgia, Howell Cobb, the Unionist candidate for governor, received 56,261 votes to 37,472 for his opponent, a prominent Southern Rights man; in the legislature the Unionists captured 101 of the 127 seats. After the same election the congressional delegation of Alabama consisted of two secessionists and five Union supporters. In the Calhoun stronghold of Mississippi, where Jefferson Davis was the best-known spokesman for the Southern Rights movement, Davis was defeated for the governorship, 28,738 to 27,729, by his Unionist opponent, Henry S. Foote. Even in fire-eating South Carolina itself, the anti-Calhoun forces won overwhelmingly, 25,045 to 17,710.

By the time of the Kansas-Nebraska Act of 1854, the Whig party had all but disappeared, the victim of a widening sectional schism. Bereft of its traditional political organization, southern Unionism was, for the time, almost voiceless, but it was not dead. In the election of 1860, it reappeared in the shape of the Constitutional Union party. Its candidate was John Bell of Tennessee, an old-line Whig and staunch Unionist who, in order to prevent disruption of the nation, made his platform the Union itself. That year, in a four-party race, the Constitutional Unionists were the effective second party to the southern Democrats; for Stephen A. Douglas, the candidate of the northern Democrats, received few votes outside the border states, and Lincoln was not even on a ballot in ten of the fifteen slave states.

The Constitutional Unionists gave the dominant Democratic party a hot fight in every southern state. Of the upper southern states, Virginia, Kentucky, and Tennessee went to Bell outright, while Maryland gave him forty-five percent and North Carolina forty-seven percent of their votes.

Bell's showing in the Deep South was not as strong as in the upper South, but it nonetheless demonstrated that those southerners still willing to be counted for the Union were a large minority in almost all of the states. From the whole South, Bell received forty percent of the popular vote to southern Democrat Breckinridge's forty-five.

A clear indication of the continuity of Unionism from the days of the Whigs to the election of 1860 is that Bell's support in the Deep South centered in the same general areas where the Whigs had been most powerful in the 1840s. Many of the delta counties along the Mississippi River—in Arkansas, Mississippi, and Louisiana—which were always strongholds of Whiggery, went for Bell. Whig votes had always been conspicuous in the black belt counties of central Alabama and Georgia, and so were Bell's in 1860.

Surprisingly enough, the wealthy, slaveholding counties of the South were more often Whig than Democratic in the years before the war. Ever since the days of Jackson, the Democracy had been predominantly the party of the small planter and non-slaveholder. Regardless of the serious threat to slavery posed by the Republican party in 1860, many slaveholders could still not bring themselves to violate their traditional political allegiances and vote for a Democratic candidate identified with states' rights.

A further test of southern Unionism was provided in the election of delegates to the state secession conventions in the winter of 1860–61. Unfortunately, the voting figures do not tell us as much as we would like to know. To most southerners at the time, the issue was not simply the Union versus the right of a state to secede; more often it was whether secession was expedient, with little thought about its constitutionality. Therefore, those delegates who favored a course other than immediate secession did not necessarily support the Union under all and every circumstance.

Nevertheless, these voting returns make clear that even on the verge of secession, tens of thousands in all the states of the Deep South were still opposed to a break with the Union. In Alabama, for example, 28,200 voted against immediate secession to 35,700 for; furthermore, one third of the delegates of the convention refused to sign the secession ordinance because it would not be submitted to the people. In Georgia, 37,123 were against secession to 50,243 in favor; in Louisiana the Unionists were an even larger minority: 17,296 against secession, 20,448 for. In Texas, despite much intimidation of Unionists, twenty-two percent of the voters still opposed secession.

Before Sumter was fired upon and Lincoln called for volunteers, the states of the upper South refused to join the seceding states. Early in 1861, the people of Tennessee voted against having a secession convention, 68,282 to 59,449; the vote of the people of Arkansas against secession in February 1861 was 22,000 to 17,000. North Carolina, in a popular vote, also turned down a call for a secession convention. As late as April 4, the Virginia convention voted down a proposal to draw up an ordinance of secession by an almost two-to-one majority. Even after Sumter, when the upper South states did secede, it is clear that loyalty to the Union was still a powerful sentiment.

Throughout the war southern Unionists were active in opposition to the Confederacy. Areas of strong Unionist feeling, like eastern Tennessee, western Virginia, northern Alabama, and the mountain counties of Arkansas, quickly come to mind. In eastern Tennessee, for example, Unionist sentiment was so widespread and deep-felt that for a large part of the war, the courts of the Confederacy in that area could not function without military support and not always even then. After the war broke out, Charles Galloway, a staunch Unionist who had opposed secession in Arkansas, led two companies of his fellow southerners to Springfield, Missouri, where they were mustered into the Union army. Galloway then led his men back to Arkansas to fight the Confederates. Some 48,000 white southern Unionists, it has been estimated, served voluntarily in the army of the United States. In northern Alabama and Georgia in 1863 and after, peace societies, replete with secret grips, passwords, and elaborate security precautions, worked to encourage desertion from the Confederate army.

A recent study of the Southern Claims Commission provides the most explicit and detailed evidence of the character of southern Unionism during the war. The commission was set up by the United States government at the end of hostilities in order to reimburse those southerners who had sustained certain kinds of property losses because of their loyalty to the Union. (Only actual material losses incurred by loyal southerners in behalf of the Union armies were to be honored; acts of charity or mercy, or losses occasioned by Confederate action, for example, were not included.) Since all claimants first had to offer ironclad proof of loyalty before their losses could even be considered, those who did file claims may well be taken as the hard core of southern

Unionism. There must have been thousands more who, because they lacked the opportunity or the substance to help the Union armies, went uncounted. Still others may not have been able to meet the high standards set for proof of loyalty, though their devotion to the Union was unquestioned. Under these circumstances, 22,298 claimants is an impressive number.

One of the striking facts that emerges from a study of the records of the commission is the great number of southern Unionists who were people of substance. The total amount of the claims was $22.5 million, and 701 claims were for losses of $10,000 or more—a very substantial sum in the 1860s. The wealthy claimants were mainly planters, owners of great plantations and large numbers of slaves. Despite their wealth, or perhaps because of it, they stood with the Union when the storm of secession broke upon them—though to do so often meant obloquy and harassment at the very least, and not infrequently confiscation of property and personal danger.

Southern Unionism also played its part in the complicated history of Reconstruction. Tennessee, for example, probably escaped radical congressional Reconstruction because of the large number of Unionists in the state. William "Parson" Brownlow, an old Whig and Unionist turned Republican, was able to gain control of the state after the war, and under his leadership Tennessee managed to avoid the military occupation that was the retribution visited upon its more recalcitrant neighbors.

In Louisiana, the first Republican governor, Michael Hahn, was also a lifelong Unionist, though originally a Democrat; he had opposed secession and during the war refused to take a pledge of loyalty to the Confederacy. About a third of the members of the Mississippi legislature during Reconstruction were so-called scalawags; but far from being the disreputable persons usually associated with that label, most of them were actually respectable former Whig Unionists turned Republican.

This shift in allegiance from Whig to Republican—by no means a rarity in the Reconstruction South—is not so strange when it is recalled that Lincoln, the first Republican president, was once a confirmed Whig. Indeed, to many former southern Whigs it must have seemed that the Republican party—the party of business, national authority, sound money, and internal improvements—was a most fortunate reincarnation of Henry Clay's old organization. And now that slavery was no more, it seemed that southerners could once again divide politically as their interests dictated.

The opportunity, however, proved to be short-lived, for to resist effectively the excesses of the Radicals during Reconstruction, all southerners of consequence became Democrats as a matter of necessity. But though they may have been Democrats in name, in principles they were Whigs and as such worked quite easily with northern Republicans to end Reconstruction and to bring new railroads and industry to the South in the 1880s.

Most Americans assume that between 1830 and 1860 all southerners favored slavery. This is not so. In the earlier years of the Republic, the great Virginians had not defended the institution but only excused it as an undeniable evil that was exceptionally difficult to eradicate. It was not until the 1830s that it began to be widely upheld as something to be proud of, a positive good. Here too, as in the nullification controversy, Calhoun's thought dominated the southern mind. He had been among the first prominent southerners to shake off the sense of guilt over slavery and to proclaim it a "great moral revolution." At the same time, however, many men and women in the South continued to doubt the utility, the wisdom, and the justice of slavery. These, too, constituted another South.

Although there were some southerners who opposed slavery for reasons of Christian ethics, many more decried it for economic and political reasons. Cassius Marcellus Clay of Kentucky, a cousin of the more famous Henry, was prominent among those who abominated slavery because it retarded the economic growth of the South. The son of a wealthy slaveholder, Clay was educated at Yale, where his future is supposed to have been decided by hearing William Lloyd Garrison present an abolitionist lecture. Regardless of the cause for Clay's subsequent antislavery views, he emancipated his slaves in 1833, soon after his graduation, and devoted himself to ridding his state of slavery. Despite his proclaimed hostile sentiments on the subject, Clay gained a large following in state and national politics.

The nature of Clay's objections to slavery were made clear in a speech he delivered before the Kentucky legislature in 1841:

Gentlemen would import slaves "to clear up the forests of the Green River country." Take one day's ride from this capital and then go and tell them what you have seen. Tell them that you have looked upon the once most lovely and fertile lands that nature ever formed; and have seen it in fifty years worn to the rock. . . . tell them of the depopulation of the country and the consequent ruin of the towns and villages; tell them that the white Kentuckian has been driven out by slaves, by the unequal competition of unpaid labor; tell them that the mass of our people are uneducated; tell them that you have heard the children of white Kentuckians crying for bread, whilst the children of the African was [sic] clothed, and fed, and laughed! And then ask them if they will have blacks to fell their forests.

The troublesome race question effectively prevented some antislavery southerners from taking any concrete steps to end slavery; others saw a threat in the possibility of a large free Negro population. To many, the return of former slaves to Africa seemed the necessary first step in any movement toward emancipation. Cassius Clay was both more radical and more realistic. He recognized that colonization was as illusory a solution to the evils of slavery and the Negro problem as it actually proved to be; many more Negroes were born each year than could possibly be sent to Liberia in a generation. Instead, Clay boldly advocated gradual emancipation, with the owners of the slaves being compensated by the state.

Hinton Rowan Helper is better known today as an antislavery southerner than Clay, though the latter was certainly more prominent at the time. Helper was the son of a poor North Carolina farmer; with the publication of his book, *The Impending Crisis of the South,* in 1857, he became a nationally known figure. In an effort to demonstrate the material and cultural backwardness of the slave states, Helper brought together statistics from the Census of 1850—compiled by that most indefatigable southern publicist, J. D. B. De Bow, and therefore unimpeachable in southern eyes—to show that in a number of libraries, newspapers, and schools, as well as in wealth, manufactures, population, and commerce, the North far outdistanced the South. Helper pointed out that even in agriculture, the vaunted specialty of Dixie, northern production exceeded southern. Almost contemptuously, he observed that the value of the Cotton Kingdom's chief staple was surpassed by that of the North's lowly hay crop. The cause for these discrepancies, Helper contended, was slavery.

Helper's indictment of slavery was sufficiently telling to arouse violent southern attacks. He also serves to illustrate the variety of motives underlying the southern antislavery movement. He was more disturbed about what slavery did to the poor white man than about what it did to the Negro. Many antislavery men felt the same, but Helper went further; his concern for the white man was coupled with an almost pathological hatred of the black.

Not its economic disadvantages, but its essential incompatibility with the genius of America, was the more compelling argument against slavery for some southerners. The great Virginians of the eighteenth century—men like Washington, Marshall, Patrick Henry, Madison, Jefferson, and Monroe—all felt that it somehow contradicted their ideal of a new republic of freemen. Echoes of this view were heard by Frederick Law Olmsted when he traveled through the back country of the South in the 1850s. One mountain dweller told Olmsted that he "was afraid that there was many a man who had gone to the bad world, who wouldn't have gone if he hadn't had any slaves."

Though less moralistic in his conclusions, Henry Clay was of much the same opinion. "I am no friend to slavery," he wrote to an Alabaman in 1838. "I think it is an evil; but I believe it better that slaves should remain slaves than to be set loose as free men among us. . . ." For Clay, as for many antislavery southerners, it was difficult to believe that emancipated Negroes and whites could live together peacefully in the same country. This deep-seated belief in the incompatibility of the two races constituted the great dilemma in the minds of antislavery southerners; often it paralyzed all action.

The effects of this dilemma were certainly evident in the course of the remarkable debate on slavery in the Virginia legislature in 1832.

The event which precipitated it was a brief but violent uprising of slaves in Southampton County on August 21, 1831. Led by Nat Turner, a slave preacher given to visions and prophecies, the insurrectionists deliberately killed some sixty white people, mainly women and children. But even the rapidity and efficiency with which the might of the white man had been mobilized against the runaway slaves did not assuage the fear that surged through the minds of southerners everywhere. And so it was that on January 11, 1832, there began one of the most searching debates on slavery ever held by the elected representatives of a slave-holding people. For two weeks the venerable institution was subjected to the frankest kind of criticism.

Three quarters of the members of the House of Delegates held slaves, yet more than half of that body spoke out against the institution in one fashion or another. In analyzing the statements and the notes of the members, one historian concluded that 60 of the 134 delegates were consistently antislavery, working for legislation that would eventually terminated Negro bondage in Virginia. Twelve more, whom he calls the compromisers, were antislavery in belief but were not prepared to vote for any measure which would, at that time, commit the state to emancipation. It was this latter group, in league with the sixty or so defenders of the *status quo,* who defeated the efforts to initiate gradual emancipation in 1832.

Though individual opponents of slavery remained in the South right up to the Civil War, it is impossible to ascertain their numbers. However, a glimpse into the mind of one such southerner has been afforded by the publication of the diary of Mary Minor Blackford. Mrs. Blackford lived in Fredericksburg, Virginia, across the street from a slave trader's house, a location which permitted her to see slavery at its worst. And it was slavery as a moral evil rather than as an economic fallacy which troubled her: how could people otherwise good and humane, kind and Christian, hold fellow human beings in bondage? For unlike some northern abolitionists, she knew slave owners too well to think them innately evil. Her answer was not surprising: material self-interest morally blinded them.

The tragedy of the South's history was woven into the fabric of Mary Minor Blackford's life. Despite her long opposition to slavery, she proudly saw five of her sons serve in the Confederate army. Yet with its defeat, she could still write early in 1866: "A New Era has dawned since I last wrote in this book. Slavery has been abolished!!!"

Other individual opponents of slavery in the South could be cited, but perhaps it would be best to close by mentioning an antislavery organization. The American Colonization Society, founded in 1817 by southern and northern antislavery men, always included prominent southerners among its leaders. In the course of its half century of operations, the society managed to send more than six thousand Negroes to its African colony in Liberia.

The society was strongest in the South; indeed, it was anathema to the New England and middle western abolitionists. Though it is true that antislavery was never a popular cause in the South, it was never a dead one either, so long as thousands of southerners refused to view slavery as anything but an evil for their region.

As we have seen, the South was even less united on nullification and secession than it was on the question of slavery. In fact, it is now clear that if a majority of southerners ever did support secession—and there is real doubt on this—it was never a big majority, and it was not achieved until the very eve of the Civil War. In short, the South, rather than being a monolith of undivided opinion, was not even of one mind on the two most vital issues of the thirty years that led up to the war.

10

Cavalier and Yankee: Synthetic Stereotypes

William R. Taylor

By 1859 the plantation legend and its complement the southern cavalier had become the dominant images shaping southern social psychology. Though critical to the development of incipient southern nationalism, the South's psychological construction of the "cavalier image" was to be but one of a cluster of images which were eventually to emerge supporting the view that southerners were a distinct people. The important void yet to be filled on the historical landscape was a counter-image—the "yankee" stereotype. William R. Taylor, Professor of History at the University of New York, Stony Brook, delineates the political and psychological forces responsible for the emergence of Cavalier *and* Yankee as contending symbols of alien cultures North and South. Following a coalition of historical circumstances—particularly John Brown's raid at Harper's Ferry in October of 1859 and the election of Abraham Lincoln as President in November of 1860—the "incompatability of temper" evident in political matters now began to manifest itself psychologically. John Brown's "private war" served to reinforce the predatory Yankee image, thus maximizing psychological and political tensions. Lincoln's election, given the South's erroneous image of him as a tool of the abolitionists, worked to the same end. The quest for an independent and uncontaminated South was now largely completed. A whole new set of assumptions had emerged and taken hold, so forcefully in fact that even after the war images of Cavalier and Yankee would continue to engage the imaginations of southerners and northerners alike.

By the summer of 1861 the subdued, candid and reasonable exchange of views which had taken place between Jefferson and John Adams some 45 years before seemed to belong to another, faraway age.[1] Early that year, as every schoolboy knows, a separate Southern government had been organized in Montgomery, Alabama. Fort Sumter had fallen in April, a peace conference in Washington had collapsed and by July the United States were at war with themselves. Historians agree that the vast majority of people in the North and South had not wanted secession, to say nothing of war, but events swept them up in a whirlwind of excitement and pre-cipitant action over which no one, finally, could exercise control.

In the South the move to separate had at first received massive support. Of those who hung back, some, perhaps most, were genuinely undecided, others confused or indifferent, and still others afraid to acknowledge their secret convictions. Little recourse was left open for moderation. The choice, to use the language of the time, lay between "secession" and "sub-mission." The insurgents, capitalizing on the fears inspired by Lincoln's election and emboldened by their confidence in the invincibility of the united South, had moved ahead, heedless of dissenting views.

One by one the "erring sisters" had departed "in peace"—South Caro-lina on December 20; Mississippi, Alabama, Georgia, and Louisiana dur-ing the month of January, and Texas on February 1. Not until late spring or early summer did Tennessee, North Carolina, and Arkansas finally secede. Only on April 17, and after Lincoln had called upon her for her militia, did Virginia, the historical leader of Southern opinion, pass an ordinance of secession. Missouri, Maryland, and Kentucky, although tragically divided, chose to remain with the Union.

Along this middle tier of states, which separated New England and the Northwest from the lower South, a resolution of conflicting loyalties was arrived at only after agonizing and prolonged reflection and debate. Lincoln correctly gauged the mood which existed in these still uncommitted parts of the South when he inserted into his Inaugural Address, delivered in March of that year, a pointed reference to Hamlet's Third Act soliloquy. Was the South, he asked, contemplating suicide?

Will you hazard so desperate a step while there is any possibility that any portion of the ills you fly from have no real existence? Will you, while the certain ills you fly to are greater than all the real ones you fly from, will you risk the commission of so fearful a mistake?[2]

[1] [For an interesting letter on secession] See Representative David Clopton of Alabama to Senator Clement C. Clay, Dec. 13, 1860, in Clement Eaton, *A History of the Southern Confederacy* (New York, 1954), p. 12.

[2] Richard Hofstadter (ed.), *Great Issues in American History: A Documentary Record* (New York, 1958), p. 392.

In the state capitals, county seats, in village assemblies and in individual families, anguishing, seldom unanimous, decisions were made, and by midsummer the peoples of the North and South, sometimes with reluctance and sometimes in a fever of excitement, were beginning to array themselves on opposite sides of the battle lines. In a poem written that year, one of the Union's warmest advocates caught the sense of the moment in a few lines of verse.

> Beat! beat! drums!—blow! bugles! blow!
> Make no parley—stop for no expostulation,
> Mind not the timid—mind not the weeper or prayer. . . .[3]

The most memorable war in American history was about to begin.

Historians have long debated the causes which precipitated this rapid series of events, and doubtless they always will. Much has been learned about the subtle shifts of opinion which occurred within various Southern states between John Brown's raid on Harper's Ferry in October, 1859, and Lincoln's fateful decision in April, 1861, to send supplies to the beleaguered garrison at Fort Sumter. Careful studies have been made of the parochial political circumstances which heightened the sensitivity of parts of the South to sectional issues and made the election of Abraham Lincoln, as the Northern President backed by a Northern party, a nightmarish prospect. The list of Southern grievances against the federal government, it has been made clear, had been growing since the debates over Missouri in 1819–20; and the constitutional arguments employed at the time of secession have a history almost as long as the Union itself. The growth of the Southern movement for independence has been traced back to the statements of its earliest proponents in the thirties. It is the importance of this idea of Southern nationality, the popular supposition that Southerners and Northerners were distinct and different peoples, which has prompted the present study. If this idea had not been firmly embedded in the consciousness of extremists on both sides and vaguely present in the thinking of countless others, it seems doubtful that secession and Civil War would have taken place at the time and in the way that they did.

No one, of course, will ever be able to recapture in their totality the elusive feelings of individual Southerners in the face of these bewildering events, but it is clear that a significant shift in attitude took place after 1859. For a time during the early fifties the threat of open rebellion seemed to have disappeared. Problems there were, and some of them very grave, but concessions had been made. The South was enjoying flush times with

[3] Walt Whitman, "Beat! Beat! Drums!" *Complete Poetry and Selected Prose and Letters* (ed.), Emory Holloway (London, n.d.), p. 260.

cotton and slave prices at an all-time high, and Democrats responsive to Southern opinions were in control of the government in Washington. Then came the brief rehearsal for civil war, between Northerners and Southerners fighting over the corpse of "bleeding Kansas," the appearance on the scene of a sectional party with growing strength, a sudden and disastrous economic depression and Lincoln's highly publicized "House Divided" speech, made during his senatorial campaign in 1858. Lincoln himself conceded that some kind of crisis lay ahead, and a great many people who saw eye to eye with him on little else were inclined to agree. Then, in quick succession, came two events which shattered what little complacency remained in the South. Miscalculation of the significance of these dramatic moments was in the spirit of the times, rumors consciously launched grew rapidly out of control and genuinely conciliatory gestures on the part of the North slipped by unnoticed.

The first shock was provided by John Brown's Private War, as C. Vann Woodward has called it. This brief but highly publicized skirmish began near Harper's Ferry on the night of October 16, 1859, when Brown and 18 cohorts captured a federal arsenal. The struggle was of short duration, and it collapsed in a matter of hours. It left in its wake some 15 dead, a great mass of documents compromising Brown's supporters in the North and one of the most controversial prisoners ever to be arrested and executed by an American state. For many Southerners who took the documents at face value and let their imaginations play over the potential consequences of a massive conspiracy of this kind, John Brown personified Northern predatory intentions which they all along had suspected lurked behind the reasonable and accommodating gestures of Northern statesmen. His name evoked almost everything hateful about the Yankee character: destructiveness, conspiracy, and hypocrisy. Upon this one man for a time were focused the emotions which for close to 30 years had been gathering around the figure of the Yankee. Brown's defense by a few New Englanders such as Emerson and Thoreau, who looked upon him as a saint and a martyr, only quickened Southern response. The possibility that he may have been mad was dismissed by his attackers and supporters alike. The fact that certain of his defenders, like the Reverend Theodore Parker of Boston, were actively implicated in his conspiracy led to gross exaggerations of his real support in New England and the magnitude of his enterprise generally. Although not a single slave rose in rebellion and Brown's action was deplored in Washington by all but a few extremists in the North, the South in a matter of weeks was thrown into a state of panic and one of the worst witch-hunts in American history occurred as eccentrics and "suspicious characters" of all kinds, many of them innocent strangers passing through, were mobbed, beaten, and tarred and feathered in a vigilante effort to root out Yankees and potential Southern subversives.

No relaxation of tension followed. Rumors of slave insurrections swept the South during the next year. Finally, the election of Lincoln, who was popularly believed to be the pawn of abolitionists, and the anticipated prominence in his coming administration of William Seward of "Irrepressible Conflict" fame provided the finishing touches to the picture of a Northern conspiracy about to be launched against the South.[4]

The state of feeling that existed in the South during these fateful months can be suggested in a series of brief tableaux. In Washington Southern congressmen, and in the South, federal judges, began to resign their offices; some like Senator James H. Hammond with hesitation, some with feelings of vindictiveness and triumph. Northerners who happened to be stranded in the South were threatened, mistreated, and even mobbed, and most of them rapidly headed for home. Daniel Hundley, a Southerner living in Chicago, fled the city under cover of night out of fear for his life. There was in fact a general exodus of Southerners from Northern cities. On December 22, 1859, a trainload of students from Philadelphia arrived in Richmond, marched past the stately capitol designed by Jefferson, and assembled before the governor's mansion to hear a speech from Governor John A. Wise on Southern self-sufficiency. "Let Virginia call home her children!" the governor told them, and he went on to advocate self-sacrifice and austerity. "Let us," he said, "dress in the wool raised on our own pastures. Let us eat the flour from our own mills, and if we can't get that, why let us go back to our old accustomed corn bread."[5] Troops of "Minute Men" wearing the blue cockade drilled before admiring Negroes who caught only the holiday spirit of color and display. Everywhere the hated Yankee became a figure of ridicule and contempt. He was a conspirator and a hypocrite, but he was also a coward. He would never fight, and he could certainly never win.

The move to dissociate the South from every contaminating northern influence had reached almost hysterical proportions by the time of Lincoln's inauguration. The capital was almost empty of its former official occupants. Southern politicians and their ladies, including many of the city's most prominent hostesses, had departed for home, leaving the incoming Northern administration to run the country and—such as it was—Washington society. It was all a little mad, Senator Hammond, himself once an ardent secessionist, frankly conceded—and suicidal too. "It is an epidemic and very foolish," he wrote in December, 1860. "It reminds me of the Japanese who when insulted rip open their own bowels."[6]

[4] C. Vann Woodward, "John Brown's Private War," *The Burden of Southern History* (Baton Rouge, 1960), pp. 41–68.

[5] Eaton, *Confederacy,* p. 1.

[6] *Ibid.,* pp. 9–10.

By the following summer, then, communications between North and South had broken down—even the mail had stopped moving across the Potomac—and many leading spokesmen of both sections now regarded one another suspiciously and hostilely as symbols of alien cultures. To Mrs. Chesnut, who was inclined to see things somewhat melodramatically and—like Lincoln—in familial terms, it was also a question of a divided household and a marriage gone bad. "We separated," she wrote in her diary, "because of incompatibility of temper; we are divorced, North from South, because we have hated each other so."[7] "And for so long a time," she might have added without greater exaggeration than she had already employed, since the hatred to which she referred had been slowly intensifying for over 30 years, and along with it the awakening sense of a divided culture.

Two English astronomers, Charles Mason and Jeremiah Dixon, in an effort to settle a boundary dispute, had run a line between Pennsylvania and Maryland in the 1760s, but no one had then conceived of such a boundary as dividing a North from a South. Jefferson had seen the danger of such a distinction at the time of the Missouri Compromise, but a popular belief in a precise demarcation between North and South was a development of the decades which followed, and the frontier was still indistinct even after secession. Maryland, immediately south of the line, remained loyal and other so-called slave states like Missouri and Kentucky, both of them in some measure Southern in their traditions and style of life, remained officially in the North. If there was a line, and increasingly Americans agreed that there was, it possessed no geographical definition. It was a psychological, not a physical division, which often cut like a cleaver through the mentality of individual men and women everywhere in the country.

The shift in attitude which occurred during the fifties and the alignment which rapidly appeared during the tense months following Lincoln's election in 1860, much as they owe to particular contemporary events, are deeply rooted in an equally significant but much less easily defined reorientation of American mentality which had been taking place at least since the thirties. If separation as a political and social fact was the immediate result of the political pressures, miscalculations and excited activism of these tumultuous months, the idea of a coherent South, of a distinct and different Southern civilization was not new in 1850, to say nothing of 1859; yet it was an idea which would have startled both Jefferson and Adams in 1816, and did in fact alarm Jefferson when he caught the first intimation of it in 1820.

[7] Mary Boykin Chesnut, *A Diary from Dixie* (Boston, 1949), p. 20; cited by Eaton, *Confederacy*, p. 17.

Neither Jefferson nor Adams, furthermore, had thought of the natural aristocrat—their choice for the republican leader—as possessing any particular regional traits. Neither, certainly, would have localized either lower-class villainy or aristocratic honor and virtue in any North or South which they knew. Adams, with his alertness to the danger of a false aristocracy in New England and with his keen sense of fallibility, saw evil and ambition lurking in every man's heart. He probably would have found the fully developed idea of the Yankee laughable and yet a little appealing, but he scarcely would have looked for better human materials south of the Potomac. Jefferson would have looked upon the full-blown Cavalier ideal with something like loathing and seen in its currency the undoing of much that he had worked to accomplish. Yet some three decades were sufficient to bring about these changes and to usher in a whole new set of assumptions concerning the history, cultural background, and racial composition of the two regions from which these two men had sprung—and for which they had made themselves the spokesmen. The nature of these changes is implicit in the preceding chapters, but the pattern of change is a somewhat complicated one and perhaps deserves brief reiteration.

The Southern Cavalier Redivivus

The first quarter of the nineteenth century had not passed before a significant number of Americans in both the North and the South had begun to express decided reservations about the direction progress was taking and about the kind of aggressive, mercenary, self-made man who was rapidly making his way in their society. In everyone's eyes this type of parvenu came to express a worrisome facet of the national character, to symbolize, in fact, both the restless mobility and the strident materialism of new world society. In the face of the threat which seemed to be posed by this new man, Americans—genteel and would-be genteel—began to develop pronounced longings for some form of aristocracy. They longed for a class of men immune to acquisitiveness, indifferent to social ambition and hostile to commercial life, cities, and secular progress. They sought, they would frankly have conceded, for something a little old-fashioned.

Writers like Cooper, Sarah Hale, and Paulding, themselves representative spokesmen of a much larger group, were particularly attracted by the idea of a conservative country gentry such as England possessed—or, at least, had possessed—only purer and better. The equalitarian character of life in the North provided an unsuitable terrain in which to locate, even in fantasy, an aristocracy of this kind. By the 1830s the legendary Southern planter, despite reservations of one kind or another, began to seem almost perfectly suited to fill the need. His ample estates, his spacious style of life, his Cavalier ancestry and his reputed obliviousness to money matters gained him favor in the eyes of those in search of a native American aristocracy. More and more, he came to be looked upon *the* characteristic expression of life in the South. Meanwhile, the acquisitive man, the man on the make, became inseparably associated with the North and especially with New England. In the end, the Yankee—for so he became known—was thought to be as much the product of the North as the planter-Cavalier of the South. By 1850 these two types—the Cavalier and the Yankee—expressed in the popular imagination the basic cultural conflict which people felt had grown up between a decorous, agrarian South and the rootless, shifting, money-minded North.

No such absolute division, of course, ever really existed between the North and the South. Southerners engaged in business, speculated on real estate, sought profits, lived in towns and cities, voted for the same national parties and subscribed to many of the same ideals and values as other Americans. What differences they developed, as over the issue of Negro slavery, did not lead many of them to formulate a totally different set of social objectives; these differences simply complicated their response to objectives which they already in large measure had accepted. Thus, in crying out against the Yankee North, Southerners who did so were, in a sense, striking out at part of themselves. By 1860 they had become self-divided, frustrated in their hopes and wishes, increasingly unrealistic in their social aspirations and ripe for some kind of bloody showdown.

The problem for the self-conscious South finally lay in the need which it felt to isolate—to quarantine—itself from the contaminating influence of the Yankee North, which it both feared and envied—and which, finally, was so much a part of itself. The result was the creation of an exclusively Southern historical, and even racial, heritage. Outvoted or overruled in national affairs, outgrown in population, outproduced and, as many Southerners at least secretly felt, outraged on the justice of slavery, the South in 1860 sought some kind of redemption in separateness, only to set up a Confederate government which was not essentially different, even in its constitutional details, from the federal republic from which it had just seceded.

The "Southern" problem was, then, for these men a condition of paralysis brought on by conflicting loyalties—they finally could not believe in either their own regional ideals or those of the country as a whole. Belief in the one conflicted with belief in the other; the result was confusion, indecision, and a kind of gnawing dispiritedness. By the 1850s, certainly, they no longer believed wholeheartedly in the effectiveness of the Cavalier gentleman, since they, too, came to measure achievement by financial success and the gentleman planter was, almost by definition, born to fail. But neither could they worship success, since it was measured in dollars and cents rather than in honor and cultural elevation. The improvident, generous-hearted gentleman planter for them became increasingly a symbol of a Lost Cause—an insurgent, a dueler, a fighter against overwhelming odds—in short, a figment of a utopian social world which was doomed to be submerged under a tide of middle-class materialism.

Without quite acknowledging it, many Southerners during these years had been waging a kind of war with themselves. Increasingly their ideal of a stable social order came into conflict with the social and political realities with which they were confronted. The lowly, whether white or black, gave clear evidence that they did not wish to remain lowly and feudally dependent upon the planter's goodwill. Even women were beginning to speak out in their own names, and some of the things they said represented a distinct challenge to the patriarchal role which the planter had assumed for himself and to many of the values which he thought of himself as embodying. Meanwhile, in the larger sphere of political events, the planter class in the Southern states, divested of the support of the West and challenged at home by its own yeomanry, found its power threatened both in Washington and in state legislatures. And what was an aristocrat who did not possess the power to order his own home, to say nothing of ruling over the national councils, especially when he was beginning to question some of the sanctions upon which his power had been based?

The Alabaman, Daniel Hundley,[8] for example, expressed his ambivalent attitude toward the force of the Cavalier ideal in his *Social Relations in our Southern States,* the book which he published on the eve of the war. In it he drew an ominous picture of the aristocrat in the South surrounded by predatory, or at least more forceful, social types, who seemed destined to overthrow his cultural and political domination. His book contained chapters devoted to the Southern Yankee, the southern bully, the poor white, and the enterprising and forward-looking representative of the new middle class. While he argued for the aristocratic ethos of the Southern gentleman, his confidence in his effectiveness clearly wavered before the vision of a rising Southern bourgeoisie.

Few figures in Southern history exemplify better than Edmund Ruffin the tensions and frustrations felt by those who had long battled for the Lost Cause. Ruffin, for years one of the South's leading agricultural scientists and an advocate of a diversified farm economy, was never reconciled to the defeat of the Cavalier ideal. Toward the end of his life, weary and partly deaf, he became obsessed by the idea of an independent, uncontaminated South and fought every inroad of what he regarded as Yankeeism. Dressed—rather conspicuously—in coarse Southern homespun; or,

---

[8] Hundley is discussed at greater length in another section.

in 1859, at the age of 63, attending John Brown's hanging clad in the uniform of a VMI cadet; or, as a volunteer in the Palmetto Guards, pulling the lanyard that sent one of the first shells toward Fort Sumter, he became a kind of Lanny Budd of the Old South, his every act a symbolic representation of Southern intransigeance before the Yankee North.

Few men more keenly sensed or more deeply resented the obstacles with which true Southernism was confronted within the South itself; no one, certainly, lashed out at the Yankee with greater bitterness or, finally expressed his feelings of frustration and self-defeat more melodramatically. As an agitator he repeatedly faced indifferent Southern audiences and, poor speaker that he was, he constantly reproached himself for his failure to bring the South to a boil. Virginia he early abandoned as reprobate; he was appalled to find the large planters in Kentucky holding strong Unionist views; and even South Carolina constantly disappointed him by her unwillingness, as in 1850, to take deliberate action. On a visit to White Sulphur Springs in August, 1859, he was astonished to find himself virtually alone among some 1600 Southern guests in calling for secession. For a time after John Brown's raid he hoped "the sluggish blood of the South" would be stirred,[9] and he personally sent pikes with which Brown had intended to arm the slaves to the governors of all the Southern states; but once again he was disappointed in his expectations. Even when confronted with the virtual certainty of Lincoln's election, no state except South Carolina expressed a willingness to take the initiative in seceding. The election of 1860, in which the more moderate Bell triumphed over Breckinridge within the South by a majority of 136,875, only confirmed his fear that the South would never act.

Then, as Southern states began to pass ordinances of secession, his hopes soared one final time. After a lifetime of ceaseless struggle, his dream of an independent South seemed about to become a reality. Once the exciting days of Fort Sumter were over, even these hopes were dashed as Jefferson Davis neglected former secessionists and formed a government dominated by moderates and men Ruffin regarded as would-be reunionists. Davis himself, furthermore, seemed slow to move and indecisive, and left Southern extremists generally dissatisfied with his leadership. But for Ruffin—as for most Southerners—the most crushing blow, one which destroyed for all time the myth of Southern invincibility, was the military defeat of the South by the Northern armies that swarmed across his beloved Virginia, destroying his plantation "Beechwood" and leaving obscene graffiti scrawled on the walls of his house. His plantation a shambles, deserted

[9] Avery Craven, *Edmund Ruffin Southerner: A Study in Secession* (New York, 1932), p. 171.

by his slaves, his hearing gone, and the alien North on his very doorstep, he had little left to him that he valued save his sense of honor, his bitterness, and his pride, to which he regularly gave expression in a diary kept through these trying years.

On June 17, 1865, after he had digested the news from Appomattox, he made this entry in the diary:

> I here declare my unmitigated hatred to Yankee rule—to all political, social and business connections with the Yankees and to the Yankee race. Would that I could impress these sentiments, in their full force, on every living Southerner and bequeath them to every one yet to be born! May such sentiments be held universally in the outraged and downtrodden South, though in silence and stillness, until the now far-distant day shall arrive for just retribution for Yankee usurpation, oppression and atrocious outrages, and for deliverance and vengeance for the now ruined, subjugated and enslaved Southern States! . . . And now with my latest writing and utterance, and with what will be near my latest breath, I here repeat and would willingly proclaim my unmitigated hatred to Yankee rule—to all political, social and business connections with Yankees, and the perfidious, malignant and vile Yankee race.[10]

Almost before the ink of this entry had dried the old man performed his most symbolic act. Seating himself erectly in his chair, he propped the butt of his silver-mounted gun against a trunk at his feet, placed the muzzle in his mouth and, as his son reported in a letter to members of the family, "pulled the trigger with a forked stick."[11]

Coda

With Edmund Ruffin's suicide and the collapse of the Confederacy which it symbolized, the Old South as a concrete entity passed beyond history and into legend. One prolonged attempt to establish and sustain an aristocratic ideal in the face of obstacles of the kind invariably thrown up by American circumstances had ended. It was not the first such attempt, as colonial historians have shown,[12] nor was it to be the last, as those

---

[10] *Ibid.*, p. 259. The information about Ruffin, except for the details of his death, derives entirely from Professor Craven's biography.

[11] Edmund Ruffin, Jr., to his sons, June 20, 1865, in "Death of Edmund Ruffin," *Tyler's Quarterly Historical and Genealogical Magazine,* V (January, 1924), 193.

[12] Bernard Bailyn, "Politics and Social Structure in Virginia," *Seventeenth-Century America: Essays in Colonial History* (ed.), James Morton Smith (Chapel Hill, 1959), pp. 90–115.

familiar with elitist groups at the end of the century can testify;[13] but perhaps, because of its bearing on the course of American history before 1861 and because of its more general consequences for the development of our cultural self-awareness, it has been the most important.

The Cavalier ideal was predestined to fail, as some of its earliest proponents secretly knew. The men who originated it were not aristocrats in any sense which Europeans would have recognized. Often they themselves were self-made men, provincial in their outlook and historically naïve, who possessed no sure sense of any cultural tradition. I have spoken, principally as a matter of convenience, of "the South" and "the planter class" in assigning a specific locus to the kind of thinking which I have been describing; but at no time, I suspect, was the Cavalier ideal as it was defined by Beverley Tucker, for example, widely understood or embraced by Southern planters in general, to say nothing of other people living within the South. Such an ideal was significant because it exemplified an important American cultural problem and because it defined a tendency in Southern thought which ultimately affected political events.

As it moved toward implementation, of course, the ideal was repeatedly and necessarily compromised. The constitution of no Southern state, not even that of South Carolina, provided for anything more than a kind of modified planter oligarchy; most of the older states within the South yielded to democratic pressures before the war; and the newer states of the Southwest were no more exclusive in their political arrangements than comparable states in the North. The Confederate constitution, finally, despite its explicit recognition of slavery, was in no sense meant to set up an aristocracy, and in certain ways it provided more assurance of popular government than the federal Constitution.

The legacy left behind by the Cavalier ideal is a little difficult to define; a careful consideration of it would require a study in itself. The close of the war did not mean, certainly, that some kind of aristocratic ideal ceased to form a part of Southern thinking, nor did it mean, once Reconstruction was over, that some kind of planter class ceased to dominate Southern politics. Quite the contrary. The century had virtually ended before the old dominant groups in the South and their new business allies received any substantial challenge from the majority of Southerners, whose affairs they had historically directed. After the war, as everyone knows, the legend, far from dying away, was given a new lease on life and, in the North, probably enjoyed greater popularity and evoked more interest than at any other time. Its vitality, it seems apparent enough, has not yet

[13] Barbara Miller Solomon, *Ancestors and Immigrants: A Changing New England Tradition* (Cambridge, Mass.; 1956); Arthur Mann, *Yankee Reformers in The Urban Age* (Cambridge, Mass., 1954).

exhausted itself today after more than a century of discussion and dramatic reembodiment. The nostalgia felt by Americans for the antebellum South and for the drama of the Civil War is a phenomenon which continues to startle those unfamiliar with our culture, with our collective anxieties about the kind of civilization we have created, and with our reservations concerning the kind of social conformity which, it appears, it has been our destiny to exemplify before the world. Some of our greatest writers—Henry Adams and Henry James within the nineteenth century—have employed the Cavalier legend as a means of defining and measuring the failures and limitations of our culture at large. It seems scarcely necessary to add that this same concern has characteristically engaged the imagination of William Faulkner. But for the great mass of Americans, even those who take their impression exclusively from popular novels, television plays, and Civil War centennials, the Old South has also become an enduring part of our sense of the past. At odd moments probably even the most skeptical of us allow our thoughts to play over this lingering social image, and to concede with mingled pride and wonderment: "Once it was *different* down there."

11

The Confederate Myth

Frank E. Vandiver

To the minds of most, the War Between the States represents the
greatest watershed and psychodrama of the national experience. It
represents as well the most acute trauma in southern historical
consciousness. The southern mind and its mystique are clearly
wedded in the Civil War. To Frank E. Vandiver, Professor of
History and Provost at Rice University, Houston, the impact of
the war and the consequent emergence of the Confederate States
of America had been debilitating as regards the social imagination
of the South. It was the war experience that reinforced the "pseudo-
past" of the Old South. It was by virtue of "the crusade of the
planters" that a related, but nonetheless new, mythical edifice
began to emerge from the ashes of Shiloh, Vicksburg, and Chattanooga. Ironically, however, it was not the mythologized Confederate leadership which functioned as principle architects of the
"Confederate Myth," but rather future idolaters with an appetite for
historical romance. In the wake of civil war, Confederate political
and military leaders continued at the cutting edge of historical
change. They stood in the vanguard of a New South, a redeemed
South based on economic progress. It would be subsequent generations who would function as the mythmakers and falsifiers of history—seeing the revolutionary generation as strict state righters,
blind patriots to a "lost cause," and preservers of southern racial integrity. As has often been the case in other political circumstances,
it was "enterprising conservatives" who led a historical pilgrimage
to the shrine of dead radicals.

This essay first appeared in the *Southwest Review,* 46 (Summer 1961), 199–204. © 1961 by
Frank Vandiver.

In the states of the old Confederacy the Centennial celebration of the Civil War is to be largely a refurbishing of the Confederate myth. The Confederate myth is a vital part of life in the South. According to this legend, sanctified southern ancestors fought valiantly against virtually hopeless odds to sustain a "way of life" peculiar to the section of long, hot summers, and Negro field hands. This "way of life" never seemed to be wholly understood, but it found description in various paeans of nostalgia and in the self-image of all southerners. Key elements in the southern mode of living were tradition, dedication to the protocols of lineage, land, cotton, sun, and vast hordes of blacks. Tending southern life were a special breed represented by the planters. Not everybody by any means was a planter, but the myth holds that everybody wanted to be and that all had the same chance to rise to that pinnacle of grace—all save the noncitizens with dark skin. The planters came to hoard their status with a certain grim zeal. Under increasing pressure throughout the 1830's, 40's, and 50's, they turned to all types of protection—censorship, intimidation, propaganda, open hostility to fellow-Americans.

But their tactics were glossed by myth into a creditable struggle for self-determination against a tide of urban nationalism which threatened extinction of the "way of life" so happy and so alien to the time.

The crusade of the planters spread to a campaign for Southern Rights, and hence the small farmer, the town merchant, the southern clergy found themselves sharing the planter's war. What was good for the planter was good for the South.

War, according to the myth, may not have been the only way to save the social and economic order, but it showed how deeply dedicated were the southerners to their inarticulated "rights." Against forces most formidable the southerner pitted himself, his small fortune, his Lilliputian industry, his life, and his girded honor. He lost, but lost magnificently. He lost wholly, utterly, but out of the ashes of his homes, his cities, his broken generation, he salvaged his sacred honor. And with this scrap of victory he could build the myth that has sustained him, has shackled him to a false image, and has convinced him of a lasting difference between himself and the rest of the United States.

Marshall Fishwick, in a brave and controversial essay, "Robert E. Lee: The Guardian Angel Myth" (*Saturday Review,* March 4, 1961), points out that Lee's noble virtues, peerless leadership, and heroic acceptance of defeat fixed in the southern mind the meaning of the Lost Cause. That cause represented the true acme of southern achievement: for it died the flower of the South, and those who yielded up their blood were such southerners as all those who came since would like to be. They were the shining model, the marble image, the men above men who lived a brief moment as destiny's chosen. They were the South.

They still are the South, for they stand above, around, and beyond what the South now is, and loom as silent prophets to lesser men in troubled times. And so they are God and curse, inspiration and death. Their stone faces look from countless shafts to the past, and their sons, grandsons, and great-grandsons look with them. They are different from the present; they were alien to their time. So, too, the modern southerner who points to difference, to his ageless "white man's burden" and his genteel poverty. His ancestors lurking from musty picture frames stood against the leviathan state and its leveling tendencies. He, too, stands with his own perception of past obligations and future duties. If the rest of the nation has lost its agrarian innocence, the southerner remembers. He, at least, is faithful to a dim Jeffersonian image and to a Greek democracy ideal which came, was fleetingly touched by life and sustained by blood, and faded to the pantheon of lost glories. But the brief blood bath lent a strange endurance and gave hope to generations held tight in inertia, fear, poverty, and the horror of a lost dream and a shattered mirror. The broken image had to be conjured again, and when it came it was twisted into a grotesque sort of plaster beauty which satisfied its designers and doomed the past it seemed to limn to a hundred years of distortion.

Distorting Civil War southerners was not easy. They lived larger than most, fought, raged, cowed, bled, spoke, and died with the nobility of desperation. They were, like their northern brethren, touched with timeless animation. They were unique and so should have been immune to the myth-makers and falsifiers of history. But myth-makers are determined and their works often approved by necessity. So the Confederate changed from a human, striving, erring being to something much different. All Confederates automatically became virtuous, all were defenders of the rights of states and individuals, all were segregationists, all steadfast, all patriotic.

Like all lasting myths, this one had enough validity to sound good. The Lost Cause came on to the present as the last American resistance against the Organization State, against racial indistinction, against mass and motor.

And while post-Civil War southerners were pushing as fast as they could into the New South, were grasping Yankee dollars with enthusiasm, they purified their motives in the well of Lost Causism. Politicians found it a bottomless source of bombast and ballots, preachers found it balm and solace to somewhat reluctant middle-class morals, writers found it a noble and salable theme. What the South had been could be the touchstone for the future, could be the fundament of a section going into the industrial age with part of its heart and holding firm to the past with the other.

Lost Causism came to fulfil a role similar to that of the pro-slavery argument in ante-bellum times. It offered justification for resistance to the leveling tendencies continued by harsh Reconstruction measures. It cloaked the lawless Klansman and lent license to the segregating Christian. It was, finally, the cornerstone of the New South.

The tragedy is that the Confederate myth is so wrong. That the Confederacy could come to represent in the present things it never represented in its lifetime is an irony of the present southern dilemma.

What, then, are some of the axioms of the Confederate myth?

First: The Confederate States represented the unified nationalistic yearning of all the state rights advocates in the South.

Wrong. State righters were not unified and there is considerable doubt that they were in the majority when the Confederacy took form in February, 1861. Certain it is that they failed to gain control of the government under Jefferson Davis, and although they did much to impede the Confederate war effort, they did not dominate the high councils.

Second: The Confederacy was defended to the last by gaunt gray heroes who went with Lee and Johnston and others to the bitterest end.

Wrong again. There was probably more per capita desertion from Confederate ranks than from the ranks of the Union. Far more Rebel troops were absent from roll call at the end of the war than were with the colors. Much bravery, even shining, incredible heroism the southern men did display, but that they were all blind patriots is demonstrably untrue.

Third: Any Confederate could lick ten Yankees.

Possibly, but in the end the Rebels were "overwhelmed."

Fourth: Everyone behind the Confederate lines showed the same dauntless dedication to oblivion as the soldiery. Men, women, and children all served the cause to the last shred of cloth, the last window weight, the last crust of bread.

Not so. While there were many magnificent examples of fate-defying loyalty by southern civilians, there were also many examples of petty speculation, wanton brigandage, Unionism, criminal selfishness, and treason. Defection behind the lines, open resistance to Confederate laws, became a matter of national scandal before the conflict ended.

Fifth: All Confederate leaders were unswervingly dedicated to the cause and would have preferred to perish rather than survive under a despised and crushing victor.

Still wrong. Many Confederate leaders, including Davis, Stephens, Lee, and Stonewall Jackson, looked on secession with a jaundiced eye. Legal they thought it to be, but they doubted its practicality. And when the war ended only a few of the leaders who survived buried themselves in the past. Davis did, and so did lasting disservice to the section he strove to defend. Lee, on the other hand, put the war behind him and worked unsparingly for a prosperous New South sharing fully the destiny of a re-United States. His example set the tone for most veterans. Numbers of former generals, to be sure, used their combat records to gain some personal advantage, but most wanted that advantage to further a career in business or politics and hence partook of the new industrial age.

Sixth: The Confederacy fought not only for state rights, but also and especially to preserve racial integrity. The government and the people of the embattled southern states were solidly against letting down racial barriers and understood that a northern victory would mean abolition. The Negro was kept in his place in the Confederacy, was used only for agricultural and menial tasks, and what was good enough for the Confederates is good enough for us.

False, and this is false on two levels. During the war the South did attempt for a time to shore up the bonds of servitude, but when the pressure of defeat grew grim, various southern leaders, including Lee and Davis, came to advocate the use of slaves in the army; some even suggested freedom in return for service. And after the war, on the level of special pleading, the South engaged in a long paper conflict with northern historians about the causes of the fighting. A point which the southerners strove staunchly to sustain was that the war had not been fought to preserve slavery, but to preserve the "Southern Way of Life," of which slavery was only an aspect. Finally some argued that the war had been fought solely to gain independence, and cited the offer to England in March, 1865, of total freedom in exchange for recognition as proof.

Seventh: The Confederate government was a supreme, unsullied example of a state rights organization that remained loyal to the principles of Calhoun, even in the face of defeat.

This is the wrongest of all assumptions. Davis and his administration tried for a while to do what seemed constitutional under the narrow southern view of law, but war and a curiously unnoticed strain of mind in the South changed the course of governmental conduct.

Union sentiment, long-standing in many parts of the South, united with conservative Democratic sentiment and with latent Whiggery to introduce a new element in southern politics. Men who looked on violent change with repugnance banded together to prevent the secessionists from carrying the Confederacy to revolutionary excesses. These men, including Davis himslf, kept the Montgomery Convention in hand, saw to it that the trend toward vast, ruinous upheaval was halted by moderate counsel. The result of moderate control at Montgomery was a Confederate constitution much like that of the Union, a government based on established and familiar federal principles, and a president who had not camped with the fire-eaters. Many with these cautious views were elected to the various Confederate congresses and so held some authority through the war.

Caution and the natural conservatism of some Democrats and Whigs did not mean that these members of the Confederate Congress were unwilling to fight a hard war. Most of these southern moderates were men dedicated to strong central government as the main bulwark of law and order. They hated disturbance and resisted disruption of the Union. But when it came, they "went with their state," they stayed with family and land. They stayed, too, with principles of steady government, strong law, and established order. Consequently they stood for power in the hands of the executive, power in the federal government, and a stern war effort.

It was these Whiggish moderates who came to represent the Confederate "left" and to urge big government to fight a big war. They knew something of the corporate state, saw that it had virtues for organization, and urged Davis and his cabinet to centralize and command. These neo-organization men supported the growth of a large army, strict taxation (in keeping with sound Whig monetary views), conscription, impressment of private property, and finally the use of Negro slaves in the ranks—even to the point of manumission in return for service. When the war ended, these same "leftists" of the Confederacy moved into the New South.

Many became leaders in new southern industries, some went into politics and supported the coming of northern capital, most stood for sound finances, restoration of order, and the onward march of business. These moderates, these quiet men who abhorred revolution but used it when they had to, were the ones who brought about the greatest revolution of the South. They changed the Confederacy right under the eyes of the rabid secessionists from a localistic community into a small industrial power run along centralized lines. They aroused resistance from the Confederate "right"—state righters and fire-eaters—but kept control and forced their opponents to adopt modern centralist measures to resist them. When their attempt to remake the wartime South ended in defeat, they continued their efforts with the aid of Radical Republicans and ultimately achieved their goal. The Old South disappeared in the smoke of Chattanooga's and Birmingham's iron furnaces, in the dust of Alabama's coal pits, in the busy marts of Atlanta, Houston, Memphis, and New Orleans. These quiet, soft action men were the ones who set the base for the rise of a new industrial giant south of Mason and Dixon's Line, a giant whose future, according to Professor Walter Prescott Webb, is limitless because of its natural resources.

But in one salient respect these Whiggish gentlemen failed to remold their native section: this boundless potential painted by Webb and many chambers of commerce is sharply restricted by the Confederate myth. Although the moderate businessmen of the Confederate and New South were willing and partially able to set the black man free, and did break the bonds of southern agriculture, they could not unshackle the mind of the South—the Negro became a symbol of all troubles, and the Confederacy lingered as the herald of the South's greatness. The myth holds that the South was so great when it fought with piteous ardor for a twisted past and for principles aged and vestigial, that there was no future left for it. Its future lay buried with its gray dead.

This stultifying acceptance of decline is the wages of the Confederate myth. What was, was pure and better than what is, and in what was lies a sort of self-realization. While the South was transformed by Confederates into a moderately modern, progressive nation, the myth twists the achievement of the rebellious generation and dooms descendants to cheating themselves. Acceptance of the illusion of rabid Confederate racism, for instance, leads the modern Confederate to waste a vast source of manpower—a source which could be of inestimable value if the South is to move into the rosy future that some have predicted for it.

The Centennial years could best be devoted to revising the Confederate myth and bringing it up to date. Instead of standing for a pseudo-past, for false traditions and sham virtues, it should be repaired by the reality of perspective into what it has always been. Lee, Davis, members of the Confederate Congress, many soldiers who fell gallantly on scores of fields, were alert, forward-looking southerners. They were willing, for the sake of their cause, to abandon old shibboleths, to change the very nature of their body politic and body social. Instead of looking back and making war with weapons withered by age, they looked at the new ones their enemies used and copied, improved, progressed. The Confederate States of America did not have America in the name for nothing. Confederates were Americans, too, and so had no fear of challenge. The Rebels accepted challenge and almost met it. Most of them surely would regard with scorn their descendants who look backward in frustration.

12

The Tragic Legend of Reconstruction

Kenneth M. Stampp

With the afterglow of the sectional conflict still firing their imaginations, southerners and northerners collectively began the arduous process of reshaping the social and political configuration of the South. The desire to "bind up the nation's wounds," to redirect the frenetic energy of the Civil War into reconstructive channels, was a major compulsion for many in post–Civil War America. Indeed, the war for the Union had settled many issues; but it had left as many outstanding. Unfortunately for "posterity," the historical record of the dozen years of Reconstruction—in fact, that of the total postwar experience from 1865–1900 and even beyond—has been extremely difficult to assess, particularly given its intimate relationship to fundamental patterns of national public policy. Perhaps legend and myth become most debilitating when they directly affect a society's overt social and political behavior. If this is so, the legend of reconstruction qualifies as particularly tragic. Kenneth M. Stampp, Professor of History at the University of California, Berkeley, applies a revisionist lens to the era of Reconstruction in the interest of explaining American racial attitudes, past and present. Through his revisionist view of the Reconstruction "radicals," Stampp brings much weight to bear against the mythology of northern postwar brutality. It was a mythology, he finds, that was largely the product of the historical community itself, but one that nonetheless found an especially receptive audience both north and south.

In much serious history, a well as in a durable poplar legend, two American epochs—the Civil War and the Reconstruction that followed—bear an odd relationship to one another. The Civil War, though admittedly a tragedy, is nevertheless often described as a glorious time of gallantry, noble self-sacrifice, and high idealism. Even historians who have considered the war "needless" and have condemned the politicians of the 1850s for blundering into it, once they passed the firing on Fort Sumter, have usually written with reverence about Civil War heroes—the martyred Lincoln, the Christlike Lee, the intrepid Stonewall Jackson, and many others in this galaxy of demigods.

Few, of course, are so innocent as not to know that the Civil War had its seamy side. One can hardly ignore the political opportunism, the graft and profiteering in the filling of war contracts, the military blundering and needless loss of lives, the horrors of army hospitals and prison camps, and the ugly depths as well as the nobility of human nature that the war exposed with a fine impartiality. These things cannot be ignored, but they can be, and frequently are, dismissed as something alien to the essence of the war years. What was real and fundamental was the idealism and the nobility of the two contending forces: the Yankees struggling to save the Union, dying to make men free; the Confederates fighting for great constitutional principles, defending their homes from invasion. Here, indeed, is one of the secrets of the spell the Civil War has cast: it involved high-minded Americans on both sides, and there was glory enough to go around. This, in fact, is the supreme synthesis of Civil War historiography and the great balm that has healed the nation's wounds: Yankees and Confederates alike fought bravely for what they believed to be just causes. There were few villains in the drama.

But when the historian reaches the year 1865, he must take leave of the war and turn to another epoch, Reconstruction, when the task was, in Lincoln's words, "to bind up the nation's wounds" and "to do all which may achieve and cherish a just and lasting peace." How, until recently, Reconstruction was portrayed in both history and legend, how sharply it was believed to contrast with the years of the Civil War, is evident in the terms that were used to identify it. Various historians have called this phase of American history "The Tragic Era," "The Dreadful Decade," "The Age of Hate," and "The Blackout of Honest Government." Reconstruction represented the ultimate shame of the American people—as one historian phrased it, "the nadir of national disgrace." It was the epoch that most Americans wanted to forget.

Claude Bowers, who divided his time between politics and history, has been the chief disseminator of the traditional picture of Reconstruction, for his book, *The Tragic Era,* published in 1929, has attracted more readers than any other dealing with this period. For Bowers, Reconstruction was a time of almost unrelieved sordidness in public and private life; whole regiments of villains march through his pages; the corrupt politicians who dominated the administration of Ulysses S. Grant; the crafty, scheming northern carpetbaggers who invaded the South after the war for political and economic plunder; the degraded and depraved southern scalawags who betrayed their own people and collaborated with the enemy; and the ignorant, barbarous, sensual Negroes who threatened to Africanize the South and destroy its Caucasian civilization.

Most of Bowers's key generalizations can be found in his preface. The years of Reconstruction, he wrote, "were years of revolutionary turmoil, with the elemental passions predominant. . . . The prevailing note was one of tragedy. . . . Never have American public men in responsible positions, directing the destiny of the nation, been so brutal, hypocritical, and corrupt. The constitution was treated as a doormat on which politicians and army officers wiped their feet after wading in the muck. . . . The southern people literally were put to the torture . . . [by] rugged conspirators . . . [who] assumed the pose of philanthropists and patriots." The popularity of Bowers's book stems in part from the simplicity of his characters. None are etched in shades of gray; none are confronted with complex moral decisions. Like characters in a Victorian romance, the Republican leaders of the Reconstruction era were evil through and through, and the helpless, innocent white men of the South were totally noble and pure.

If Bowers's prose is more vivid and his anger more intense, his general interpretation of Reconstruction is only a slight exaggeration of a point of view shared by most serious American historians from the late nineteenth century until very recently. Writing in the 1890s, James Ford Rhodes, author of a multivolumed history of the United States since the Compromise of 1850, branded the Republican scheme of reconstruction as "repressive" and "uncivilized," one that "pandered to the ignorant negroes, the knavish white natives and the vulturous adventurers who flocked from the North." About the same time Professor John W. Burgess, of Columbia University, called Reconstruction the "most soul-sickening spectacle that Americans had ever been called upon to behold."[1] Early in the twentieth century Professor William A. Dunning, also of Columbia University, and a group of talented graduate students wrote a series of monographs that presented a crushing indictment of the

[1] James Ford Rhodes, *History of the United States from the Compromise of 1850 . . .*, 7 vols. (New York, 1893–1906), VII, p. 168; John W. Burgess, *Reconstruction and the Constitution* (New York, 1902), p. 263.

Republican reconstruction program in the South—a series that made a deep and lasting impression on American historians. In the 1930s, Professor James G. Randall, of the University of Illinois, still writing in the spirit of the Dunningites, described the Reconstruction era "as a time of party abuse, of corruption, of vindictive bigotry." "To use a modern phrase," wrote Randall, "government under Radical Republican rule in the South had become a kind of 'racket.' " As late as 1947, Professor E. Merton Coulter, of the University of Georgia, reminded critics of the traditional interpretation that no "amount of revision can write away the grievous mistakes made in this abnormal period of American history."[2] Thus, from Rhodes and Burgess and Dunning to Randall and Coulter the central emphasis of most historical writing about Reconstruction has been upon sordid motives and human depravity. Somehow, during the summer of 1865, the nobility and idealism of the war years had died.

A synopsis of the Dunning school's version of Reconstruction would run something like this: Abraham Lincoln, while the Civil War was still in progress, turned his thoughts to the great problem of reconciliation; and, "with malice toward none and charity for all," this gentle and compassionate man devised a plan that would restore the South to the Union with minimum humiliation and maximum speed. But there had already emerged in Congress a faction of Radical Republicans, sometimes called Jacobins or Vindictives, who sought to defeat Lincoln's generous program. Motivated by hatred of the South, by selfish political ambitions, and by crass economic interests, the Radicals tried to make the process of reconstruction as humiliating, as difficult, and as prolonged as they possibly could. Until Lincoln's tragic death, they poured their scorn upon him—and then used his coffin as a political stump to arouse the passions of the northern electorate.

The second chapter of the Dunning version begins with Andrew Johnson's succession to the presidency. Johnson, the old Jacksonian Unionist from Tennessee, took advantage of the adjournment of Congress to put Lincoln's mild plan of reconstruction into operation, and it was a striking success. In the summer and fall of 1865, Southerners organized loyal state governments, showed a willingness to deal fairly with their former slaves, and in general accepted the outcome of the Civil War in good faith. In December, when Congress assembled, President Johnson reported that the process of reconstruction was nearly completed and that the old Union had been restored. But the Radicals

[2] James G. Randall, *Civil War and Reconstruction* (Boston, 1937), pp. 689, 852; E. Merton, Coulter, *The South during Reconstruction, 1865–1877* (Baton Rouge, 1947), p. xi.

unfortunately had their own sinister purposes: they repudiated the governments Johnson had established in the South, refused to seat southern senators and representatives, and then directed their fury against the new president. After a year of bitter controversy and political stalemate, the Radicals, resorting to shamefully demagogic tactics, won an overwhelming victory in the congressional elections of 1866.

Now, the third chapter and the final tragedy. Riding rough-shod over presidential vetoes and federal courts, the Radicals put the South under military occupation, gave the ballot to Negroes, and formed new southern state governments dominated by base and corrupt men, black and white. Not satisfied with reducing the South to political slavery and financial bankruptcy, the Radicals even laid their obscene hands on the pure fabric of the federal Constitution. They impeached President Johnson and came within one vote of removing him from office, though they had no legal grounds for such action. Next, they elected Ulysses S. Grant president, and during his two administrations they indulged in such an orgy of corruption and so prostituted the civil service as to make Grantism an enduring symbol of political immorality.

The last chapter is the story of ultimate redemption. Decent southern white Democrats, their patience exhausted, organized to drive the Negroes, carpetbaggers, and scalawags from power, peacefully if possible, forcefully if necessary. One by one the southern states were redeemed, honesty and virtue triumphed, and the South's natural leaders returned to power. In the spring of 1877, the Tragic Era finally came to an end when President Hayes withdrew the federal troops from the South and restored home rule. But the legacy of Radical Reconstruction remained in the form of a solidly Democratic South and embittered relations between the races.

This point of view was rarely challenged until the 1930s, when a small group of revisionist historians began to give new life and a new direction to the study of Reconstruction. The revisionists are a curious lot who sometimes quarrel with each other as much as they quarrel with the disciples of Dunning. At various times they have counted in their ranks Marxists of various degrees of orthodoxy, Negroes seeking historical vindication, skeptical white southerners, and latter-day northern abolitionists. But among them are numerous scholars who have the wisdom to know that the history of an age is seldom simple and clear-cut, seldom without its tragic aspects, seldom without its redeeming virtues.

Few revisionists would claim that the Dunning interpretation of Reconstruction is a pure fabrication. They recognize the shabby aspects of this era: the corruption was real, the failures obvious, the tragedy undeniable. Grant is not their idea of a model president, nor were the southern carpetbag governments worthy of their unqualified praise. They understand that the Radical Republicans were not all selfless patriots, and that southern white men were not all Negro-hating rebels. In short, they have not turned history on its head, but rather, they recognize that much of what Dunning's disciples have said about Reconstruction is true.

Revisionists, however, have discovered that the Dunningites overlooked a great deal, and they doubt that nobility and idealism suddenly died in 1865. They are neither surprised nor disillusioned to find that the Civil War, for all its nobility, revealed some of the ugliness of human nature as well. And they approach Reconstruction with the confident expectation that here, too, every facet of human nature will be exposed. They are not satisfied with the two-dimensional characters that Dunning's disciples have painted.

What is perhaps most puzzling in the legend of Reconstruction is the notion that the white people of the South were treated with unprecedented brutality, that their conquerors, in Bowers's colorful phrase, literally put them to the torture. How, in fact, *were* they treated after the failure of their rebellion against the authority of the federal government? The great mass of ordinary Southerners who voluntarily took up arms, or in other ways supported the Confederacy, were required simply to take an oath of allegiance to obtain pardon and to regain their right to vote and hold public office. But what of the Confederate leaders—the men who held high civil offices, often after resigning similar federal offices; the military leaders who had graduated from West Point and had resigned commissions in the United States Army to take commissions in the Confederate army? Were there mass arrests, indictments for treason or conspiracy, trials and convictions, executions or imprisonments? Nothing of the sort. Officers of the Confederate army were paroled and sent home with their men. After surrendering at Appomattox, General Lee bid farewell to his troops and rode home to live his remaining years undisturbed. Only one officer, Captain Henry Wirtz, was arrested; and he was tried, convicted, and executed, not for treason or conspiracy, but for "war crimes." Wirtz's alleged offense, for which the evidence was rather flimsy, was the mistreatment of prisoners of war in the military prison at Andersonville, Georgia.

Of the Confederate civil officers, a handful were arrested at the close of the war, and there was talk for a time of trying a few for treason. But none, actually, was ever brought to trial, and all but Jefferson Davis were released within a few months. The former Confederate president was held in prison for nearly two years, but in 1867 he too was released. With a few exceptions, even the property of Confederate leaders was untouched, save, of course, for the emancipation of their slaves. Indeed, the only penalty imposed on most Confederate leaders was a temporary political disability provided in the Fourteenth Amendment. But in 1872 Congress pardoned all but a handful of southerners; and soon former Confederate civil and military leaders were serving as state governors, as members of Congress, and even as cabinet advisers of presidents.

What, then, constituted the alleged brutality that white southerners endured? First, the freeing of their slaves; second, the brief incarceration of a few Confederate leaders; third, a political disability imposed for a few years on most Confederate leaders; fourth, a relatively weak military occupation terminated in 1877; and last, an attempt to extend the rights and privileges of citizenship to southern Negroes. Mistakes there were in the implementation of these measures—some of them serious—but brutality almost none. In fact, it can be said that rarely in history have the participants in an unsuccessful rebellion endured penalties as mild as those Congress imposed upon the people of the South, and particularly upon their leaders. After four years of bitter struggle costing hundreds of thousands of lives, the generosity of the federal government's terms was quite remarkable.

If northern brutality is a myth, the scandals of the Grant administration and the peculations of some of the southern Reconstruction governments are sordid facts. Yet even here the Dunningites are guilty of distortion by exaggeration, by a lack of perspective, by superficial analysis, and by overemphasis. They make corruption a central theme of their narratives, but they overlook constructive accomplishments. They give insufficient attention to the men who transcended the greed of an age when, to be sure, self-serving politicians and irresponsible entrepreneurs were all too plentiful. Among these men were the humanitarians who organized Freedmen's Aid Societies to help four million southern Negroes make the difficult transition from slavery to freedom, and the missionaries and teachers who went into the South on slender budgets to build churches and schools for the freedmen. Under their auspices the Negroes first began to learn the responsibilities and obligations of freedom. Thus the training of Negroes for citizenship had its successful beginnings in the years of Reconstruction.

In the nineteenth century most white Americans, North and South, had reservations about the Negro's potentialities—doubted that he had the innate intellectual capacity and moral fiber of the white man and assumed that after emancipation he would be relegated to an inferior caste. But some of the Radical Republicans refused to believe that the Negroes were innately inferior and hoped passionately that they would confound their critics. The Radicals then had little empirical evidence and no scientific evidence to support their belief—nothing, in fact, but faith. Their faith was derived mostly from their religion: all men, they said, are the sons of Adam and equal in the sight of God. And if Negroes are equal to white men in the sight of God, it is morally wrong for white men to withhold from Negroes the liberties and rights that white men enjoy. Here, surely, was a projection into the Reconstruction era of the idealism of the abolitionist crusade and of the Civil War.

Radical idealism was in part responsible for two of the most momentous enactments of the Reconstruction years: the Fourteenth Amendment to the federal Constitution which gave Negroes citizenship and promised them equal protection of the laws, and the Fifteenth Amendment which gave them the right to vote. The fact that these amendments could not have been adopted under any other circumstances, or at any other time, before or since, may suggest the crucial importance of the Reconstruction era in American history. Indeed, without Radical Reconstruction, it would be impossible to this day for the federal government to protect Negroes from legal and political discrimination.

If all of this is true, or even part of it, why was the Dunning legend born, and why has it been so durable? Southerners, of course, have contributed much to the legend of Reconstruction, but most northerners have found the legend quite acceptable. Many of the historians who helped to create it were Northerners, among them James Ford Rhodes, William A. Dunning, Claude Bowers, and James G. Randall. Thus the legend cannot be explained simply in terms of a southern literary or historiographical conspiracy, satisfying as the legend has been to most white southerners. What we need to know is why it also satisfies northerners—how it became part of the intellectual baggage of so many northern historians. Why, in short, was there for so many years a kind of national, or intersectional, consensus that the Civil War was America's glory and Reconstruction her disgrace?

The Civil War won its place in the hearts of the American people because, by the end of the nineteenth century, Northerners were willing to concede that southerners had fought bravely for a cause that they believed to be just; whereas southerners, with few exceptions, were willing to concede that the outcome of the war was probably best for all concerned. In an era of intense nationalism, both northerners and southerners agreed that the preservation of the federal Union was essential to the future power of the American people. Southerners could even say now that the abolition of slavery was one of the war's great blessings—not so much, they insisted, because slavery was an injustice to the Negroes but because it was a grievous burden upon the whites. By 1886, Henry W. Grady, the great Georgia editor and spokesman for a New South, could confess to a New York audience: "I am glad that the omniscient God held the balance of battle in His Almighty hand, and that human slavery was swept forever from American soil—the American

Union saved from the wreck of war." Soon Union and Confederate veterans were holding joint reunions, exchanging anecdotes, and sharing their sentimental memories of those glorious war years. The Civil War thus took its position in the center of American folk mythology.

That the Reconstruction era elicits neither pride nor sentimentality is due only in part to its moral delinquencies — remember, those of the Civil War years can be overlooked. It is also due to the white American's ambivalent attitude toward race and toward the steps that Radical Republicans took to protect the Negroes. Southern white men accepted the Thirteenth Amendment to the Constitution, which abolished slavery, with a minimum of complaint, but they expected federal intervention to proceed no further than that. They assumed that the regulation of the freedmen would be left to the individual states; and clearly most of them intended to replace slavery with a caste system that would keep the Negroes perpetually subordinate to the whites. Negroes were to remain a dependent laboring class; they were to be governed by a separate code of laws; they were to play no active part in the South's political life; and they were to be segregated socially. When Radical Republicans used federal power to interfere in these matters, the majority of southern white men formed a resistance movement to fight the radical-dominated state governments until they were overthrown, after which southern whites established a caste system in defiance of federal statutes and constitutional amendments. For many decades thereafter the federal government simply admitted defeat and acquiesced; but the South refused to forget or forgive those years of humiliation when Negroes came close to winning equality. In southern mythology, then, Reconstruction was a horrid nightmare.

As for the majority of northern white men, it is hard to tell how deeply they were concerned about the welfare of the American Negro after the abolition of slavery. If one were to judge from the way they treated the small number of free Negroes who resided in the northern states, one might conclude that they were, at best, indifferent to the problem — and that a considerable number of them shared the racial attitudes of the South and preferred to keep Negroes in a subordinate caste. For a time after the Civil War the Radical Republicans, who were always a minority group, persuaded the northern electorate that the ultimate purpose of southern white men was to rob the North of the fruits of victory and to re-establish slavery and that federal intervention was therefore essential. In this manner Radicals won approval of, or acquiescence in, their program to give civil rights and the ballot to southern Negroes. Popular support for the Radical program waned rapidly, however, and by the middle of the 1870s it had all but vanished. In 1875 a Republican politician confessed that northern voters were tired of the "wornout cry of 'southern outrages,' " and they wished that "the 'nigger' the 'everlasting nigger' were in—Africa." As northerners ceased to worry about the possibility of another southern rebellion, they became increasingly receptive to criticism of radical reconstruction.

The eventual disintegration of the radical phalanx, those root-and-branch men who, for a time, seemed bent on engineering a sweeping reformation of southern society, was another important reason for the denigration of reconstruction in American historiography. To be sure, some of the Radicals, especially those who had been abolitionists before the war, never lost faith in the Negro, and in the years after Reconstruction they stood by him as he struggled to break the intellectual and psychological fetters he had brought with him out of slavery. Other Radicals, however, lost interest in the cause—tired of reform and spent their declining years writing their memoirs. Still others retained their crusading zeal but became disenchanted with Radical Reconstruction and found other crusades more attractive: civil service reform, or tariff reform, or defense of the gold standard. In 1872 they repudiated Grant and jointed the Liberal Republicans; in subsequent years they considered themselves to be political independents.

This latter group had been an important element in the original Radical coalition. Most of them were respectable, middle-class people in comfortable economic circumstances, well educated and highly articulate, and acutely conscious of their obligation to perform disinterested public service. They had looked upon Senator Charles Sumner of Massachusetts as their political spokesman and upon Edwin L. Godkin of the New York *Nation* as their editorial spokesman. Like most radicals they had believed that the Negro was what slavery had made him; give the Negro equal rights and he would be quickly transformed into an industrious and responsible citizen. With the Radical Reconstruction program fairly launched, they had looked forward to swift and dramatic results.

But Reconstruction was not as orderly and the Negro's progress was not nearly as swift and dramatic as these reformers had seemed to expect. The first signs of doubt came soon after the Radicals won control of Reconstruction policy, when the *Nation* warned the Negroes that the government had already done all it could for them. They were now, said the *Nation,* "on the dusty and rugged highway of competition"; henceforth "the removal of white prejudice against the Negro depends almost entirely on the Negro himself." By 1870 this bellwether of the reformers viewed with alarm the disorders and irregularities in the states governed by Negroes and carpetbaggers; by 1871 it proclaimed: "The experiment has totally failed. . . . We owe it to human nature to say that worse governments have seldom been seen in a civilized country." And three years later, looking at South Carolina, the *Nation* pronounced the ultimate epithet: "This is . . . socialism." Among the former Radicals associated with *Nation* in these years of tragic disillusionment were three prewar abolitionists: Edmund Quincy of Massachusetts, James Miller McKim of Pennsylvania, and the Reverend O. B. Frothingham of New York.

Finally, in 1890, many years after the Reconstruction governments had collapsed, the *Nation,* still accurately reflecting the state of mind of the disenchanted reformers, made a full confession of its past errors. "There is," said the *Nation,*

> a rapidly growing sympathy at the North with Southern perplexity over the negro problem. . . . Even those who were not shocked by the carpet-bag experiment . . . are beginning to "view with alarm" the political prospect created by the increase of the negro population, and by the continued inability of southern society to absorb or assimilate them in any sense, physical, social, or political. . . . The sudden admission to the suffrage of a million of the recently emancipated slaves belonging to the least civilized race in the world . . . was a great leap in the dark, the ultimate consequences of which no man now living can foresee. No nation has ever done this, or anything like this for the benefit of aliens of any race or creed. Who or what is . . . [the Negro] that we should put the interests of the 55,000,000 whites on this continent in peril for his sake?

Editor Godkin answered his own question in a letter to another one-time Radical: "I do not see . . . how the negro is ever to be worked into a system of government for which you and I would have much respect."

Actually, neither the obvious shortcomings of Reconstruction nor an objective view of the Negro's progress in the years after emancipation can wholly explain the disillusionment of so many former Radicals. Rather, their changed attitude toward the Negro and the hostile historical interpretation of Reconstruction that won their favor were in part the product of social trends that severely affected the old American middle classes with whom most of them were identified. These trends had their origin in the industrial revolution; they were evident in the early nineteenth century but were enormously accelerated after the Civil War. Their institutional symbols were the giant manufacturing and railroad corporations.

In a new age of industrial enterprise there seemed to be no place for the old families with their genteel culture and strong traditions of disinterested public service. On the one hand, they were overshadowed by new and powerful industrial capitalists whose economic strength brought with it vast political influence. Legislative bodies became arenas in which the political vassals of oil, steel, and railroad barons struggled for special favors, while the interest of the public — and the old middle classes liked to think of themselves as *the public* — counted for nothing. On the other hand, they were threatened by the immigrants who came to America to work in the mines and mills and on the railroads — Italians, Slavs, and Jews from Poland and Russia. The immigrants crowded into the tenements of eastern cities, responded to the friendly overtures of urban political bosses, and used their ballots to evict the old middle-class families from power. Here was a threat to the traditional America that these families had loved — and dominated — to that once vigorous American nationality that was Protestant, Anglo-Saxon, and pure. Henry James commented bitterly about the people he met on Boston Common during a stroll one Sunday afternoon: "No sound of English, in a single instance escaped their lips; the greater number spoke a rude form of Italian, the others some outland dialect unknown to me. . . . The types and faces bore them out; the people before me were gross aliens to a man, and they were in serene and triumphant possession."

Soon the new immigrant groups had become the victims of cruel racial stereotypes. Taken collectively it would appear that they were, among other things, innately inferior to the Anglo-Saxons in their intellectual and physical traits, dirty and immoral in their habits, inclined toward criminality, receptive to dangerous political beliefs, and shiftless and irresponsible.

In due time, those who repeated these stereotypes awoke to the realization that what they were saying was not really very original — that, as a matter of fact, these generalizations were *precisely* the ones that southern white men had been making about Negroes for years. And, in their extremity, the old middle classes of the North looked with new understanding upon the problems of the beleaguered white men of the South. Perhaps all along southerners had understood the problem better than they. Here, then, was a crucial part of the intellectual climate in which the Dunning interpretation of Reconstruction was written. It was written at a time when xenophobia had become almost a national disease, when the immigration restriction movement was getting into high gear, when numerous northern cities (among them Philadelphia and Chicago) were seriously considering the establishment of racially segregated schools, and when Negroes and immigrants were being lumped together in the category of unassimilable aliens.

Several other attitudes, prevalent in the late nineteenth century, encouraged an interpretation of Reconstruction that condemned Radical Republicans for meddling in southern race relations. The vogue of

Social Darwinism discouraged governmental intervention in behalf of Negroes as well as other underprivileged groups; it encouraged the belief that a solution to the race problem could only evolve slowly as the Negroes gradually improved themselves. A rising spirit of nationalism stimulated a desire for sectional reconciliation, and part of the price was a virtual abdication of federal responsibility for the protection of the Negro's civil and political rights. An outburst of imperialism, manifested in the Spanish-American War and the annexation of the Hawaiian Islands, found one of its principal justifications in the notion that Anglo-Saxons were superior to other peoples, especially when it came to politics. In the words of Senator Albert J. Beveridge of Indiana: "God has not been preparing the English-speaking and Teutonic people for a thousand years for nothing but vain and idle self-admiration. No! He has made us the master organizers of the world to establish system where chaos reigns. . . . He has made us adept in government that we may administer government among savages and senile peoples." What folly, then, to expect Italians and Slavs to behave like Anglo-Saxons—or to accept the sentimental doctrine that Negroes deserve to be given the same political rights as white men!

Finally, at this critical juncture, sociologists, anthropologists, and psychologists presented what they regarded as convincing evidence of innate racial traits—evidence indicating that Negroes were intellectually inferior to whites and had distinctive emotional characteristics. The social scientists thus supplied the racists of the late nineteenth and early twentieth centuries with something that antebellum proslavery writers had always lacked: a respectable scientific argument. When, in 1916, Madison Grant, an amateur cultural anthropologist, published *The Passing of the Great Race,* his racism was only a mild caricature of a point of view shared by numerous social scientists. Examining the history of the United States, Grant easily detected her tragic blunder:

Race consciousness . . . in the United States, down to and including the Mexican War, seems to have been very strongly developed among native Americans, and it still remains in full vigor today in the South, where the presence of a large negro population forces this question upon the daily attention of the whites. . . . In New England, however . . . there appeared early in the last century a wave of sentimentalism, which at that time took up the cause of the negro, and in so doing apparently destroyed, to a large extent, pride and consciousness of race in the North. The agitation over slavery was inimical to the Nordic race, because it thrust aside all national opposition to the intrusion of hordes of immigrants of inferior racial value, and prevented the fixing of a definite American type. . . . The native American by the middle of the nineteenth century was rapidly becoming a distinct type. . . . The Civil War, however, put a severe, perhaps fatal, check to the development and expansion of this splendid type, by destroying great numbers of the best breeding stock on both sides, and by breaking up the home ties of many more. If the war had not occurred these same men with their descendants would have populated the Western States instead of the racial nondescripts who are now flocking there.[3]

In this social atmosphere, armed with the knowledge of race that the social scientists had given them, historians exposed the folly of Radical Reconstruction. At the turn of the century, James Ford Rhodes, that intimate friend of New England Brahmins, gave his verdict on Negro suffrage — one that the Dunningites would soon develop into the central assumption, the controlling generalization, of the Reconstruction legend. "No large policy in our country," concluded Rhodes, "has ever been so conspicuous a failure as that of forcing universal negro suffrage upon the South. . . . From the Republican policy came no real good to the negroes. Most of them developed no political capacity, and the few who raised themselves above the mass did not reach a high order of intelligence. . . . The negro's political activity is rarely of a nature to identify him with any movement on a high plane. . . . [He] has been politically a failure and he could not have been otherwise."[4]

In the course of time the social scientists drastically revised their notions about race, and in recent years most of them have been striving to destroy the errors in whose creation their predecessors played so crucial a part. As ideas about race have changed, historians have become increasingly critical of the Dunning interpretation of Reconstruction. These changes, together with a great deal of painstaking research, have produced the revisionist writing of the past generation. It is dangerous, of course, for a historian to label himself as a revisionist, for his ultimate and inevitable fate is one day to have his own revisions revised.

But that has never discouraged revisionists, and we may hope that it never will, especially those who have been rewriting the history of the Reconstruction era. One need not be disturbed about the romantic nonsense that still fills the minds of many Americans about their Civil War. This folklore is essentially harmless. But the legend of Reconstruction is another matter. It has had serious consequences, because it has exerted a powerful influence upon the political behavior of many white men, North and South.

[3] Madison Grant, *The Passing of the Great Race* (New York, 1916), pp. 77–79.
[4] Rhodes, *History of the United States*, VII, pp. 168–70.

13

The Religion of the Lost Cause

Charles Reagan Wilson

Religion, broadly defined, rests at the heart of southern culture and what is means to be a southerner. Southerners, it has been said, are those Americans most "haunted by God." The central theme of southern culture, others have added, is religion, at least in the sense that to be southern is most often to see oneself as having an unequivocal dependence upon God. Current public opinion polls disclose that nine out of every ten southerners declare themselves Protestants with nearly four out of every five of these Baptists, Methodists, or Presbyterians. Thus most observers of southern culture—sooner or later—come to terms with the region's religiosity. As religion continues to permeate the southern character and southern culture, it could not have worked other than to have structured southern history and southern mythology. According to the findings of Charles Reagan Wilson, of the University of Mississippi and Center for the Study of Southern Culture, religion and mythology much affected the shaping of southern attitudes regarding Confederate defeat in the Civil War. As the vanquished South felt the trauma of defeat and discovered its cause to be "lost," it sought its reconstruction with the collective sense that the region had been "baptized in blood." Thus did the Myth of the Lost Cause, like most every antecedent southern myth, resonate with religious undercurrents and find expression in religious vocabulary and religious imagery. Moreover, rituals celebrating the Lost Cause not only exploited the southern talent for ceremonial style, to which the region was already given, but made it clear that longstanding

From the *Journal of Southern History,* 46 (May 1980), 220–38. Copyright 1980 by the Southern Historical Association. Reprinted by permission of the Managing Editor.

southern myth (as with any myth) could best be sustained in public consciousness through symbolic remembrance. Through the introduction of such social rituals as Confederate Memorial Day and Confederate reunions, the southern past—particularly as canonized by the United Confederate Veterans and the United Daughters of the Confederacy—became imaginatively reunited with its tragic present. Southern mythology was becoming institutionalized as a kind of theology—a Civil Religion.

Scholars have long noted the importance of religion in the South. The predominant evangelical Protestantism and the distinct regional church structures have been key factors in a "southern identity" separate from that of the North. Historians of southern religion have noted the close ties between religion and southern culture itself. Denominational studies have pointed out the role of the churches in acquiescing to the area's racial orthodoxy and in imposing a conservative, moralistic tone on the South since the late nineteenth century, while other works have posited the existence of two cultures in Dixie, one of Christian and one of southern values. At times, it is clear, the churches have been in "cultural captivity," rather than maintaining a judgmental distance, to southern values. The ties between religion and culture in the South have actually been even closer than has so far been suggested. In the years after the Civil War a pervasive southern civil religion emerged. This common religion of the South, which grew out of Confederate defeat in the Civil War, had an identifiable mythology, ritual, and organization. C. Vann Woodward noted long ago that the southern experience of defeat in the Civil War nurtured a tragic sense of life in the region, but historians have overlooked the fact that this profound understanding has been expressed in a civil religion which blended Christian and southern values.[1]

The religion of the Lost Cause originated in the antebellum period. By

[1]Kenneth K. Bailey, *Southern White Protestantism in the Twentieth Century* (New York, 1964); Rufus B. Smith, *At East in Zion: Social History of Southern Baptists, 1865–1900* (Nashville, 1967); Hunter D. Farish, *The Circuit Rider Dismounts: A Social History of Southern Methodism, 1865–1900* (Richmond, 1938); Ernest T. Thompson, *Presbyterians in the South,* 3 vols. (Richmond, 1963–1974); Samuel S. Hill, Jr., *Southern Churches in Crisis* (New York, 1966); Hill *et al., Religion and the Solid South* (Nashville and New York, 1972); John L. Eighmy, *Churches in Cultural Captivity: A History of the Social Attitudes of Southern Baptists* (Knoxville, 1972); H. Shelton Smith, *In His Image, but . . . . : Racism in Southern Religion, 1780–1910* (Durham, N.C., 1972); C. Vann Woodward, *The Burden of Southern History* (Baton Rouge, 1960), especially chap. 1.

1860 a religious culture had been established wherein a religious outlook and tone permeated southern society. The popular sects (Methodists, Baptists, and Presbyterians) provided a sense of community in the individualistic rural areas, which helped to nurture a southern identity. At a time when northern religion was becoming increasingly diverse, the southern churches remained orthodox in theology and, above all, evangelical in orientation. Despite a conversion-centered theology, ministers played a key role in defending the status quo, and by 1845 the Methodists and the Baptists had split from their northern counterparts, supplying an institutionalized foundation for the belief in southern distinctiveness. The proslavery argument leaned more heavily on the Bible and Christian ministers than on anything else, thus tying churches and culture close together. Because of the religious culture, southern life seemed so Christian to the clerics that they saw threats to their society as challenges to the last bastion of Christian civilization in America.

During the Civil War religion played a vital role in the Confederacy. Preachers nourished Confederate morale, served as chaplains to the southern armies, and directed the intense revivals in the Confederate ranks. As a result of the wartime experience the religious culture became even more deeply engrained in the South. Preachers who had been soldiers or chaplains became the celebrants of the Lost Cause religion after the war. By 1865 conditions existed for the emergence of an institutionalized common religion that would grow out of the antebellum-wartime religious culture.[2]

Judged by historical and anthropological criteria, the civil religion that emerged in the postbellum South was an authentic expression of religion. The South faced problems after the Civil War which were cultural but also religious—the problems of providing meaning to life and society amid the baffling failure of fundamental beliefs, offering comfort to those suffering poverty and disillusionment, and encouraging a sense of belonging in the shattered southern community. Anthropologist Anthony F. C. Wallace argues that religion originates "in situations of social and cultural stress," and for postbellum southerners

[2]Hill, *Southern Churches*, 12–14, 52, 56–59; John B. Boles, *The Great Revival, 1787–1805: The Origins of the Southern Evangelical Mind* (Lexington, Ky., 1972); Boles, *Religion in Antebellum Kentucky* (Lexington, Ky., 1976), 123–45; Dickson D. Bruce, Jr., "Religion, Society and Culture in the Old South: A Comparative View," *American Quarterly*, XXVI (October 1974), 399–416; Donald G. Mathews, *Religion in the Old South* (Chicago and London, 1977). For the wartime role of the churches there is no synthesis, but see James W. Silver, *Confederate Morale and Church Propaganda* (Tuscaloosa, Ala., 1957); Herman Norton, *Rebel Religion: The Story of Confederate Chaplains* (St. Louis, 1961); John Shepard, Jr., "Religion in the Army of Northern Virginia," *North Carolina Historical Review*, XXV (July 1948), 341–76; and the special issue of *Civil War History*, VI (December 1960).

such traditional religious issues as the nature of suffering, evil, and the seeming irrationality of life had a disturbing relevance. Scholars stress that the existence of a sacred symbol system and its embodiment in ritual define religion. As Clifford James Geertz has said, the religious response to the threat of disorder in existence is the creation of symbols "of such a genuine order of the world which will account for, and even celebrate, the perceived ambiguities, puzzles, and paradoxes in human experience." These symbols create "long-lasting moods and motivations," which lead men to act on their religious feelings. Mythology, in other words, is not enough to launch a religion. Ritual is crucial because, as Geertz has said, it is "out of the context of concrete acts of religious observance that religious conviction emerges on the human plane." As Wallace concisely expresses it, "The primary phenomenon of religion is ritual." Not all rituals, to be sure, are religious. The crucial factors are rhetoric and intent: whether the language and motivation of a ritual are religious. The constant application of biblical archetypes to the Confederacy and the interpretation of the Civil War experience in cosmic terms indicated the religious importance of the Lost Cause.[3]

The southern civil religion assumes added meaning when compared to the American civil religion. Sociologist Robert Neelly Bellah's 1967 article on the civil religion and his subsequent work have focused scholarly discussion on the common religion of the American people. Bellah argued that "an elaborate and well-institutionalized civil religion" existed that was "clearly differentiated" from the denominations. He defined "civil religion" as the "religious dimension" of a "people through which it interprets its historical experience in the light of transcendent reality." Like Sidney Earl Mead, Bellah saw it as essentially prophetic, judging the behavior of the nation against transcendent values. Will Herberg has suggested that the civil religion has been a folk religion, a common religion emerging out of the life of the folk. He argues that it grew out of a long social and historical experience that established a heterogeneous society. The civil religion came to be the American Way of Life, a set of beliefs that were accepted and revered by Protestants, Catholics, and Jews. "Democracy" has been the fundamental concept of this civil religion. Scholars have identified the sources of the American public faith in the Enlightenment tradition and in the secularized Puritan and Revivalist traditions. It clearly was born during

---

[3]A. F. C. Wallace, *Religion: An Anthropological View* (New York, 1966), 30 (first quotation), 102 (fifth quotation); Clifford J. Geertz, "Religion as a Cultural System," in Michael Banton, ed., *Anthropological Approaches to the Study of Religion* (New York, 1966), 4 (third quotation), 8–12, 14, 23 (second quotation), 28 (fourth quotation). See also Andrew M. Greeley, *The Denominational Society: A Sociological Approach to Religion in America* (Glenview, Ill., 1972), 23; and Mircea Eliade, *Myth and Reality* (New York and Evanston, 1963), 8, 17–18.

the American Revolution, but the American civil religion was reborn, with the new theme of sacrifice and renewal, in the Civil War.[4]

In the post–Civil War South the antebellum religious culture evolved into a southern civil religion, differing from the national faith. A set of values arose that could be designated a Southern Way of Life. Dixie's value system differed from that Herberg discussed—southerners undoubtedly were less optimistic, less liberal, less democratic, less tolerant, and more homogeneously Protestant. In their religion southerners stressed "democracy" less than the conservative concepts of moral virtue and an orderly society. Though the whole course of southern history provided the background, the southern civil religion actually emerged from the Civil War experience. Just as the revolution of 1776 caused Americans to see their historical experience in transcendent terms, so the Confederate experience led southerners to a profound self-examination. They understood that the results of the war had clearly given them a history distinct from the northern one. Southerners thus focused the mythic, ritualistic, and organizational dimensions of their civil religion around the Confederacy. Moreover, the Enlightenment tradition played virtually no role in the religion of the Lost Cause, but the emotionally intense, dynamic Revivalist tradition and the secularized legacy of idealistic, moralistic Puritanism did shape it.

As a result of emerging from a heterogeneous, immigrant society, the American civil religion was especially significant in providing a sense of belonging to the uprooted immigrants. As a result of its origins in Confederate defeat, the southern civil religion offered confused southerners a sense of meaning, an identity in a precarious but distinct culture. One central issue of the American public faith has been the relationship between church and state, but, since the Confederate quest for political nationhood failed, the southern civil religion has been less concerned with that question than with the cultural issue of identity.

The mythology of the American civil religion taught that Americans are a chosen people, destined to play a special role in the world as representatives of freedom and equality. The religion of the Lost Cause rested on a mythology that focused on the Confederacy. It was a creation myth, the story of the attempt to create a southern nation. According to

[4]Robert N. Bellah, "Civil Religion in America," in Russell E. Richey and Donald G. Jones, eds., *American Civil Religion* (New York, 1974), 21–44 (first two quotations on p. 21); Bellah, *The Broken Covenant: American Civil Religion in Time of Trial* (New York, 1975), 3 (last two quotations); Mead, "The 'Nation with the Soul of a Church',." in Richey and Jones, eds., *American Civil Religion,* 45–75; Will Herberg, "America's Civil Religion: What It Is and Whence It Comes," *ibid.* 76–88; Herberg, *Protestant-Catholic-Jew: An Essay in American Religious Sociology* (Garden City, NY., 1955); Catherine L. Albanese, *Sons of the Fathers: The Civil Religion of the American Revolution* (Philadelphia, 1976); James H. Moorhead, *American Apocalypse: Yankee Protestants and the Civil War, 1860–1869* (New Haven, 1978).

the mythmakers, a pantheon of southern heroes, portrayed as the highest products of the Old South civilization, had appeared during the Civil War to battle the forces of evil as symbolized by the Yankees. The myth enacted the Christian story of Christ's suffering and death with the Confederacy at the sacred center. But in the southern myth the Christian drama of suffering and salvation was incomplete. The Confederacy lost a holy war, and there was no resurrection.[5]

As Mircea Eliade has said, "it is not enough to *know* the origin myth, one must *recite* it. . . ." While other southern myths could be seen in literature, politics, or economics, the Confederate myth reached its true fulfillment after the Civil War in a ritualistic structure of activities that represented a religious commemoration and celebration of the Confederacy. One part of the ritualistic liturgy focused on the religious figures of the Lost Cause. Southern Protestant churches have been sparse in iconography, but the southern civil religion was rich in images. Southern ministers and other rhetoricians portrayed Robert Edward Lee, Thomas Jonathan ("Stonewall") Jackson, Jefferson Davis, and many other wartime heroes as religious saints and martyrs.[6] They were said to epitomize the best of Christian and southern values. Their images pervaded the South, and they were especially aimed at children. In the first two decades of this century local chapters of the United Daughters of the Confederacy undertook successfully to blanket southern schools with portraits of Lee and Davis. Lee's birthday, January 19, became a holiday throughout Dixie, and ceremonies honoring him frequently occurred in the schools.[7]

[5]For the political, economic, intellectual, and literary aspects of the Lost Cause myth see Rollin G. Osterweis, *The Myth of the Lost Cause, 1865–1900* (Hamden, Conn., 1973); Daniel Aaron, *The Unwritten War: American Writers and the Civil War* (New York, 1973); Paul M. Gaston, *The New South Creed: A Study in Southern Mythmaking* (New York, 1970); Richard M. Weaver, *The Southern Tradition at Bay: A History of Postbellum Thought* (New Rochelle, N.Y., 1968); Richard B. Harwell, "The Confederate Heritage," in Louis D. Rubin, Jr., and James J. Kilpatrick, eds., *The Lasting South: Fourteen Southerners Look at Their Home* (Chicago, 1957), 16–27; William B. Hesseltine, *Confederate Leaders in the New South* (Baton Rouge, 1950); Susan S. Durant, "The Gently Furled Banner: The Development of the Myth of the Lost Cause, 1865–1900" (unpublished Ph.D. dissertation, University of North Carolina, 1972); and Sharon E. Hannum, "Confederate Cavaliers: The Myth in War and Defeat" (unpublished Ph.D. dissertation, Rice University, 1965).

[6]Eliade, *Myth and Reality,* 17; "Robert E. Lee" and "Innocence Vindicated," Atlanta *Christian Index,* October 20, 1870, p. 162; August 23, 1866, p. 135; "Robert E. Lee," Richmond *Southern Churchman,* January 19, 1907, p. 2; T. V. Moore, "Memorial Discourse on the Death of General Robert E. Lee" and "Jefferson Davis," in Nashville *Christian Advocate,* November 5, 1870, p. 2; December 12, 1889, p. 8; and James P. Smith, "Jackson's Religious Character: An Address at Lexington, Va.," Southern Historical Society *Papers,* XLIII (September 1920), 67–75. The *Papers* will be cited hereinafter as *SHSP.*

[7]United Daughters of the Confederacy, *Minutes of the Fourteenth Annual Convention*

An explicit link between Confederate images and religious values was made in the stained-glass windows placed in churches to commemorate Confederate sacrifices. One of the earliest of these was a window placed in Trinity Church, Portsmouth, Virginia, in April 1868, while federal troops still occupied the city. The window portrayed a biblical Rachel weeping at a tomb, on which appeared the names of the members of the congregation who had died during the war. In Mississippi, Biloxi's Church of the Redeemer, "the Westminster of the South," was particularly prominent in this endeavor at the turn of the century. St. Paul's Episcopal church in Richmond, which had been the wartime congregation of many Confederate leaders, established a Lee Memorial Window, which used an Egyptian scene to connect the Confederacy with the stories of the Old Testament. Even a Negro Presbyterian church in Roanoke, Virginia, dedicated a Stonewall Jackson memorial window. The pastor had been a pupil in Jackson's Sunday school in prewar Lexington, Virginia.[8]

Wartime artifacts also had a sacred aura. Bibles that had been touched by the Cause were especially holy. The United Daughters of the Confederacy kept under lock and key the Bible used when Jefferson Davis was sworn in as president of the Confederacy. More poignantly, a faded, torn overcoat belonging to a young Confederate martyr named Sam Davis was discovered in 1897, and when shown to a United Daughters of the Confederacy meeting the response was, said an observer, first "sacred silence" and then weeping. Presbyterian preacher James Isaac Vance noted that, "like Elijah's mantle of old, the spirit of the mighty dwells within it." Museums were sanctuaries containing such sacred relics. The Confederate Museum in Richmond, which had been the White House of the Confederacy, included a room for each seceding state. These rooms had medals, flags, uniforms, and weapons from the Confederacy, and the Solid South Room displayed the Great Seal of the Confederate States.[9]

. . . 1907 (Opelika, Ala., 1908), 6; ibid., 1915 (Charlotte, N.C., n.d.), 357; "The South's Tribute to General Lee," Confederate Veteran, XXII (February 1914), 62. The minutes of conventions of the United Daughters of the Confederacy will hereinafter be cited as UDC, Minutes along with the proper years. The Confederate Veteran will hereinafter be cited as CV.

8"The Memorial Window in Trinity Church, Portsmouth, Va., to the Confederate Dead of Its Congregation," SHSP, XIX (January 1891), 207–12; "Pegram Battalion Association," ibid., XVI (January–December 1888), 194–206; J. William Jones, "The Career of General Jackson," ibid., XXXV (January–December 1907), 97; "A Memorial Chapel at Fort Donelson," CV, V (September 1897), 461; Elizabeth W. Weddell, St. Paul's Church, Richmond, Virginia . . ., 2 vols. (Richmond, 1931), I, frontispiece, 224–25.

9CV, VIII (November 1900), 468; "Sermons before the Reunion," ibid., V (July 1897), 351 (quotation); ibid., XXII (May 1914), 194; Herbert and Marjorie Katz, Museums, U.S.A.: A History and Guide (Garden City, N.Y., 1965), 181.

The southern civil religion had its reverent images and its sacred artifacts, and it also had its hymns. One group of hymns sung at postwar Confederate gatherings was made up of Christian songs straight from the hymnal. "Nearer My God to Thee," "Abide with Me," and "Praise God from Whom All Blessings Flow" were popular, but the favorite was "How Firm a Foundation." Another group of Confederate sacred songs was created by putting new words to old melodies. The spirit of "That Old-Time Religion" was preserved when someone retitled it "We Are Old-Time Confederates." J. B. Stinson composed new verses for the melody of "When the Roll Is Called up Yonder I'll Be There." A change from the original lyric was the phrase "let's be there," rather than "I'll be there," indicating a more communal redemption in the Lost Cause version. The song used Confederates as evangelical models of behavior: "On that mistless, lonely morning when the saved of Christ shall rise, / In the Father's many-mansioned home to share; / Where our Lee and Jackson call to us [sic] their homes beyond the skies, / When the roll is called up yonder, let's be there."[10] Of special significance was the hymn "Let Us Pass over the River, and Rest under the Shade of the Trees," which was officially adopted by the Southern Methodist church. The words in the title were the last words spoken by the dying Stonewall Jackson. Two other hymns, "Stonewall Jackson's Requiem" and "Stonewall Jackson's Way," made a similar appeal. At some ceremonial occasions choirs from local churches sang hymns. In 1907 southerners organized the United Confederate Choirs of America, and soon the young belles from Dixie, clad in Confederate gray uniforms, were a popular presence at ritual events.[11]

These liturgical ingredients appeared during the ritualistic expres-

[10]United Confederate Veterans (hereinafter UCV), *Minutes of the Ninth Annual Meeting and Reunion . . . 1899* (New Orleans, 1900), 17, 32; UCV, *Minutes of the Twenty-first Annual Meeting and Reunion . . . 1911* (New Orleans, n.d.), 111; UCV, *Minutes of the Nineteenth Annual Meeting and Reunion . . . 1909* (New Orleans, n.d.), 64; UDC, *Minutes . . . 1912* (Jackson, Tenn., n.d.), 321, 407; UDC, *Minutes . . . 1914* (Raleigh, N.C., 1915), 406; UDC, *Ritual of the United Daughters of the Confederacy* (Austin, Tex., n.d.); "Burial of Margaret Davis Hayes," *CV,* XVII (December 1909), 612; "Old Time Confederates," *ibid.,* VIII (July 1900), 298; Joseph M. Brown, "Dixie," *ibid.,* XII (March 1904), 134; "Memorial Ode," *ibid.,* IX (December 1901), 567.

[11]*CV,* IX (April 1901), 147; UDC, *Minutes . . . 1909* (Opelika, Ala., 1909), 56. See also C. H. Scott, "The Hymn of Robert E. Lee," *SHSP,* II (September 1915), 322; A. W. Kercheval, "The Burial of Lieutenant-General Jackson: A Dirge," *New Eclectic,* V (November 1869), 611; "The Ohio Division," *CV,* XXVI (August 1918), 368; Harold B. Simpson, *Hood's Texas Brigade in Reunion and Memory* (Hillsboro, Tex., 1974), 76; "The Confederate Choir No. 1," *CV,* XV (April 1907), 154–55; "United Confederate Choirs of America," *ibid.,* XV (July 1907), 304; "Stonewall Jackson's Way," *ibid.,* XXV (November 1917), 528–29; "Our Confederate Veterans," *ibid.,* V (August 1897), 439; *ibid.,* VI (November 1898), cover.

sions of the Lost Cause. In the years immediately after the war, southern anguish at Confederate defeat was most apparent during the special days appointed by the denominations or the states for humiliation, fasting, prayer, or thanksgiving. These special days could be occasions for jeremiads calling prodigals back to the church, prophesying future battles, or stressing submission to God's mysterious providence in the face of seemingly unwarranted suffering.[12] Southerners, however, usually ignored the national Thanksgiving Day, complaining that northerners used the day to exploit the war issue and to wave the bloody shirt. D. Shaver, the editor of the *Christian Index*, a Baptist newspaper in Atlanta, noted in 1869 that such days too often evoked in the Yankee "the smell (if they do not wake the thirst) of blood." He characterized the northern Christian's behavior on Thanksgiving Day as like that of a Pharisee of old who stood "pilloried through the ages as venting a self-complacent but empty piety." Southerners did celebrate thanksgiving days designated by their denominations, but in general the days of humiliation, fasting, and prayer were more appropriate to the immediate postwar southern mood.[13]

Southern reverence for dead heroes could be seen in the activities of yet another ritual event—Confederate Memorial Day. Southern legend has it that the custom of decorating the graves of soldiers arose in Georgia in 1866 when Mrs. Charles J. Williams, a Confederate widow, published an appeal to southerners to set apart a day "to be handed down through time as a religious custom of the South to wreathe the graves of our martyred dead with flowers." Like true Confederates, southern states could not at first agree among themselves as to which day to honor, but by 1916 ten states had designated June 3, Jefferson Davis's birthday, as Memorial Day. Women played a key role in this ritual since they were in charge of decorating the graves with flowers and of organizing the day's events. It was a holy day, "the Sabbath of the South." One southern woman compared her sisters to the biblical Mary and Martha, who "last at the cross and first at the grave brought their offerings of love. . . ." Another southern woman noted that the aroma of flowers on Memorial

[12]Southern Presbyterian General Assembly, *Minutes of the General Assembly of the Presbyterian Church in the United States* (Columbia, S.C., 1867), 137; Stephen Elliott, "Forty-fifth Sermon: On the State Fast-day," in Elliott, *Sermons by the Right Reverend Stephen Elliott . . .* (New York, 1867), 497, 505, 507; "Day of Fasting, Humiliation and Prayer," Atlanta *Christian Index*, March 9, 1865, p. 3.

[13]"Thanksgiving Day: Its Afterclaps," Atlanta *Christian Index*, December 16, 1869, p. 2. See also "Day of Thanksgiving," Columbia (S.C.) *Southern Presbyterian*, November 14, 1872, p. 2; "The Two Proclamations," Atlanta *Christian Index*, November 22, 1866, p. 1; and Elliott's sermon "On the National Thanksgiving-day," in Elliott, *Sermons*, 514–15.

Day was "like incense burning in golden censers to the memory of the saints."[14]

A third ritual was the funeral of a wartime hero. The veterans attending the funerals dressed in their gray uniforms, served as active or honorary pallbearers, and provided a military ceremony. Everything was done according to the "Confederate Veteran's Burial Ritual," which emphasized that the soldier was going to "an honorable grave." "He fought a good fight," said the ritual, "and has left a record of which we, his surviving comrades, are proud, and which is a heritage of glory to his family and their descendants for all time to come." These ceremonies reiterated what southerners heard elsewhere—that despite defeat the Confederate experience provided that they were a noble, virtuous people. Moreover, the Confederate funeral included the display of the Confederate flag, the central symbol of southern identity. Often, it was dramatically placed over the hero's casket just before the box was lowered into the ground, while at other times the folded battle flag was removed from the coffin and placed at the head of the grave. Even after Southerners began again to honor the American flag, they continued to cherish the Stars and Bars as well.[15]

The dedication of monuments to the Confederate heroes was the fourth ritualistic expression of the Lost Cause. In 1914 the *Confederate Veteran* magazine revealed that over a thousand monuments existed in the South, and by that time many battlefields had been set aside as pilgrimage sites with holy shrines. Preachers converted the innumerable statues dotting the southern countryside into religious objects, almost idols, that quite blatantly taught Christian religious and moral lessons. "Our cause is with God" and "In hope of a joyful resurrection" were among the most directly religious inscriptions on monuments, but they were not atypical ones. El Dorado, Arkansas, erected a marble drinking fountain to the Confederacy, and its publicity statement said—in a phrase culled from countless hymns and sermons on the sacrificial Jesus—that the water in it symbolized "the loving stream of blood" that was shed by the southern soldiers. Drinkers from the fount were thus

[14]James H. M'Neilly, "Jefferson Davis: Gentleman, Patriot, Christian," *CV,* XXIV (June 1916), 248; "Our Memorial Day," *ibid.,* XXII (May 1914), 195; Lizzie Rutherford Chapter, UDC, *A History of the Origin of Memorial Day . . .* (Columbus, Ga., 1898), 24 (first quotation); Mrs. A. M'D. Wilson, "Memorial Day," *CV,* XVII (April 1919), 156 (second and third quotations); UDC, *Minutes . . . 1901* (Nashville, 1902), 112.

[15]UCV, Texas Division, James J. A. Barker Camp, No. 1555, *Burial Ritual* (n.p., n.d.); "Burial Ritual for Veterans," *CV,* III (February 1895), 43 (first and second quotations); "Burial Ritual, Suitable for Confederates Everywhere," *ibid.,* XVII (May 1909), 214; Arthur B. Kinsolving, *Texas George: The Life of George Herbert Kinsolving . . .* (Milwaukee and London, 1932), 130; "Rev. Romulus Morris Tuttle," *CV,* XII (June 1904), 296–97; and "Sumner Archibald Cunningham," *ibid.,* XXII (January 1914), 6–8.

symbolically baptized in Confederate blood. The dedication of such monuments became more elaborate as the years went on. Perhaps the greatest monument dedication came in 1907, when an estimated 200,000 people gathered in Richmond for the dedication of a statue to Jefferson Davis on Monument Boulevard. Richmond was the Mecca of the Lost Cause, and Monument Boulevard was the sacred road to it, containing statues of Lee, James Ewell Brown ("Jeb") Stuart, George Washington, and Stonewall Jackson, as well as Davis.[16]

Rituals similar to these existed as part of the American civil religion. In both instances, they were, to use Claude Lévi-Strauss's categories, partly commemorative rites that re-created the mythical time of the past and partly mourning rites that converted dead heroes into revered ancestors. Both civil religions confronted the precariousness and instability of collective life. They were ways for communities to help their citizens meet their individual fears of death. As sociologist William Lloyd Warner has said: "Whenever the living think about the deaths of others they necessarily express some of their own concern about their own extinction." By the continuance of the community, the citizens in it achieve a measure of immortality. For southerners the need for such a symbolic life was even greater than for northerners. Union soldiers sacrificed, but at least the success of their cause seemed to validate their deaths. Postwar southerners feared that the defeat of the Confederacy had jeopardized their continued existence as a distinctively southern people. By participating in the Lost Cause rituals, southerners tried to show that the Confederate sacrifices had not been in vain. Similar rituals existed to honor the Grand Army of the Republic, but the crucial point was that southern rituals began from a very different starting point and had a different symbolic content. Thus, within the United States there was a functioning civil religion not dedicated to honoring the American nation.[17]

[16]"The Monumental Spirit of the South," *CV,* XXII (August 1914), 344; Confederate Monumental Association, *Tennessee Confederate Memorial* (Nashville, n.d.), 44; "Dedicatory Prayer of Monument," *CV,* IX (January 1901), 38; "Confederate Monument at San Antonio," *ibid.,* VII (September 1899), 399 (first quotation); "Confederate Monument at Bolivar, Tenn.," *ibid.,* VIII (August 1900), 353 (second quotation); "Fourth Report of Monumental Committee," UCV, *Minutes of the Twenty-first Annual Meeting and Reunion,* 52; Bettie Emerson, comp., *Historic Southern Monuments: Representative Memorials of the Heroic Dead of the Southern Confederacy* (Washington and New York, 1911), 53–54 (third quotation), 133, 265, 426–27; UCV, *Minutes of the Seventeenth Annual Meeting and Reunion . . . 1907* (Richmond, 1907), 118–27; Mary B. Poppenheim *et al., The History of the United Daughters of the Confederacy* (2 vols. in 1, Raleigh, N.C., 1956), I, 49–51.

[17]William Lloyd Warner, *The Living and the Dead: A Study of the Symbolic Life of Americans* (New Haven, 1959), 280. See also Claude Lévi-Strauss, *The Savage Mind* (Chicago, 1962), 236–37; Warner, "An American Sacred Ceremony," in Richey and Jones, eds., *American Civil Religion,* 89–111; Catherine Albanese, "Requiem for

The permanence of the Lost Cause religion could be seen in its structural-functional aspect. Three institutions directed its operations, furnishing ongoing leadership and institutional encouragement. One organizational focus was the Confederate veterans' groups. Local associations of veterans existed in the 1870s and 1880s, but southerners took a step forward in this activity with the establishment of the United Confederate Veterans in New Orleans in 1889. The heirs of the Lost Cause formed another group in 1896, the United Sons of Confederate Veterans, which supplied still more energy for the movement. The local chapters of these organizations held frequent meetings, which were an important social activity for southerners, especially those in rural areas. They also had their sacred elements, mostly in the rhetoric used in orations. The highlight of the year for the veterans was the annual regionwide reunion, which was held in a major southern city. It was one of the most highly publicized events in the South. Railroads ran special trains, and the cities gave lavish welcomes to the grizzled old men and their entourage of splendidly dressed young women sponsored by the local chapters. Tens of thousands of people flocked into the chosen city each year to relive the past for a few days. The earliest reunions were boisterous gatherings, but that spirit did not subdue an equally religious tone, especially as the veterans aged. In 1899 the reunion was in Charleston, and a city reporter noted that the veterans were lighthearted at times but that they also were as devout as any pilgrim going "to the tomb of the prophet, or Christian knight to the walls of Jerusalem."[18]

Each day of the reunion began with a prayer, which usually reminded the aging Confederates that religion was at the heart of the Confederate heritage. Presbyterian clergyman Peyton H. Hogue, in a prayer at the tenth reunion in 1900, was not subtle in suggesting his view of the typical Confederate's afterlife. He prayed that those present "may meet in that Heavenly Home where Lee, Jackson and all the Heroes who have gone before are waiting to welcome us there."[19] A hymn was usually sung after the invocation. One favorite was the "Doxology," which ended

Memorial Day: Dissent in the Redeemer Nation," *American Quarterly,* XXVI (October 1974), 386–98; Conrad Cherry, "Two American Sacred Ceremonies: Their Implications for the Study of Religion in America," *ibid.,* XXI (Winter 1969), 739–54.

[18]For background on the veterans groups see William W. White, *The Confederate Veteran* (Tuscaloosa, Ala., 1962). The reporter's quotation was in UCV, *Minutes of the Ninth Annual Meeting and Reunion,* 8.

[19]UCV, *Minutes of the Tenth Annual Meeting and Reunion . . . 1900* (New Orleans, 1902), 70 (quotation). For examples of this revealing theme in other forums see UCV, *Minutes of the Twelfth Annual Meeting and Reunion . . . 1902* (New Orleans, n.d.), 10; "The Confederate Dead of Mississippi: Prayer," *SHSP,* XVIII (January-December 1890), 297; "The Monument to General Robert E. Lee: The Prayer," *ibid.,* XVII (January-December 1889), 301–2.

with the explicitly Christian reference, "Praise Father, Son, and Holy Ghost." A memorial service was held each year at a local church as part of the official reunion program, and it was here that the most direct connections were made between Christianity and the Confederacy. At the 1920 reunion, for example, the Baptist cleric B. A. Owen compared the memorial service to the Christian sacrament, the Holy Communion. In the Communion service, he said, "our hearts are focused upon Calvary's cross and the dying Lamb of God," and in the Confederate sacrament "we hold sweet converse with the spirits of departed comrades." In order to coordinate their work at memorial services and elsewhere, the ministers of the Lost Cause organized a Chaplains' Association before the Atlanta reunion in 1898.[20]

The Nashville reunion of 1897 was probably the single most religiously oriented Confederate meeting. The veterans met that year at the downtown Union Gospel Tabernacle, later known as Ryman Auditorium, the home of southern music's Grand Old Opry. A new balcony was added to the tabernacle for the 1897 convention, and it was dedicated as a Confederate memorial. Sitting on hard church pews facing the altar and the permanent baptismal font, the veterans had a rollicking but reverent time in 1897 in the sweltering summer heat of the poorly ventilated tabernacle. Each reunion ended with a long parade, and the 1897 procession was one of the most memorable. The reviewing stand was set up on the campus of the Methodists' Vanderbilt University, where the old veterans paused before continuing their march. The reunion coincided with Tennessee's centennial celebration and included the unveiling in Nashville's new Centennial Park of the Parthenon, the replica of the ancient Greek temple, and a mammoth statue to the goddess Athena. The Confederate parade ended in Centennial Park, and as the old soldiers entered the grounds the bells from a nearby tower chimed the old hymn "Shall We Gather at the River?" Apparently unintentionally, the ceremony evoked comparisons with the annual Panathenaic procession in ancient Athens from the lower agora to the Acropolis and then to the Parthenon, the temple of Athena.[21]

[20]For hymns at the reunions see UCV, *Minutes of the Seventh Annual Meeting and Reunion . . . 1897* (New Orleans, 1898) 15; UCV, *Minutes of the Tenth Annual Meeting and Reunion*, 40; UCV, *Minutes of the Thirteenth Annual Meeting and Reunion . . . 1903* (New Orleans, n.d.), 50. For the memorial services see UCV, *Minutes of the Tenth Annual Meeting and Reunion*, 95–101; UCV, *Minutes of the Seventeenth Annual Meeting and Reunion*, 110; UCV, *Minutes of the Thirtieth Annual Meeting and Reunion . . . 1920* (New Orleans, n.d.), 41 (quotations); and "Reunion of Confederate Chaplains," *CV*, VI (June 1898), 244.

[21]"The Reunion: The Seventh Annual Convention of the U.D.C.," *CV*, V (July 1897), 338–39; *ibid.*, V (June 1897), 243; "Comment on Nashville Reunion," *ibid.*, V (September 1897), 463; "About the Nashville Reunion," *CV*, V (August 1897), 427–28.

If religion pervaded the United Confederate Veterans, it saturated the United Daughters of the Confederacy. The importance of Christianity to the Daughters could be seen in the approved ritual for their meetings. It began with an invocation by the president: "Daughters of the Confederacy, this day we are gathered together, in the sight of God, to strengthen the bonds that unite us in a common cause; to renew the vows of loyalty to our sacred principles; to do homage unto the memory of our gallant Confederate soldiers, and to perpetuate the fame of their noble deeds into the third and fourth generations. To this end we invoke the aid of our Lord." The members responded, "From the end of the Earth will I cry unto Thee, when my heart is overwhelmed; lead me to the rock that is higher than I." After similar chanting exchanges, the hymn "How Firm a Foundation" was sung, followed by the reading of a prayer composed by Episcopal bishop Ellison Capers of South Carolina, who had been a Confederate general before entering the ministry. After the prayer the president then read the Lord's Prayer, and the meeting or convention began its official business.[22]

The Daughters provided an unmatched crusading zeal to the religion of the Lost Cause. The members rarely doubted that God was on their side. Cornelia Branch Stone entitled her 1912 pamphlet on Confederate history *U. D. C. Catechism for Children,* a title that suggested the assumed sacred quality of its contents. The Daughters took an especially aggressive role in preserving the records of the southern past. These were sacred documents that were viewed by the women in a fundamentalist perspective. Mrs. M. D. Farris of Texas urged the organization in 1912 to guard its records and archives, "even as the children of Israel did the Ark of the Covenant."[23]

The Christian churches formed the second organizational focus for the southern civil religion. The postwar development of the religion of the Lost Cause was intimately related to developments in the churches themselves. Before the war an evangelical consensus had been achieved in the South, but it had not been institutionalized. Not until after the war did church membership become pervasive. The evangelical denominations that profited from this enormous expansion of what Samuel Smythe Hill, Jr., calls a "single-option religious culture" taught an inward, conversion-centered religion. Fundamental beliefs on such matters as

[22]UDC, *Ritual of the United Daughters of the Confederacy,* 1–2 (quotations); UDC, *Minutes . . . 1905* (Nashville, 1906), 265–66. Local women's groups in 1900 formed an organization similar to the U.D.C., the Confederated Memorial Associations of the South. See *History of the Confederated Memorial Associations of the South* (New Orleans, 1904), 32–34.

[23]Poppenheim, *History,* 1–12; Cornelia Branch Stone, *U.D.C. Catechism for Children* (n.p., 1912); UDC, *Minutes . . . 1912,* p. 398.

sin, guilt, grace, judgment, the reality of heaven and hell, and the loving Jesus were agreed upon by all without regard to denominational boundaries. The concept of a civil religion at first glance seems contrary to this inward theology, but the southern churches were not so otherworldly as to ignore society entirely. A southern social gospel existed, as did successful attempts to establish moral reform through state coercion. The combination of a societal interest and the dynamic growth of an evangelical Protestantism was not antithetical to the development of a civil religion.[24]

Unlike the American civil religion, the religion of the Lost Cause did not entirely stand apart from the Christian denominations. They taught similar religious-moral values, and the southern heroes had been directly touched by Christianity. The God invoked in the Lost Cause was a distinctly biblical, transcendent God. Prayers at veterans' gatherings appealed for the blessings of, in John William Jones's words, the "God of Israel, God of the centuries, God of our forefathers, God of Jefferson Davis and Sidney Johnston and Robert E. Lee, and Stonewall Jackson, God of the Southern Confederacy." Prayers invariably ended in some variation of "We ask it all in the name and for the sake of Christ our dear Redeemer." At the 1907 veterans' reunion, the Reverend Randolph Harrison McKim, like other preachers before and after him, invoked the third person of the Christian godhead, praying for "the blessing of the Holy Ghost in our hearts." The references to Christ and the Holy Ghost clearly differentiated the southern civil religion from the more deistic American civil religion. The latter's ceremonies rarely included such Christian references because of potential alienation of Jews, who were but a small percentage of the southern population. In the South, in short, the civil religion and Christianity openly supported each other.[25]

Certainly, the most blatant connections between Christianity and the Confederacy were made during Confederate rituals. Though they praised their society and its customs, it is clear that in their normal Christian

[24]Hill et al., Religion and the Solid South, 18–19, 26–28, 36–37 (quotation on p. 37); Hill, Southern Churches, xvii, 18, 201; Bailey, Southern White Protestantism, 2–3.

[25]"Chaplain Jones' Prayer," UCV, Minutes of the Eighteenth Annual Meeting and Reunion . . . 1908 (New Orleans, n.d.), 49–50 (first quotation); UCV, Minutes of the Twentieth Annual Meeting and Reunion . . . 1910 (New Orleans, n.d.), 53–54, 121; "Prayer," UCV, Minutes of the Seventeenth Annual Meeting and Reunion . . . 1907, 64 (third quotation). See also "The Confederate Dead in Stonewall Cemetery, Winchester, Va." SHSP, XXII (January-December 1894), 42; "Unveiling of the Soldiers' and Sailors' Monument: Dr. Hoge's Prayer," ibid., 352–53; "Confederate Dead of Florida . . . ," ibid., XXVII (January-December 1899), 112. The failure to make specifically Christian references is noted by Bellah, "Civil Religion in America," and Martin E. Marty, "Two Kinds of Civil Religion," in Richey and Jones, eds., American Civil Religion, 23, 28, 148; and by Conrad Cherry, God's New Israel: Religious Interpretations of American Destiny (Englewood Cliffs, N.J., 1971), 9–10.

services southerners did not worship the Confederacy. Nevertheless, southern religious journals, books, and even pulpits were the sources of Lost Cause sentiments. Church buildings were the most frequently used sites for Memorial Day activities, funerals of veterans, and memorial observances when prominent Confederates died. Such gatherings were interdenominational, with pastors from different religious bodies participating. A spirit of interdenominationalism had existed in the wartime Confederate armies, and it survived in the postbellum South in the ceremonies of the Lost Cause. The overwhelmingly Protestant character of southern religion facilitated the growth of an ecumenical Lost Cause religion. It, in turn, furthered Protestant ecumenicism. Although predominantly Protestant, southern religion was not manifested in any one denomination but was ecclesiastically fragmented. The Lost Cause offered a forum for ministers and laymen from differing churches to participate in a common spiritual activity. References to particular denominational beliefs were occasionally made, but since southerners shared so many of the same doctrines, there was a basis for cooperation.[26] Moreover, despite the Protestant orientation of the Lost Cause, Catholics and Jews were not excluded from it. Members of these faiths joined the Confederate groups, and rabbis and priests occasionally appeared at Lost Cause events. Undoubtedly, with some discomfort, Catholics and Jews accepted the Protestant tinge of the southern civil religion and made their own contributions to it.[27]

The southern churches proved to be important institutions for the dissemination of the Lost Cause. Despite the opposition of some clerics, on Sunday morning November 27, 1884, congregations across the South contributed to a well-promoted special collection to finance a Robert E. Lee monument in Richmond. The denominational papers approvingly published appeals of Confederate organizations for support, editorially endorsed Lost Cause fund raising, recommended Confederate writings, and praised the Lost Cause itself. The Confederate periodicals, in turn, printed stories about Christianity seemingly unrelated to the usual focus on the Civil War. Richmond was the center of Lost Cause activity, and

[26]For examples of the interdenominational character of the Lost Cause see John L. Johnson, *Autobiographical Notes* (Boulder, Colo., 1958), 279; Moses D. Hogue to Peyton Hogue, May 22, 1891; January 20, 1893, Moses Drury Hogue Papers (Historical Foundation of the Presbyterian and Reformed Churches, Montreat, N.C.); "Gordon Memorial Service at Nashville," *CV,* XII (June 1904), 293; J. William Jones, *The Davis Memorial Volume; or, Our Dead President, Jefferson Davis, and the World's Tribute to His Memory* (Waco, Tex., 1890), 590–91, 595, 598.

[27]For examples of Catholic and Jewish involvement in the Lost Cause see "Monument to Father Ryan in Mobile," *CV,* XXI (October 1913), 489–90; "The Reunion," *ibid.,* V (July 1897), 340–41; "Address of Rabbi J. K. Gutheim," *SHSP,* X (June 1882), 248–50; "Sir Moses Ezekiel," *CV,* XXV (May 1917), 235–36.

the city was also a religious publishing center. The Episcopalians, Baptists, Methodists, and Presbyterians all published periodicals there, and the Southern Presbyterian Publishing House was located in the Confederate capital. Nashville was a religious publishing center as well, and it had the same Confederate-Christian mixture. The *Confederate Veteran* magazine, the most important organ of the Lost Cause after 1890, had its offices in and was published by the Publishing House of the Southern Methodist Church in the city.[28]

The close connection between the churches and the Confederate organizations could be seen in terms of the central experience of southern Protestantism—evangelism. Confederate heroes were popular choices to appear at southern revivals. The most influential southern evangelist, iconoclastic Georgia Methodist Samuel Porter ("Sam") Jones, was a master at having Confederates testify to the power of Christianity in their lives, preferably its inspirational effect on the battlefield. At the same time, a significant feature of the religious rhetoric of the reunions was the insistence on a response by the veterans. The invitation to follow Christ, which was made during the memorial services, was also an invitation to follow once again Robert E. Lee, Stonewall Jackson, and Jefferson Davis. Some reunions thus resembled vast revivals, with tens of thousands of listeners hearing ministers remind them of the imminence of death for the aged veterans and of the need to ensure everlasting life.[29]

The third organizational embodiment of the Lost Cause, the educational system, directed the effort to pass the Lost Cause religion on to future generations. Confederate veterans and their widows and daughters dominated the schools, serving as teachers and administrators, and they had no reticence in teaching the southern tradition. The year 1907 was especially observed in the southern schools. It was the centennial of General Lee's birth, and state boards of education issued pamphlets providing guidelines to encourage appropriate celebrations in the schools. In addition, the latter-day Confederates were sought to maintain a prosouthern interpretation of the Civil War in the textbooks used in southern schools. The United Daughters of the Confederacy directed this endeavor, pressuring school boards to adopt textbooks from an

[28]Thomas L. Connelly, *The Marble Man: Robert E. Lee and His Image in American Society* (New York, 1977), 45; "Appeal to the South," Atlanta *Christian Index*, February 28, 1884, p. 4; *CV*, V (July 1897), 359; Edward P. Humphrey, "Moses and the Critics," *Southern Bivouac*, n.s., I (August 1885), 134–39; "Bishop John James Tigert," *CV*, XV (January 1907), 25; *ibid.*, V (August 1897), 401.

[29]Laura M. Jones and Walt Holcomb, *The Life and Sayings of Sam P. Jones . . .* (Atlanta, 1907), 142–48, 447–48; George C. Rankin, *The Story of My Life . . .* (Nashville and Dallas, 1912), 227; J. William Jones, *Personal Reminiscences, Anecdotes and Letters of Gen. Robert E. Lee* (New York, 1874), 333; UCV, *Minutes of the Tenth Annual Meeting and Reunion*, 102–4, 108.

approved list compiled by the organization. The same concern motivated the later southern Fundamentalists who campaigned to keep the doctrine of evolution out of textbooks. The most direct Christian-Confederate connections were not in the public schools but in the private academies, particularly in the denominational schools. Typical of these were the Episcopal High School of Alexandria, Virginia, and the Stonewall Jackson Institute, a Presbyterian female academy in Abingdon, Virginia. Confederate leaders like Lee and Jackson were the explicit models of behavior for the students, and the ex-Confederate teachers served as living models of virtue. The students wore Confederate-style uniforms and drilled on campus, and the advertisements for these religious schools played upon the Confederate theme to attract young people. The United Daughters of the Confederacy supported the Stonewall Jackson Institute by financing scholarships to the school.[30]

Two colleges existed as major institutional shrines of the Lost Cause. The first was the University of the South, an Episcopal college located like an isolated retreat in the mountains at Sewanee, Tennessee. Bishop Leonidas Polk, who would later die at the Battle of Pine Mountain in Georgia while serving as a brigadier general, founded the school in the sectionally divisive 1850s, conceiving of it in part as a place to educate young southerners in regional as well as Christian values. The nascent institution was all but destroyed during the Civil War, but Bishop Charles Todd Quintard, himself a Confederate chaplain and active member of postwar Confederate veterans' groups, resurrected it. The most potent Lost Cause influence came from the faculty he assembled. They were "a body of noble men," said Sarah Barnwell Elliott, daughter of Bishop Stephen Elliott, in 1909, "with the training, education, and traditions of the Old South and whose like we shall never see again." They included William Porcher DuBose, a captain in Lee's Army of Northern Virginia and later a respected theologian; Major George Rainsford Fairbanks of the Army of Tennessee; Brigadier General Francis Asbury Shoup of Florida; Brigadier General Josiah Gorgas, the Confederacy's chief of ordinance; and General Edmund Kirby Smith, commander of the Trans-Mississippi Department of the Confederate armies, who had the honor of being known as the last general to

---

[30] A. D. Mayo, "The Woman's Movement in the South," *New England Magazine*, n.s., V (October 1891), 257; White, *Confederate Veteran*, 59–60; UDC, *Minutes . . . 1901* (Nashville, 1902), 127–28; J. William Jones, *School History of the United States* (Baltimore, 1896); Arthur B. Kinsolving, *The Story of a Southern School: The Episcopal High School of Virginia* (Baltimore, 1922), 79–80, 102, 132; C. D. Walker, "A Living Monument," *CV,* VIII (July 1900), 334; advertisement for Stonewall Jackson Institute, *ibid.,* XII (July 1904), back cover; *ibid.,* XXV (July 1917), back cover; UDC, *Minutes . . . 1915* (Charlotte, N.C., n.d.), 142.

surrender. Women also contributed to the inculcation of Lost Cause religious values. The University of the South gave free tuition to the children of Confederate widows who boarded college students. The Sewanee matrons purposely chose names to connect their homes to the South; thus, one could find a Palmetto Hall, a Magnolia Hall, and an Alabama Hall. They re-created and fostered the culture of the Old South that had produced the heroes of the war.[31]

Sewanee was also an institutional center for Lost Cause orations, dedications, and other rituals. These events adapted Lost Cause themes to the student audience. When Lee died in 1870, for example, the Episcopal bishop of Louisiana, Joseph Pere Bell Wilmer, preached a sermon on the general's moral and religious virtues for the edification of the students. Moreover, when one of the heroes on campus died, regional attention concentrated on Sewanee, prompting the appearance of the ritualistic trappings of the civil religion. Confederate monuments and plaques still dot the campus, serving as devotional points on the holy ground.[32]

Washington and Lee University reflected a different aspect of the southern civil religion than that at the University of the South. Located at Lexington in the Virginia valley, it was more Virginian in its Confederate orientation, and its Christian influence was predominantly Presbyterian. Stonewall Jackson had taught in Lexington at the Virginia Military Institute before the war, and the town provided recruits for his famed Stonewall Brigade. Washington College itself, like Sewanee, suffered during the war, but the choice in 1865 of Robert E. Lee to head the school gave it a new start and a new fame as a center of the Lost Cause. In a sermon, Baptist preacher Edwin Theodore Winkler described the sacred atmosphere of the campus in evocative phrases: "Lexington is the parable of the great Virginia soldiers. In that quiet

[31]Arthur B. Chitty, "Heir of Hopes: Historical Summary of the University of the South," *Historical Magazine of the Protestant Episcopal Church*, XXIII (September 1954), 258–60; Chitty, *Reconstruction at Sewanee: The Founding of the University of the South and Its First Administration, 1857–1872* (Sewanee, Tenn., 1954), 45, 54–55, 73, 83; George R. Fairbanks, *History of the University of the South at Sewanee, Tennessee* (Jacksonville, Fla., 1905), 38–59, 70, 394; Richard Wilmer, *In Memoriam: A Sermon in Commemoration of the Life and Labors of the Rt. Rev. Stephen Elliott . . .* (Mobile, 1867), 13–14; Elliott, *An Appeal for Southern Books and Relics for the Library of the University of the South* (Sewanee, 1921), no pagination (quotation); Moultrie Guerry, *Men Who Made Sewanee* (Sewanee, Tenn., 1932), 73–89, 92, 49–71; Queenie W. Washington, "Memories"; Louise Finley, "Magnolia Hall"; and Monte Cooper, "Miss Sada," in Lily Baker *et al., S* eds., *Sewanee* (Sewanee, Tenn., 1932), 61–63, 100–101, 142–43.

[32]Wilmer, *Gen'l. Robert E. Lee: An Address Delivered before the Students of the University of the South, October 15, 1870* (Nashville, 1872), 5, 9–12; "Funeral of Gen. E. Kirby-Smith," *CV*, I (April 1893), 100–101; "Monument of Gen. F. A. Shoup," *ibid.*, XI (July 1903), 311.

scholastic retreat, in that city set upon a hill and crowned with martial trophies, they, being dead, yet speak."[33]

The presence of prominent Confederates was again the key factor in fostering a Lost Cause aura in Lexington. Among the residents of the town were Colonel William Preston Johnston, son of the martyred General Albert Sidney Johnston; Colonel William Nelson, chief ordnance officer for Stonewall Jackson's command; John Letcher, wartime governor of Virginia; Confederate Judge John White Brockenbrough; General Francis Henney Smith, superintendent of Virginia Military Institute; Colonel John Mercer Brooke, builder of the *Merrimac;* Commander Matthew Fontaine Maury, famed geographer who taught at the institute; and Brigadier General William Nelson Pendleton, rector of the Grace Memorial Episcopal Church, where Lee worshiped. The Lost Cause religious orientation came most directly from the influence of one man—Lee. A deeply religious man himself, he encouraged spiritual activities, including revivalism, at his school. He helped launch the town's Young Men's Christian Association, supervised the erection of a chapel on campus, organized daily interdenominational devotionals conducted by the town's pastors, and invited preachers from across the South to deliver baccalaureate sermons.[34]

As at Sewanee, Lexington was a focus for orations, dedications, and funerals. The chapel was one of the most holy of all Lost Cause shrines. Lee was buried there in a limestone mausoleum, and the site was marked by a recumbent statue of white marble resting on a sarcophagus. The unveiling of the monument on June 23, 1883, was a media event throughout the South. In 1907, the year of the centennial of Lee's birth, the entire region looked to Lexington for the major commemoration of the birth. Stonewall Jackson was also buried in the town, in the cemetery of the Presbyterian church. Lexington came to be so full of Lost Cause shrines that one could take an organized walking tour, which bore some

[33]The Winkler quotation is in Jones, *Personal Reminiscences,* 130–31. See also Henry A. White, *The Scotch-Irish University of the South: Washington and Lee* (Lexington, Va.(?); 1890), 21–22; W. G. Bean, *The Liberty Hall Volunteers; Stonewall's College Boys* (Charlottesville, Va., 1964); Walter C. Preston, *Lee, West Point and Lexington* (Yellow Springs, Ohio, 1934), 48–51, 53–57; Ollinger Crenshaw, *General Lee's College: The Rise and Growth of Washington and Lee University* (New York, 1969), 152–54.

[34]Franklin L. Riley, ed., *General Robert E. Lee after Appomattox* (New York, 1922), 19–20, 22–23, 62; Marshall W. Fishwick, "Robert E. Lee Churchman," *Historical Magazine of the Protestant Episcopal Church,* XXX (December 1961), 251–58, 260–63; Archibald T. Robertson, *Life and Letters of John Albert Broadus* (Philadelphia, 1910), 224–26; Francis H. Smith, *The Virginia Military Institute, Its Building and Rebuilding* (Lynchburg, Va., 1912); and Susan P. Lee, *Memoirs of William Nelson Pendleton* (Philadelphia, 1893), 422–38.

resemblance to a medieval processional of the Stations of the Cross.[35]

All these rituals and institutions dealt with a profound problem. The southern civil religion emerged because defeat in the Civil War had created the spiritual and psychological need for southerners to reaffirm their identity, an identity which came to have outright religious dimensions. Each Lost Cause ritual and organization was tangible evidence that southerners had made a religion out of their history. As with all ritualistic repetition of archetypal actions, southerners in their institutionalized Lost Cause religion were trying symbolically to overcome history. By repetition of ritual, they recreated the mythical times of their noble ancestors and paid tribute to them.[36] Despite the bafflement and frustration of defeat, southerners showed that the time of the myth's creation still had meaning for them. The Confederate veteran was a living incarnation of an idea that southerners tried to defend at the cultural level after Confederate defeat had made political success impossible. Every time a Confederate veteran died, every time flowers were placed on graves on Southern Memorial Day, southerners relived and confronted the death of the Confederacy. The religion of the Lost Cause was a cult of the dead, which dealt with essential religious concerns. Having lost what they considered to be a holy war, southerners had to face suffering, doubt, guilt, a recognition of what seemed to be evil triumphant, and above all death. Through the ritualistic and organizational activities of their civil religion, southerners tried to overcome their existential worries and to live with their tragic sense of life.

[35]*Ceremonies Connected with the Inauguration of the Mausoleum and the Unveiling of the Recumbent Figure of General Robert Edward Lee at Washington and Lee University, Lexington, Va., June 28, 1883* (Richmond, 1883); Thomas N. Page, *The Old South: Essays Social and Political* (New York, 1894), 3, 51–54; Crenshaw, *General Lee's College,* 282–89; Charles F. Adams, *Lee's Centennial: An Address* (Boston, 1907), 2, 6–8, 14, 57; "The Old Virginia Town, Lexington," *CV,* I (April 1893), 108.

[36]Mircea Eliade, *Patterns in Comparative Religion* (New York, 1958), 216–35.

Bibliography

Bibliography

Abbott, Shirley, "Southern Women and the Indispensable Myth," *American Heritage,* 34 (December 1982), 82–91.

Adams, Richard P., "Faulkner and the Myth of the South," *Mississippi Quarterly,* 14 (1961), 131–37.

Alden, John R., *The First South* (Baton Rouge, 1961).

Alexander, Thomas B., Stanley Engerman, Forrest McDonald, Grady Mc-Whiney, and Edward Pessen, "Antebellum North and South in Comparative Perspective: A Discussion," *American Historical Review,* 85 (1980), 1150–66.

————, "Persistent Whiggery in the Confederate South, 1860–1877," *Journal of Southern History,* 27 (1961), 305–29.

Atkinson, Maxine P., and Jacqueline Boles, "The Shaky Pedestal: Southern Ladies Yesterday and Today," *Southern Studies,* 24 (1985), 398–406.

Axtell, James, "White Legend: The Jesuit Missions in Maryland," *Maryland Historical Magazine,* 81 (1986), 1–7.

Ballard, Michael B., *A Long Shadow: Jefferson Davis and the Final Days of the Confederacy* (Jackson, Miss., 1986).

Bargainnier, Earl F., "The Myth of Moonlight and Magnolias," *Louisiana Studies,* 15 (1976), 5–20.

Belz, Herman, "Twentieth-Century American Historians and the Old South: A Review Essay," *Civil War History,* 31 (1985), 171–80.

Berlin, Ira, "Time, Space, and the Evolution of Afro-American Society on British Mainland North America," *American Historical Review,* 85 (1980), 44–78.

Berry, Mary F. and John W. Blassingame, *Long Memory: The Black Experience in America* (New York, 1982).

Berthoff, Rowland, "Celtic Mist over the South," *Journal of Southern History,* 52 (1986), 523–46.

Bickley, R. Bruce, Jr., "Joel Chandler Harris and the Old and New South: Paradoxes of Perception," *Atlanta Historical Journal,* 30 (1986), 9–31.

Blassingame, John W., *Black New Orleans, 1860–1880* (Chicago, 1973).

————, *The Slave Community: Plantation Life in the Antebellum South* (rev. ed., New York, 1979).

————, "Using the Testimony of Ex-Slaves: Approaches and Problems," *Journal of Southern History,* 41 (1975), 473–92.

Boles, John B., and Evelyn Thomas Nolen, *Interpreting Southern History: Historiographical Essays in Honor of Sanford W. Higginbotham* (Baton Rouge, 1987).

Boney, F. N., "The South's Peculiar Intuition," *Louisiana Studies,* 12 (1973), 565–77.

———, *Southerners All* (Macon, Ga., 1984).

Boorstin, Daniel J., "The Vision and the Reality," in *The Americans: The Colonial Experience* (New York, 1966).

Boskin, Joseph, *Sambo: The Rise and Demise of an American Jester* (New York and Oxford, 1986).

Bradford, M. E., "What We Can Know for Certain: Frank Owsley and the Recovery of Southern History," *Sewanee Review,* 78 (1970), 664–69.

Breen, T. H., "'Making a Crop': Tobacco and the Tidewater Planters on the Eve of Revolution," *Virginia Cavalcade,* 36 (1986), 53–65.

Bridenbaugh, Carl, *Myths and Realities: Societies of the Colonial South* (New York, 1963).

Brooks, Cleanth, "Faulkner and History," *Mississippi Quarterly,* 25 (1972), 3–14.

Brownell, Blaine A., "If You've Seen One, You Haven't Seen Them All: Recent Trends in Southern Urban History," *Houston Review,* 1 (1979), 63–80.

Byrd, Edward L., "The Old South as a Modern Myth: An Interpretive Essay," *Red River Valley Historical Review,* 1 (1974), 55–65.

Campbell, Edward D. C., *The Celluloid Society: Hollywood and the Southern Myth* (Knoxville, 1981).

Censer, Jane Turner, "Planters and the Southern Community: A Review Essay," *Virginia Magazine of History and Biography,* 94 (1986), 387–408.

Cider, Gerald, "When Parrots Learn to Talk, and Why They Can't: Domination, Deception, and Self-Deception in Indian-White Relations," *Comparative Studies in Society and History,* 29 (1987), 3–23.

Clinton, Catherine, *The Plantation Mistress: Woman's World in the Old South* (New York, 1982).

Cobb, James C., "From Muskogee to Luckenbach: Country Music and the 'Southernization' of America," *Journal of Popular Culture,* 16 (1982), 81–91.

Cole, Wayne S., "America First and the South," *Journal of Southern History,* 22 (1956), 36–47.

Connelly, Thomas L., *The Marble Man: Robert E. Lee and His Image in American Society* (New York, 1977).

———, and Barbara L. Bellows, *God and General Longstreet: The Lost Cause and the Southern Mind* (Baton Rouge, 1982).

Cords, Nicholas, and Patrick Gerster, eds., "The Mythology of the South," in *Myth and the American Experience,* vol. 1 (New York, 1978), 88.

Cotterill, Robert S., "The Old South to the New," *Journal of Southern History,* 15 (1949), 3–8.

Cressy, David, "Elizabethan America: 'God's Own Latitude?," *History Today,* 36 (1986), 44–50.

Cunliffe, Marcus, *Soldiers and Civilians: The Martial Spirit in America, 1775–1865* (Boston, 1968), 335–84.

Current, Richard N., "Fiction as History: A Review Essay," *Journal of Southern History,* 52 (1986), 77–90.

Danoff, Clarence H., "Four Decades of Thought on the South's Economic Problems," in Melvin Greenhut and W. Tate Whitman, eds., *Essays in Southern Economic Development* (Chapel Hill, 1964), 7–68.

Davenport, Garvin F., Jr., *The Myth of Southern History: Historical Consciousness in Twentieth-Century Southern Literature* (Nashville, 1970).

————, "Thomas Dixon's Mythology of Southern History," *Journal of Southern History,* 36 (1970), 350–67.

David, Paul A., Herbert Gutman, Richard Such, Peter Temin, and Gavin Wright, *Reckoning with Slavery: A Critical Study in the Quantitative History of American Negro Slavery* (New York, 1976).

Davis, David Brion, *The Problem of Slavery in the Age of Revolution, 1770–1823* (Ithaca, 1975).

————, *The Problem of Slavery in Western Culture* (Ithaca, 1966).

————, *Slavery and Human Progress* (New York, 1984).

Davis, Michael, *The Image of Lincoln in the South* (Knoxville, 1972).

Dawson, Jan C., "The Puritan and the Cavalier: The South's Perception of Contrasting Traditions," *Journal of Southern History,* 44 (1978), 597–614.

Dazey, Mary Ann, "Truth in Fiction and Myth in Political Rhetoric: The Old South's Legacy," *Southern Studies,* 25 (1986), 305–10.

DeConde, Alexander, "The South and Isolationism," *Journal of Southern History,* 24 (1958), 332–46.

Degler, Carl, "Dawn without Noon," in *Out of Our Past: The Forces That Shaped Modern America* (New York, 1984), 228–57.

————, "The Foundations of Southern Distinctiveness," *Southern Review,* 13 (1977), 225–39.

————, *Neither Black nor White: Slavery and Race Relations in Brazil and the United States* (New York, 1971).

————, *The Other South: Southern Dissenters in the Nineteenth Century* (New York, 1974).

————, *Place over Time: The Continuity of Southern Distinctiveness* (Baton Rouge, 1977).

————, "Remaking American History," *Journal of American History,* 67 (1980), 7–25.

————, "Rethinking Post–Civil War History," *Virginia Quarterly Review,* 57 (1981), 250–67.

————, "The South in Southern History Textbooks," *Journal of Southern History,* 30 (1964), 48–57.

————, "Thesis, Antithesis, Synthesis: The South, the North and the Nation," *Journal of Southern History,* 53 (1987), 3–18.

————, "Why Historians Change Their Minds," *Pacific Historical Review,* 45 (1976), 167–84.

Dillon, Merton L., *Ulrich Bonnell Phillips: Historian of the Old South* (Baton Rouge, 1985).

Donald, David, "The Confederate as a Fighting Man," *Journal of Southern History,* 35 (1959).

————, "The Scalawag in Mississippi Reconstruction," *Journal of Southern History*, 10 (1944), 447–60.

Dykeman, Wilma, "The Southern Demagogue," *Virginia Quarterly Review*, 33 (1957), 558–68.

Durant, Susan S., "The Gently Furled Banner: The Development of the Myth of the Lost Cause, 1865–1900" (unpublished Ph.D. dissertation, University of North Carolina, 1972).

Durden, Robert, "A Half-Century of Change in Southern History," *Journal of Southern History*, 51 (1985), 3–14.

Eaton, Clement, *The Waning of the Old South Civilization* (New York, 1969).

Egerton, John, *The Americanization of Dixie: The Southernization of America* (New York, 1974).

Engerman, Stanley, L., "The Antebellum South: What Probably Was and What Should Have Been," *Agricultural History*, 44 (1970), 127–42.

————, "A Reconsideration of Southern Economic Growth, 1770–1860," *Agricultural History*, 49 (1975), 343–61.

————, and Eugene D. Genovese, eds., *Race and Slavery in the Western Hemisphere: Quantitative Studies* (Princeton, 1975).

Estaville, Lawrence E., Jr., "Changeless Cajuns: Nineteenth-Century Reality or Myth?," *Louisiana History*, 28 (1987), 117–40.

Evans, William McKee, "From the Land of Canaan to the Land of Guinea: The Strange Odyssey of the 'Son of Ham'," *American Historical Review*, 85 (1980), 15–43.

Evitts, William J., "The Savage South: H. L. Mencken and the Roots of a Persistent Image," *Virginia Quarterly Review*, 49 (1973), 597–611.

Faust, Drew G., "Christian Soldiers: The Meaning of Revivalism in the Confederate Army," *Journal of Southern History*, 53 (1987), 63–90.

————, *The Ideology of Slavery: Proslavery Thought in the Antebellum South, 1830–1860* (Baton Rouge, 1981).

Ferris, William, "The Dogtrot: A Mythic Image in Southern Culture," *Southern Quarterly*, 25 (1986), 72–85.

Fishwick, Marshall, "Robert E. Lee: The Guardian Angel Myth," *Saturday Review*, March 4, 1961, 17–19.

Floan, Howard R., *The South in Northern Eyes, 1831–1861* (Austin, 1958).

Fogel, Robert W., and Stanley L. Engerman, *Time on the Cross: The Economics of American Negro Slavery* 2 vols. (Boston, 1974).

Fox-Genovese, Elizabeth, "Scarlet O'Hara: The Southern Lady as New Woman," *American Quarterly*, 33 (1981), 391–411.

Franklin, John Hope, "Mirrors for Americans: A Century of Reconstruction History," *American Historical Review*, 85 (1980), 1–14.

————, "The North, the South, and the American Revolution," *Journal of American History*, 62 (1975), 5–23.

————, "Southern History: The Black-White Connection," *Atlanta Historical Journal*, 30 (1986), 7–18.

Frederickson, George, *The Black Image in the White Mind: The Debate on Afro-American Character and Destiny* (New York, 1971).

————, "Masters and Mudsills: The Role of the Planter Ideology of South

Carolina," *South Atlantic Urban Studies,* 2 (1978), 73–88.

Gaines, Francis Pendelton, *The Southern Plantation: A Study in the Development and Accuracy of a Tradition* (New York, 1924).

Gara, Larry, *The Liberty Line: The Legend of the Underground Railroad* (Lexington, 1967).

Genovese, Eugene D., *In Red and Black: Marxian Explorations in Southern and Afro-American History* (New York, 1971).

————, *Roll, Jordan, Roll: The World the Slaves Made* (New York, 1974).

————, "Yeoman Farmers in a Slaveholders' Democracy," *Agricultural History,* 49 (1975), 331–42.

————, and Elizabeth Fox-Genovese, "The Religious Ideals of Southern Slave Society," *Georgia Historical Quarterly,* 70 (1986), 1–16.

————, "The Slave Economies in Political Perspective," *Journal of American History,* 66 (1979), 7–23.

Gerster, Patrick G., and Nicholas J. Cords, "The Mythology of the South," in *Myth in American History,* (New York, 1977), 110–36.

————, "The Northern Origins of Southern Mythology," in Charles R. Wilson, ed., *The Encyclopedia of Southern Culture* (Chapel Hill, 1988).

Gilmore, Al-Tony, ed., *Revisiting Blassingame's* The Slave Community: *The Scholars Respond* (Westport, Conn., 1978).

Goldfield, David R., *Promised Land: The South since 1945* (Arlington Heights, Ill., 1987).

Gomez, Jewelle, "Black Women Heroes: Here's Reality, Where's the Fiction?," *Black Scholar,* 17 (1986), 8–13.

Govan, Thomas P., "Was the Old South Different?," *Journal of Southern History,* 21 (1955), 447–55.

Grantham, Dewey W., Jr., "The Contours of Southern Progressivism," *American Historical Review,* 86 (1981), 1009–34.

————, "Regional Imagination: Social Scientists and the American South," *Journal of Southern History,* 34 (1968), 3–32.

————, ed., *The South and the Sectional Image: The Sectional Theme since Reconstruction* (New York, 1967).

————, "South to Posterity," *Mid-West Quarterly,* 8 (1966).

————, "The Southern Bourbons Revisited," *South Atlantic Quarterly,* 60 (1961), 286–95.

Green, Fletcher, "Democracy in the Old South," *Journal of Southern History,* 12 (1946), 3–23.

————, *The Role of the Yankee in the Old South* (Athens, Ga., 1973).

————, "The South and Its History," *Current History,* 35 (1958), 287–91.

Gross, Seymour L., and Eileen Bender, "History, Politics and Literature: The Myth of Nat Turner," *American Quarterly,* 23 (1974), 487–518.

Gundersen, Joan R., "The Double Bonds of Race and Sex: Black and White Women in a Colonial Virginia Parish," *Journal of Southern History,* 52 (1986), 351–72.

Gutman, Herbert G., *The Black Family in Slavery and Freedom* (New York, 1976).

————, *Slavery and the Numbers Game* (Urbana, 1975).

————, "The World Two Cliometricians Made," *Journal of Negro History,* 60 (1975), 53–227.

Gwin, Minrose C., *Black and White Women of the Old South: The Peculiar Sisterhood in American Literature* (Knoxville, 1985).

Hackney, Sheldon, "The South as a Counter Culture," *American Scholar,* 42 (1973), 283–93.

Hagler, D. Harland, "The Ideal Woman in the Antebellum South: Lady or Farmwife?," *Journal of Southern History,* 46 (1980), 405–18.

Hall, John A., "Disillusioned with Paradise: A Southern Woman's Impression of the Rural North in 1862," *Southern Studies,* 25 (1986), 204–7.

Hanna, William F., "A Gettysburg Myth Exploded," *Civil War Times Illustrated,* 24 (1986), 43–47.

Harlan, Louis R., *Booker T. Washington: The Making of a Black Leader, 1856–1901* (New York, 1972).

————, *Booker T. Washington: The Wizard of Tuskegee, 1901–1915* (New York, 1983).

Herskovits, Melville, *The Myth of the Negro Past* (Boston, 1958).

Herring, George C., and Gary R. Hess, "Regionalism and Foreign Policy: The Dying Myth of Southern Internationalism," *Southern Studies,* 21 (1981), 247–77.

Hill, Samuel S., ed. *Encyclopedia of Religion in the South* (Macon, 1984).

————, *Southern Churches in Crisis* (New York, 1967).

————, "The South's Culture—Protestantism," *Christian Century,* 79 (1962), 1094–96.

Hines, Linda O., "White Mythology and Black Duality: George Washington Carver's Response to Racism and the Radical Left," *Journal of Negro History,* 62 (1977), 134–46.

Hobson, Fred C., Jr., *Serpent in Eden: H. L. Mencken and the South* (Chapel Hill, 1974).

Hofferber, Michael, "Bronze Heroes," *Civil War Times Illustrated,* 26 (1987), 32–37.

Hofstadter, Richard, "Ulrich B. Phillips and the Plantation Legend," *Journal of Negro History,* 29 (1944), 109–24.

Holzer, Harold, "Confederate Caricature of Abraham Lincoln," *Illinois History Journal,* 80 (1987), 23–36.

Inscoe, John C., *"The Clansman* on Stage and Screen: North Carolina Reacts," *North Carolina Historical Review,* 64 (1987), 139–61.

Issac, Rhys, "Evangelical Revolt: The Nature of the Baptists' Challenge to the Traditional Order in Virginia, 1765–1775," *William and Mary Quarterly,* 31 (1974), 345–68.

————, *The Transformation of Virginia, 1740–1790* (Chapel Hill, 1974).

Johannsen, Robert W., *To the Halls of the Montezumas: The Mexican War in the American Imagination* (New York, 1985).

Johnson, Michael P., "Mary Boykin Chesnut's Autobiography and Biography: A Review Essay," *Journal of Southern History,* 47 (1981), 585–92.

Jones, Anne Goodwyn, *Tomorrow Is Another Day: The Woman Writer in the South, 1859–1936* (Baton Rouge, 1980).

Karanikas, Alexander, *Tillers of a Myth: Southern Agrarians as Social and Literary Critics* (Madison, 1966).

Keyserling, Hermann, "The South—America's Hope," *Atlantic Monthly,* 144 (1929), 605–8.

Klement, Frank L., "Civil War Politics, Nationalism, and Postwar Myths," *Historian,* 38 (1976), 419–38.

King, Richard H., *A Southern Renaissance: The Cultural Awakening of the American South, 1930–1955* (New York, 1980).

Kirby, Jack Temple, *Media-Made Dixie: The South in the American Imagination* (Baton Rouge, 1978).

Kolchin, Peter, "Reevaluating the Antebellum Slave Community: A Comparative Perspective," *Journal of American History,* 70 (1983), 579–601.

Kondert, Nancy T., "The Romance and Reality of Defeat: Southern Women in 1865," *Journal of Mississippi History,* 35 (1973), 141–52.

Kulikoff, Allan, "The Colonial Cheseapeake: Seedbed of Antebellum Southern Culture?," *Journal of Southern History,* 45 (1979), 513–40.

———, "The Origins of Afro-American Society in Tidewater Maryland and Virginia, 1700–1790," *William and Mary Quarterly,* 35 (1978), 226–59.

———, *Tobacco and Slaves: The Development of Southern Cultures in the Chesapeake, 1680–1800* (Chapel Hill, 1986).

Land, Aubrey C., "The American South: First Epiphanies," *Journal of Southern History,* 50 (1984), 3–14.

Lemons, J. Stanley, "Black Stereotypes as Reflected in Popular Culture, 1880–1920," *American Quarterly,* 29 (1977), 102–16.

Lerche, Charles O., Jr., *The Uncertain South: Its Changing Patterns of Politics and Foreign Policy* (New York, 1964).

Leslie, Kent Anderson, "A Myth of the Southern Lady: Antebellum Proslavery Rhetoric and the Proper Place of Women," *Sociological Spectrum,* 6 (1986), 31–49.

Levesque, George A., "Biracialism, the 'Central Theme' Thesis and the Emergence of Southern Sectionalism," *Journal of Black Studies,* 6 (1975), 158–74.

Levine, Lawrence W., *Black Culture and Black Consciousness: Afro-American Folk Thought from Slavery to Freedom* (New York, 1977).

Litwack, Leon F., *Been in the Storm So Long: The Aftermath of Slavery* (New York, 1979).

Lowe, Richard, "Another Look at Reconstruction in Virginia," *Civil War History,* 32 (1986), 56–76.

McArthur, Judith N. "Myth, Reality and Anomaly: The Complex World of Rebecca Hagerty," *East Texas Historical Journal,* 24 (1986), 18–32.

McCardell, John, *The Idea of a Southern Nation: Southern Nationalists and Southern Nationalism, 1830–1860* (New York, 1979).

McDonald, Forrest, and Grady McWhiney, "The South from Self-Sufficiency to Peonage: An Interpretation," *American Historical Review,* 85 (1980), 1095–118.

———, "The Antebellum Southern Herdsman: A Reinterpretation," *Jour-*

nal of Southern History, 41 (1975), 147–66.

Mackintosh, Barry, "George Washington Carver: The Making of a Myth," *Journal of Southern History,* 42 (1976), 507–28.

McPherson, James M., "Antebellum Southern Exceptionalism: A New Look at an Old Question," *Civil War History,* 29 (1983), 230–44.

McWhiney, Grady, "Jefferson Davis—The Unforgiven," *Journal of Mississippi History,* 42 (1980), 113–27.

————, *Southerners and Other Americans* (New York, 1973).

————, and Francis Simkins, "The Ghostly Legend of the KKK," *Negro History Bulletin,* 14 (1951), 109–12.

————, and Forrest McDonald, "Celtic Origins of Southern Herding Practices," *Journal of Southern History,* 51 (1985), 165–82.

Marius, Richard, "Musing on the Mysteries of the American South," *Daedalus,* 13 (1984), 143–76.

Mathis, Ray, "Mythology and the Mind of the New South," *Georgia Historical Quarterly,* 60 (1976), 228–38.

May, Robert E., "Dixie's Martial Image: A Continuing Historical Enigma," *Historian,* 40 (1978), 213–34.

————, *"Gone with the Wind* as Southern History: A Reappraisal," *Southern Quarterly,* 17 (1978), 51–64.

Mayo, Bernard, *Myths and Men* (New York, 1963).

Middleton-Keirn, Susan, "Magnolias and Microchips: Regional Subcultural Constructions of Femininity," *Sociological Spectrum,* 6 (1986), 83–107.

Miller, John Chester, *The Wolf by the Ears: Thomas Jefferson and Slavery* (New York, 1977).

Miller, Randall M., "The Man in the Middle: The Black Slave Driver," *American Heritage,* 30 (October 1979), 40–49.

Moore, John Hebron, "Two Cotton Kingdoms," *Agricultural History,* 60 (1986), 1–16.

Morgan, Chester M., *Redneck Liberal: Theodore G. Bilbo and the New Deal* (Baton Rouge, 1985).

Morgan, Edmund S., *American Slavery-American Freedom: The Ordeal of Colonial Virginia* (New York, 1975).

Mowry, George E., *Another Look at the Twentieth-Century South* (Baton Rouge, 1973).

Nagel, Paul C. "Reconstruction: Adams Style," *Journal of Southern History,* 52 (1987), 3–18.

Napier, John Hawkins III, "The Militant South Revisited: Myths and Realities," *Alabama Review,* 33 (1980), 243–65.

Nash, Gary B., "The Image of the Indian in the Southern Colonial Mind," *William and Mary Quarterly,* 29 (1972), 197–230.

Noggle, Burl, "Variety and Ambiguity: The Recent Approach to Southern History," *Mississippi Quarterly,* 16 (1963–64) 21–35.

O'Brien, Mathew C., "John Esten Cooke, George Washington, and the Virginia Cavaliers," *Virginia Magazine of History and Biography,* 84 (1976), 259–65.

O'Brien, Michael, "C. Vann Woodward and the Burden of Southern Liberalism," *American Historical Review,* 78 (1973), 589–604.

————, *The Idea of the American South, 1920–1941* (Baltimore, 1979).

————, "The Lineaments of Antebellum Southern Romanticism," *Journal of American Studies,* 20 (1986), 165–88.

Osterweiss, Roland G., *The Myth of the Lost Cause, 1865–1900* (Hamden, Conn., 1973).

————, *Romanticism and Nationalism in the Old South* (New Haven, 1949).

Owsley, Frank L. and Harriet C. Owsley, "The Economic Basis of Society in the Lake Ante-Bellum South," *Journal of Southern History,* 6 (1940), 24–45.

Payne, Ladell, "Willie Stark and Huey Long: Atmosphere, Myth or Suggestion," *American Quarterly,* 20 (1968), 580–95.

Perry, Richard L. "The Front Porch as Stage and Symbol in the Deep South," *Journal of American Culture,* 8 (1985), 13–18.

Peskin, Allan, "Was There a Compromise of 1877?," *Journal of American History,* 60 (1973), 63–75. Reply by C. Vann Woodward, "Yes, There Was a Compromise of 1877" (same citation).

Pessen, Edward, "How Different from Each Other Were the Antebellum North and South?," *American Historical Review,* 85 (1980), 1119–49.

Peterson, Thomas Virgil, *Ham and Japheth: The Mythic World of Whites in the Antebellum South* (Metuchen, N.J., 1978).

Potter, David, "On Understanding the South," *Journal of Southern History,* 30 (1964), 451–62.

————, *The South and the Sectional Conflict* (Baton Rouge, 1968).

Pyron, Darden Asbury, "*Gone with the Wind* and the Southern Cultural Awakening," *Virginia Quarterly Review,* 62 (1986), 565–87.

Rainard, R. Lyn, "The Gentlemanly Ideal in the South, 1660–1860: An Overview," *Southern Studies,* 25 (1986), 295–304.

Reed, John Shelton, *The Enduring South: Subcultural Persistence in Mass Culture* (Chapel Hill, 1974).

————, *One South: An Ethnic Approach to Regional Culture* (Baton Rouge, 1982).

————, *Southerners: The Social Psychology of Sectionalism* (Chapel Hill, 1983).

Rogers, Gayle J., "The Changing Image of the Southern Woman: A Performer on a Pedestal," *Journal of Popular Culture,* 16 (1982), 60–67.

Roland, Charles P., *The Improbable Era: The South since World War II* (Lexington, 1975).

————, "The South, America's Will-o'-the Wisp Eden," *Louisiana History,* 11 (1970), 101–19.

Roller, David C., and Robert W. Twyman, eds., *The Encyclopedia of Southern History* (Baton Rouge, 1979).

Rozwenc, Edwin C., "Captain John Smith's Image of America," *William and Mary Quarterly,* 16 (1959), 27–36.

————, ed., *The American South: Portrait of a Culture* (Baton Rouge, 1980).

Rubin, Louis D., Jr., "The Historical Image of Modern Southern Writing,"

Journal of Southern History, 22 (1956), 147–66.

————, "The South and the Faraway Country," *Virginia Quarterly Review,* 38 (1962), 444–59.

Scarborough, William K., *The Overseer: Plantation Management in the Old South* (Baton Rouge, 1966).

Scott, Ann Firor, "The 'New Women' in the South," *South Atlantic Quarterly,* 61 (1962), 473–83.

————, "The Progressive Wind from the South, 1906–13," *Journal of Southern History,* 29 (1963), 53–70.

————, *The Southern Lady: From Pedestal to Politics* (Chicago, 1970).

————, "Women in a Plantation Culture: Or What I Wish I Knew about Southern Women," *South Atlantic Urban Studies,* II (1978), 24–33.

————, "Women's Perspectives on the Patriarchy in the 1850's," *Journal of American History,* 61 (1974), 52–64.

Seidel, Kathryn Lee, *The Southern Belle in the American Novel* (Tampa, 1985).

Sellers, Charles G., Jr., ed., *The Southerner as American* (Chapel Hill, 1960).

————, "Who Were the Southern Whigs?," *American Historical Review,* 59 (1954), 335–46.

Shapiro, Edward S., "Frank L. Owsley and the Defense of Southern Identity," *Tennessee Historical Quarterly,* 36 (1977), 75–94.

Shaw, Barton C., "Henry W. Grady Heralds 'The New South'," *Atlanta Historical Journal,* 30 (1986), 55–66.

Shore, Laurence, "The Poverty of Tragedy in Historical Writing on Southern Slavery," *South Atlantic Quarterly,* 85 (1986), 147–64.

Simkins, Francis B., "The Everlasting South," *Journal of Southern History,* 13 (1947), 307–22.

————, "The South," in Merrill Jensen, ed., *Regionalism in America* (Madison, 1951), 147–72.

————, "Tolerating the South's Past," *Journal of Southern History,* 21 (1955), 3–16.

Simpson, John A., "The Cult of the 'Lost Cause'," *Tennessee Historical Quarterly,* 34 (1975), 350–61.

Singal, Daniel Joseph, "Ulrich B. Phillips: The Old South as the New," *Journal of American History,* 54 (1977), 871–91.

Skaggs, Merrill Maguire, "Roots: A New Black Myth," *Southern Quarterly,* 17 (1978), 42–50.

Smiley, David L., "The Quest for the Central Theme in Southern History," *South Atlantic Quarterly,* 71 (1972), 307–25.

Smith, Henry Nash, *Virgin Land: The American West as Symbol and Myth* (Cambridge, 1970).

Smith, Stephen A., *Myth, Media, and the Southern Mind* (Fayetteville, 1985).

————, "The Old South Myth as a Contemporary Southern Commodity," *Journal of Popular Culture,* 16 (1982), 22–29.

Soapes, Thomas F., "The Federal Writer's Project Slave Interviews: Useful Data or Misleading Source," *Oral History Review,* (1977), 33–38.

Sosna, Morton, "The South Old and New: A Review Essay," *Wisconsin*

Magazine of History, 55 (1972), 231–35.

Spruill, Julia Cherry, *Women's Life and Work in the Southern Colonies* (New York, 1973).

Stampp, Kenneth M., "Rebels and Sambos: The Search for the Negro's Personality in Slavery," *Journal of Southern History,* 37 (1971), 367–92.

Stephenson, Wendell Holmes, "The South Lives in History," *Historical Outlook,* 23 (1932).

Tate, Allen, "Faulkner's 'Sanctuary' and the Southern Myth," *Virginia Quarterly Review,* 44 (1968), 418–27.

Thornton, Kevin Pierce, "Symbolism at Old Miss and the Crisis of Southern Identity," *South Atlantic Quarterly,* 86 (1987), 254–68.

Tindall, George B., "The Benighted South: Origins of a Modern Image," *Virginia Quarterly Review,* 40 (1964), 281–94.

————, *The Disruption of the Solid South* (New York, 1973).

————, *The Ethnic Southerner: Beyond the Mainstream* (Baton Rouge, 1976).

————, "The SunBelt Snow Job," *Houston Review,* 1 (1979), 3–13.

Trelease, Allen W., "Who Were the Scalawags?," *Journal of Southern History,* 29 (1963), 445–68.

Van Deburg, William L., *The Slave Driver: Black Agricultural Labor Supervisors in the Antebellum South* (Westport, Conn., 1979).

Vandiver, Frank E., "Jefferson Davis—Leader without Legend," *Journal of Southern History,* 43 (1977), 3–18.

Van West, Carroll, "Perpetuating the Myth of America: Scottsboro and Its Interpreters," *South Atlantic Quarterly,* 80 (1981), 36–48.

Van Steeg, Clarence L., "Historians and the Southern Colonies," in Ray A. Billington, ed., *The Reinterpretation of Early American History* (San Marino, Calif., 1966).

Walters, Ronald G., "The Erotic South: Civilization and Sexuality in American Abolitionism," *American Quarterly,* 72 (1973), 177–201.

Ward, John William, *Andrew Jackson: Symbol for an Age* (New York, 1962).

Warren, Robert Penn, *The Legacy of the Civil War: Meditations on the Centennial* (New York, 1964).

Watson, Richie Devon, Jr., *The Cavalier in Virginia Fiction* (Baton Rouge, 1985).

Whitridge, Arnold, "The John Brown Legend," *History Today,* 7 (1957), 211–20.

Williams, D. Alan, "The Virginia Gentry and the Democratic Myth," in Howard H. Quint, Dean Albertson, and Milton Cantor, eds., *Main Problems in American History* (Homewood, Ill., 1972), 25–33.

Williams, T. Harry, *Romance and Realism in Southern Politics* (Athens, Ga. 1961).

Williamson, Joel, "The Oneness of Southern Life," *South Atlantic Urban Studies,* 2 (1978), 78–89.

Wilson, Charles Reagan, *Baptized in Blood: The Religion of the Lost Cause, 1865–1920* (Athens, Ga., 1980).

————, "The Death of Bear Bryant: Myth and Ritual in the Modern

South," *South Atlantic Quarterly,* 86 (1987), 282–95.

————, ed., *The Encyclopedia of Southern Culture* (Chapel Hill, 1988).

Wood, Peter H., *Black Majority: Negroes in Colonial South Carolina from 1670 through the Stono Rebellion* (New York, 1974).

————, "'I Did the Best I Could for my Day': The Study of Early Black History during the Second Reconstruction, 1960–1976," *William and Mary Quarterly,* 35 (1978), 185–225.

————, "'Taking Care of Business' in Revolutionary South Carolina: Republicanism and the Slave Society," *South Atlantic Urban Studies,* 2 (1978), 49–72.

Woodman, Harold D., "New Perspectives on Southern Economic Development: A Comment," *Agricultural History,* 49 (1975), 374–80.

————, "Sequel to Slavery: The New History Views the Postbellum South," *Journal of Southern History,* 43 (1977), 523–41.

Woodward, C. Vann, "The Aging of America," *American Historical Review,* 82 (1977), 583–94.

————, "The Antislavery Myth," *American Scholar,* 31 (1962), 312–28.

————, "The North and South of It," *American Scholar,* 35 (1966), 647–58.

————, "Southerners versus the Southern Establishment," *Atlanta History,* 31 (1987), 4–11.

————, "Southern Mythology," *Commentary,* 42 (May 1965), 60–63.

————, *The Strange Career of Jim Crow* (New York, 1974).

————, *Thinking Back: The Perils of Writing History* (Baton Rouge, 1986).

————, "Time and Place," *Southern Review,* 22 (1986), 1–14.

————, "Why the Southern Renaissance?," *Virginia Quarterly Review,* 51 (1975), 222–39.

Wright, Gavin, "The Efficiency of Slavery: Another Interpretation," *American Economic Review,* 69 (1979), 219–26.

————, *Old South, New South: An Economic History since the Civil War* (New York, 1985).

Wright, Louis B., *The Dream of Prosperity in Colonial America* (New York, 1965).

————, "Intellectual History and the Colonial South," *William and Mary Quarterly,* 16 (1959), 214–27.

————, "Less Moonlight and Roses," *American Scholar,* 12 (1943), 263–72.

Wyatt-Brown, Bertram, *Southern Honor: Ethics and Behavior in the Old South* (New York, 1982).

Zinn, Howard, *The Southern Mystique* (New York, 1964).

Index